For Janet

SWORN TO SECRECY

by

ANNETTE SALVESEN

Annette Salvesen

PublishAmerica
Baltimore

First printing

Hardcover 978-1-4626-0121-9
Softcover 978-1-4626-0122-6
PUBLISHED BY PUBLISHAMERICA, LLLP
www.publishamerica.com
Baltimore

Printed in the United States of America

INTRODUCTION

Christmas Eve 1958—a white Christmas at that! I slipped out of the house for a walk in the snow. The peace, the quiet of the countryside, the twinkling stars overhead against the vast, black sky and in the background our beautiful country home in Surrey—how lucky I was to be alive.

Shadows fell across the snow as the moon shone down. Only the sound of my boots could be heard, crunching at each step in the crisp, white snow until the lone, mellow call of an owl hooting in the distance told me that I was not alone this lovely winter night. I was warm and cozy wearing a heavy fur coat. The hood over my head encircled my face and my breath came in little clouds as it reached the cold night air. It started to snow again. I raised my face to the sky to feel the soft flakes fall on my cheeks. Christmas Eve—such a wonderful time of year.

Returning home, on nearing the wrought-iron gate I quickened my pace. A car parked in the driveway beyond the lawn told me that our guests had arrived for cocktails and dinner. The crazy paving that ran between now sorry-looking rosebushes, was covered in a fresh layer of snow, with more on the way. Everything so sparkling clean gave a rather drab appearance to the white areas of our black and white house!

I pushed open the heavy oak door and a burst of warmth took me by surprise; a blessing as I discarded my coat revealing the delicate dinner dress. Quickly I changed my boots for evening shoes and hung the hood on a hook over my coat in the hall.

I had not seen the Gransdens for quite some time, in fact since the Singapore days, and was looking forward to meeting them again. Close friends of my mother and stepfather Jackie, they kindly invited me to stay when my parents visited Australia in 1949, and that was quite a responsibility in South East Asia. Young and very much *on the loose*, I was single and heavily involved in amateur dramatics and life was exciting, glamorous, filled with fun and the *joir de vive*.

With cheeks glowing pink from the cold, flake of snow still clinging to a lash, I joined my parents and their guests in the cozy warmth of the sitting room. It was a pretty sight with Marion and my mother sitting, talking together backed by a tall Christmas tree at the far end of the room. Johnny Gransden sat by the fire with Jackie, who at that time poured whisky from a decanter into a crystal glass. The dark liquid looked inviting as the light reflected in the facets of the beautiful piece. Jackie was proud of his crystal. It replaced so much of that which was smashed to pieces when looters ransacked his home as Singapore fell to the Japanese. There was a pause in the conversation when I entered the room with happy greetings from all around.

"You look lovely tonight Annette, as always!" Johnny grinned.

Jackie handed me a glass of sherry. "Happy Christmas, Annette. Come and sit down."

Taking the glass I sank into an empty chair by the fire and sipped my sherry and soon the two men continued to talk together quietly, pausing often, obviously deep in thought of other more distressing Christmases, not so very long ago. They had been together as Prisoners of War and had many memories to recall and share, quietly between themselves.

"That Local Purchasing job was a stroke of luck for me." Jackie laughed. "Do you remember old Northcott Green?"

Johnny nodded.

"Well he and I managed to scrounge a couple of bikes to do the rounds of the local merchants, and came back loaded in more ways than one!"

I kept very quiet, sipping my drink, listening. I watched Jackie's face as he told his tale and wondered what was coming next. I knew that one reason why Jackie had survived in Changi prison camp was due to his wonderful sense of humor. Not only was it an asset for himself but for the people around him.

My mother and Marion talked of other things little realizing what went on our end of the room; otherwise "Changi talk" might have come to an abrupt end.

Apparently Northcott Green and Jackie made the rounds of the local stores to buy whatever food they could for the officers in camp: vegetables, eggs, (when available), chickens etc. But there was a draw-back to this. The *tawkis,* local merchants, with whom Jackie dealt in his job with Guthrie & Co before the war, were so delighted to see him, they insisted on him sharing a friendly drink whilst the goods were collected together.

That was fine, but the brew, in Jackie's words, was an "absolute corker." Made from rice and some sort of juice (he never found out what,) mixed together in the scooped-out shell of a pineapple, it was left to ferment for days. Jackie and Northcott Green were then obligated to partake of this offering, as they sat on the ground with their hosts before loading the "goods" onto the bikes.

"Whew!" Jackie grinned as he recalled those times. "I tell you, we were feeling no pain as we flew down the hill to Changi jail, veggies flying in all directions! The guards would see us coming, fling open the gates and wave us in. We would collapse in a heap giggling like a couple of kids. But next day! Our heads!" Both men were laughing, and I too joined in. They must have made an extraordinary sight, not withstanding the heat, the sweat and the flies.

As Jackie puffed contentedly on his pipe, his mind seemed to drift. "Do you remember that little fellow?" he asked.

"The little one with the loud voice?" Johnny grunted and made a face. Yes, he remembered. Who didn't remember that unpleasant little character—the guard who made up for his lack of intelligence and diminutive stature with the loud voice and vicious, overbearing manner of the bully?

Jackie chuckled as he sipped his drink and recalled those moments when they were able to at least gain some amusement in getting a crack at their captors, however small the incident. "We taught him to say his name in English." Then he went on to explain that because he spoke no English at all, the nasty little man was only too eager to learn the meaning of his name. In a very short time was able to boast to one and all his prowess of the English language. "What is your name?" Jackie and his friends would taunt.

"My name is Son of a Bitch," he roared. The reply whipped out with pride from the prisoner's tormentor.

"Yes you are, you little S.O.B." Jackie whispered. His voice soft, Jackie took on a far away, almost mystic gaze synonymous with former prisoners of war.

It was Johnny who broke the silence. "What happened to 'The Bird'? Any idea what actually happened to him?"

"Whew! We were lucky not to have him," Jackie remarked, too lost in his own thoughts to answer the question direct.

"I heard he had been killed," Johnny continued.

"Hmm! I know MacArthurs's people were looking for him, but I don't know if they actually caught up with him." Jackie sounded skeptical. "It wouldn't surprise me if he just disappeared."

"Well maybe he will turn up one day" Johnny remarked as Jackie replenished his drink from the decanter.

"Maybe," said Jackie, turning back to the table to top up his own. "That little so and so, but I *am* glad we didn't have him!"

"Was Bobby Clark sent up the railway?" Johnny asked.

Jackie puffed at his pipe, "Yes. But he never returned."

"Beriberi?"

"Yes. Like so many others. Did you see any of the poor devils that returned?" Jackie asked. "Their clothes, if you can call them that—they were more like rags—just hung on them. We were thin, but those poor sods! Just skin and bone. Terrible sight."

Both men seemed lost in thought until Johnny broke the silence: "Beriberi is a terrible way to go."

Jackie looked at him. "We had it in camp."

Johnny helped himself from a plate of nuts. "You kept a diary didn't you?"

Jackie gave a little laugh. "If you can call it that! Until the paper ran out."

"Going to do anything with it? It might make interesting reading."

"No," Jackie replied, "I read it to Dorothy once in a while and we talk about it, but I don't want to write."

Looking at me, as if he became aware of my presence again, he said: "Annette may be able to do something with it some day. She writes a good letter. It might be just up her alley."

The women had paused in their friendly chatter at the other end of the room. Realizing the gist of the conversation coming from our side of the fire, my mother broke in: "Come on chaps, it's Christmas! No Changi talk tonight."

She got up from her chair and took Marion's glass. Handing it to her husband, announced firmly, "Jackie, Marion would like another drink." Turning to me, she said "Annette darling, run into the dining room and make sure the table looks perfect. Put any little finishing touches you think it needs. You always make it look so lovely."

Hiding my reluctance, I arose to comply with her request. I paused briefly, anxious to hear more of the "Changi talk" between the two men. But I was to be disappointed. The conversation was brought to a close—for the time being. I left the room to comply with my mother's wishes.

CHAPTER I
WORLD WAR II

True to our word that if the Germans attacked Poland Britain would declare war on Germany, in September 1939 when the Nazis *did* invaded Poland, we were at war! I was but a child, still thirteen years old when news of the invasion reached us in Cornwall, on the South coast of England where, with my three cousins, Vere, Betty and Helen Jenkin, summer holidays were a blissful haven.

A rambling house on top of the cliffs overlooking the sea was paradise for children let loose to play in fields of long grass dotted with golden buttercups, dandelions and pale blue cornflowers. Ragged robin and little mauve violets were tucked in the grass beneath the hedges and if we looked with care we might find tiny blooms of the scarlet pimpernel peeking out as if smiling up at us. Their precious little faces recalled the wonderful tales of their namesake, the romantic hero of the 1700s—aristocrat Sir Percy Blakeney and the members of his league—the Scarlet Pimpernel—who saved the lives of many during the Reign of Terror in France. All were brought to life through the imaginative and creative mind of Baroness Orczy.

The unceasing background orchestra of mayflies, grasshoppers and other summer insects that basked in the hot summer sun was music to our ears.

A narrow path winding through tough bracken and fern led down to our beach and the sea. The sea! Oh, how I loved the sea—my father's nautical blood still runs strong in my veins. Each of us learnt to swim in this wonderful place, diving from rocks and splashing around with the dogs—Matt, a magnificent Airedale, Mickey the Spaniel and Woolly, a longhaired, short legged, black and white lovable fellow of unknown breed.

When tired of that all played ball. Eventually exhausted, we collapsed on the sand to dry off in the sun, lulled by the sound of the waves that lapped on the shore. We slept before tucking into a spread of gastronomic delight, produced and lugged down the cliff by the ever game 'grown-ups, the girls' mother, known to me as Aunt Grace, and my cousin Dameris.

The years between twelve and eighteen are a tremendous jump in a young girl's development of life—the impressionable years when ideas are formed and memories indelibly planted on the mind.

The first time we experienced a 'dog fight' up high in the clouds was late on a dark, moonless night. Still children we did not take things as seriously as we probably should. I shall never forget the sight of Aunt Grace as she sat on the floor beneath the stairs in the dark, one arm round Helen, her youngest, endeavoring to collect the rest of her unruly brood around her. It was round about ten and blackout strictly in force. We put out the lights and threw back the drapes as the commotion started outside—the sound of excited voices from some elderly men, all dressed in home guard uniform. They gazed up as bright beams from the searchlights below crisscrossed the dark skies above.

"Look, Betty, look" I squealed as she and I danced up and down in the dark. Vere stood beside us much more restrained, as became her age but we all strained our necks to peer out.

"There they are!" The beams homed in on two planes as they dodged so close it seemed impossible to avoid a collision high above the clouds.

"Vere," Aunt Grace's voice boomed out, "come away from that window! Betty, where is your pan? Annette, *will* you put that saucepan on your head."

"It's too big Aunt Grace," I protested and tried to peer from under the wretched thing. It enveloped my head including my face, "Why do we have to wear these anyway?"

"Silly child! If something falls on the house at least your head will be protected."

If anything fell and the house came tumbling down I would probably be deafened by the clatter of debris bouncing off my headgear, but now I was busy trying to decide which was more convenient, the handle sticking out at the front or the back. Whatever way it sat I couldn't see a thing and that was no fun at all.

"Ooh, look!" Betty's voice came from somewhere out there, so I tipped back my head and the offending pan went clattering to the floor, and that gave me a splendid view of my Aunt Grace, outlined in the dark, still remonstrating from inside a colander, her dutiful eldest and her terrified youngest huddled beside her, with various sorts of kitchen utensils crowning their heads. The constant clucking from my Aunt, the crash of the saucepan landing on the floor, the squeals of delight from Betty and giggles from yours truly, was all that it took to send Mickey into raptures of delight. He thought the whole affair a wonderful game. With loud barks he pranced off in search of his ball in the dark, his long, floppy ears flying in the breeze. Having found it, he returned with a mad dash, straight into the back of our legs, sending Betty and me flying, all three of us landing together in an excited heap on the floor.

"Put your saucepans on!" bellowed my aunt, as our two little faces peered over the windowsill into the darkness beyond from where we heard a familiar young voice calling my name.

"And where do you think you're going laddy?" this from a man with a deep Cornish brogue. "Don't you know there's a war on?"

"Yes, sir. But I was going to the Jenkin's home. I want to see Annette" piped up the young voice. Betty gave a giggle and nudged me in the ribs. It was our friend Gerald.

"At this time of night, in the middle of an air-raid?" came the gruff retort.

"Yes sir," the lad pleaded, "there's a dance tomorrow night in the village hall and I want to take her out."

"Well, sonny" one of the men replied, not unkindly, "at this time of night" and glancing up, "in the middle of a dogfight, her Aunt will probably say NO. Come back tomorrow. Now off with you!" and as an afterthought "and be careful you don't put on that light. Remember, there's a war on."

"Yes sir!" and off he scampered. We two leaned out as far as we could to watch his shadowy form as it disappeared into the darkness. Suddenly there was a crash—Gerald's bike had come to grips with a pothole and both went tumbling down. Of course we collapsed into fits of unkindly mirth.

It started to drizzle again. The sweet smell of rain, for which Cornwall is famous, now mingled with the salt, sea air. Next day we heard the dogfight was all a sham. Two of our planes taking a practice run. What a let down!

First Czechoslovakia fell to the brutality of their tormentors, and with frightening speed the Nazis swept across Europe leaving destruction and misery in their wake. When France succumbed and the Battle of Britain was on. We were fighting for our very existence. Night after night waves of enemy bombers headed for London, Portsmouth and other major cities. The skies were alight from the fires below unleashed by human greed and the desire for destruction. Soon the daylight raids began, and all that Britain possessed were a handful of Spitfires and Hurricanes to combat this terrible foe. But the men? Oh yes! A few heroic young men put their lives on the line to stand between us and disaster.

Then it stopped! It suddenly stopped. London waited. Coventry and Portsmouth waited, and above all, the few remaining airmen still alive waited on the ground, ready to force their weary bodies into battle. But nothing happened—the Battle of Britain was over!

On the radio Churchill's somber voice rang out his praise. "Never in the field of human conflict, was so much, owed by so many, to so few!"

We four children did not realize at the time, just how fortunate we were compared with others of our age in the bombed out areas of our towns, not withstanding those in the occupied countries as the Nazis blasted their way through Europe. That all seemed very far away, and for us those were such happy days.

But there was work to be done—even for children and that work was known as school! On returning to England on one of her trips from her home in Singapore, my mother was devastated to find that I was well near blind in my left eye. Furious by the lack of care from those in charge, she removed me forthwith from that initial school, to join Vere at the prestigious Princess Helena College in Hertfordshire, a mere forty miles from London. It was an old country mansion set on an estate in the country-side. Only one hundred and three girls were admitted at any given time—all daughters of "fallen" British officers—so that classes were small and individual care in abundance. The staff were led by an imposing figure of the head mistress, Miss V.A. Prain, irreverently known by one and all as 'VAP'.

The blitz on London during World War II resulted in the evacuation of a number of schools and colleges to the relative safety of the country, much to the delight of many students brought up in the bustle and noise of the big cities. The acrid smell of dense winter fog for which London was so infamous, sank deep into the lungs, making breathing difficult, and smarting the eyes.

In the country they enjoyed a whole new way of life, breathing in the fresh clean air, with the sweet smell of grass and newly mown hay, pine trees in the woods, oaks and the ash, chestnut and elm. They reached out and touched wild flowers of glorious hews, growing in the hedgerows; primroses and violets, buttercups and ragged-robin; and in winter, peeping out of the snow, delicate little snowdrops. They marveled at the bird and animal life around them.

It was to such a place as this my mother deposited me, before returning to the social life of Singapore,—lifestyle that suited her so well. Her most strenuous task was to rise early in the morning, after '*Amah*' had brought her an early morning cup of tea, and pick flowers in the garden before the heat of the tropical sun forced her to retreat indoors. She arranged the flowers in vases around the house, filling the rooms with color and fragrance. Should a petal drop it was immediately swept away by an ever-watchful 'boy' who padded silently through the rooms, making sure that nothing was out of place, and that the 'Mem' had everything she needed without exerting herself unduly.

I, on the other hand, settled down to life at boarding school. As young ladies of Princess Helena College, we enjoyed an attractive uniform—basically green—dark green for the tunics and afternoon skirts, and light green and gray tweed suits and overcoats for Sunday church and outings. Our shirts were of a pale cream color, or white, and, of course, we always wore our green and gold ties, the proud colors of our school.

As there were but 103 students at any given time, the classes were small, and on the whole interesting. My mind drifted off into never-

never land whenever mathematics were in progress, but was captivated by those who taught the Scriptures, History, English and particularly Dramatic Art.

Each day, after class in the afternoons, we surged onto the Lacrosse field in order to throw and catch the ball with our Lacrosse sticks, or attack each other in, what was to me, a most uncivilized, diabolical battle from which I was only too delighted to retreat. The very fact that I was near blind in one eye and obliged to wear thick lenses glasses, made it well nigh impossible to see the wretched ball, until it either whizzed past my ear like an angry mosquito, or thundered towards me like a bolt out of the blue, aiming straight for my face and specs at break-neck speed.

So it was with great relief when nature came to my rescue on those first winter afternoons, and the heavens opened to deposit their load of good refreshing rain, forcing us away from the soggy fields for the joy of the four or five mile walks, down Hertfordshire roads and country lanes.

Because of my failing sight, it was agreed between my mother, the eye specialist and mistresses at school, that time was wasted on my attending classes when close work was required, such as algebra, geometry—in fact any form of mathematics, and I wholeheartedly agreed! During those classes it was deemed more beneficial if I were to exercise by walking across the fields and through the woods of the estate, taking mental notes of nature, returning for History, English and Drama classes and, of course, gymnastics, at which I excelled.

Thus, in the company of rabbits, horses, larks and cuckoos I became cognizant of my solitude, spending many a happy hour sitting on grassy hillocks at the edge of the woods, wrapped in the cozy warmth of a huge green cloak, marveling at the trees across the valley, a patchwork of color; greens and yellows, browns and reds as summer turned into autumn. Rabbits became used to my presence, and, if I stayed very still, would venture within a foot or two, nibbling the lush green grass, whiskers twitching, ever ready for a movement that would send them scampering away, their little white tails bobbing in the distance.

That first year the war seemed far away and of little concern to us. A bomb shelter was built underground, in the woods, which we named 'Hitler's Hall.' It was never used except by the field mice, an occasional hedgehog, and the worms. We had the usual fire drill—each one of us in turn, dangling precariously from a rope attached to the topmost window skinning our knees and sometimes our noses against the wall, as we lowered ourselves to the safety of the ground.

If we held our heads high and pushed firmly against the wall with our hands and feet in a rhythmic motion, we remained unscathed but, should those of a more nervous disposition cling to the rope in terror and gaze down to the ground, which seemed to them very far below, they were apt to spin like a top. Alas we, who had lost favor in the classroom, were now vindicated and chortled with glee to see our tormentors brought down to earth at last!

It was when rationing was introduced that the war became more evident. Our taste buds and our tummies told us that things were about to change. The food, of course, was good, but not so interesting. Butter appeared before us on individual dishes, each dish marked with a girl's name. In the center sat a weekly ration of butter, all two ounces of it mocking us as we stood round our tables, gazing at it in horror and amazement, mingled with indignation. Our eyes drifted to our sugar ration. Yes, indeed life was about to change!

Following grace said by the senior mistress at high table and we sat down in silence, with different thoughts running through each girl's head, as we eyed what was to become normal and commonplace. Some decided to go the whole hog and splurge—their butter gone within two days; perhaps there would be a miracle, the war might end by the end of the week. What a hope! Others, after careful thought, drew little lines with a knife, dividing theirs into seven portions, each portion to cover three meals a day. Meat was rationed, but thanks to the brilliance of miracle workers in the kitchen, we barely noticed.

There was plenty of bread, and vegetables were grown in the vegetable garden—until the gardeners disappeared. They were "called up" to fight the war; their place taken by older men who gave us a few hours each week, between exercise, training for the Home Guard in anticipation of the German invasion, which was very real.

One by one the maids left. They too were called up. So, at each table of six, one girl was appointed to take their place. We grew up! We became more independent. And as no miracle took place, and the war did not stop at the end of that first week, the weeks drew into months and the months into years. Then our clothes were rationed.

Books of stamps invaded our lives. Stamps for food, stamps for petrol, stamps for clothes. Our most valued possessions became our ration books—full of stamps. And these we guarded as if our lives depended on them. Yes! There was a war on, and we were all in this together.

As the raids on London grew more intense, the sound of enemy planes overhead became more frequent, and on a few occasions we were roused in the middle of the night by the staff, visiting each dormitory, calling urgently but quietly so as not to alarm us unduly. We donned our slippers and our robes, grabbed our pillows and made for the cellars below. As we ran down the cellar stairs our momentum gathered, and we raced with glee towards our allotted hammocks, slung between pillars. With practice and a little skill we could dive into them in a certain way that would cause them to spin a couple of times, and with a little help, they deposit us in laughing heaps upon the floor. Finally, order restored by the staff, we would drift into sleep in our hammocks the right way up, as the planes droned overhead on their way to London.

Not once did the enemy waste a bomb on us, nor were they careless enough to release one by mistake. Far from it! When the fires from London lit up the night skies, they headed for the light and dropped their diabolical loads, adding fuel to the blaze. Fortunately not even a stray bomb was left for us.

The monotonous drone of planes increased on their return until they were overhead. Once again, all held their breath. But no chink of light showed through our heavy blackout drapes and we remained invisible to the enemy above. Hitler's Hall was not visited that night nor any other night for that matter, for the planes had released their death and destruction on the people of London.

Soon the eerie sound of owls hooting to one another in the woods could be heard once again, and the night creatures resumed their life on the ground undisturbed in the shadows, amongst the leaves and beneath the bushes.

"Quietly, girls, quietly!" called the mistresses voices breaking through our laughter. "Back to the dormitories. Quickly, no pushing! And don't shout."

"Take your blankets," V.A.P's eagle eye never missed a thing, "Joan you've forgotten your pillow.

Those girls on the floor of our cellars beneath the hammocks, crawled out of their blankets and bid a hasty retreat as we, in our comfortable containers, tumbled onto anyone unlucky enough to break our fall below. And so we climbed the stairs to the upper regions, in organized disarray, for no one wished to be alone in spooky cellars at midnight The mind of a child can imagine many a ghost of the knights of the Crusades who built that place. Who knows? They may still be there, missing an arm, or a leg, or even a head!

"To bed, girls, to bed." Humm…in my case to bed, if not to sleep.

Sleep was evasive for me those winter months of 1941. My mind so occupied by academic classes during the mornings, and afternoons of winter games, I had no time to think about my mother and Jackie in Singapore, and the war in Southeast Asia. But nighttime was different altogether. As I lay there gazing into the darkness, my friends breathing peacefully in their beds around me, I pictured my mother and Jackie in their beautiful home with their two magnificent young bull terriers, Boxer and Nobby. I was worried, for weeks had passed without letters or news from them.

What little news there was came from the radio in the main hall where we gathered before the evening meal. Girls grouped and talked together in twos and threes to while away the time, before filing into the dining hall. But a few of us gathered around the radio to listen to the 6 o'clock news, read in a dreary monotone as was the fashion of British newscasters in those days.

The Japanese had taken Siam. They were advancing down the Malay Peninsula at breakneck speed through the jungle. Past masters of jungle warfare, they soon overcame any and all resistance, and the gap between them and Singapore decreased at an alarming pace. Attack from the mainland was never anticipated. The guns and defenses of Singapore faced out to sea. No one was ready for the onslaught that was to come and when it came I again heard about it on the radio, from that cold, unfeeling voice. The others were sitting or standing in groups, chatting and laughing, unaware of the horror now taking place.

Suddenly I felt alone in the midst of all those people, afraid and physically sick. But I lined up with the rest to file into supper, taking my usual place at table, eating little, saying nothing, oblivious to the chatter of the girls around me.

That night as I lay in bed and gazed into the darkness, tears ran quietly down my face until, exhausted, blessed sleep released me from the conscious world.

But unknown to me I was not alone those anxious days following the collapse of Singapore. The staff and VAP were keeping a watchful and kindly eye upon me.

One quiet afternoon, alone on my way to the gym, VAP's voice called some distance away,

"Annette, answer the phone at the end of the passage. It's your mother! She is safe and well."

With a whoop of joy I raced full tilt the rest of the way crying aloud, "She's alive, she's alive!"

The staff room door opened. "Annette! No running in the passages! You're shouting…" The voice of a horrified mistress died away at the extraordinary sight of VAP actually laughing at this shocking display and lack of discipline. "It's alright Miss Evens! Let her shout! Her mother is safe. Dorothy Wainwright is on the phone, calling from Australia."

Indeed she *was* calling from Australia. Her voice was faint and she sounded very far away. But it was her own sweet voice telling me she was alive and safe. She was coming home as soon as she could get a passage that she wanted to see me again so very much, and hold me close in a great big hug. No, Jackie was not with her. He was still in Singapore.

With childish lack of tact, I asked if he was ail right.

"I expect so, darling." There was a break in her voice, then "I am longing to see you sweetheart. Take good care of your eyes."

My eyes seemed very unimportant at that moment, there was so much more to say, but the line cracked hopelessly. It was difficult to make out what she was saying and I wanted to catch every word.

"It will take a while to get home, Annette. I have to get a passage on one of the boats and everything is chaos out here with the war and..." The crackling got worse.

"Goodbye darling, goodbye. I am coming home..." her voice crackled again, then faded away.

"Goodbye Mummy," I called. The line went dead, and I stood gazing foolishly at the earpiece in my hand.

I closed my eyes for a moment and breathed a deep sigh of relief before slowly replacing the earpiece on the hook. My own sweet mother was alive and coming home!

Miss Prain was careful to explain to me that it would take time. These were anxious days. There were arrangements to be made, for ships were few and far between, and the journey from Australia would not be easy. "Remember, there is a war on." How could I forget?!.

What she did not tell me was that my mother now had nothing other than what she had managed to throw into a kit bag, and the clothes she had on her back. But again, she did have tremendous courage and pluck, and wonderful friends in England, ready to help in whatever way possible, pulling together to get her home, and through this terrible ordeal. All in all she was more fortunate than some.

After two days of excitement, floating on air with my head in the clouds, I gradually descended to the meaning of work. But this time it took on a more enjoyable aspect.

My eyes had improved, thanks to the care of Dr. Duke Elder and a high protein diet, in spite of rationing. I graduated to the use of a blue crayon, intended to enlarge my writing. But this backfired somewhat. Such was my delight to put crayon to paper after so many months, I got somewhat carried away. The crayon wore down, in need of sharpening after two lines but I failed to stop for so small a detail. In the end the page became a blurry, blue illegible mess. Now it was the turn of any poor, unfortunate staff member to suffer the headaches as they became positively cross-eyed, endeavoring to mark and correct my never ending, almost illegible essays.

CHAPTER II
CAPITULATION OF SINGAPORE

It did indeed take time for my mother to get a passage from Australia where she landed from one of the last ships to leave Singapore. But her numerous and very good friends were only too willing to rally round and offer a helping hand. Some who had escaped the ravages of war in Singapore sailed direct to England. Others who already lived here opened their hearts, their homes and their pocket-books to lend a hand in whatever way they could. Those who escaped the Japanese onslaught found they were not without friends in this country. But some did not make it.

There was a mad, frenzied rush to save what they could during those last terrible days, as wave after wave of bombers dived low to drop their devastating loads. At such times, what comes to mind but the things one loves the most? In her case, my mother tore pictures from walls, scooped others from furniture tops, all landing together in a kit bag, with seven or eight cumbersome photo albums. (Oh! Those memories to be preserved!) Then, common sense taking over as always in any emergency in that sharp mind of hers, jewelry, a couple of dresses and shoes followed, and whatever else she could grab and stuff into the corners of the flexible canvas bag before pulling the cords and closing it tight. All the while agonizing over the dogs—dear wonderful Boxer, and Nobby, and Pushty the cat, who early on had disappeared as cats will do, hopefully to hide in a safe nook or cranny until the horrible racket had ceased. Poor Pushty! He must have hidden for a long, long time before emerging, if he was lucky enough to make it out alive, only to find his world as he knew it, turned upside down.

Hating the noise, Boxer managed to crawl under the couch—how, my mother never could tell. It was so low on the floor, only in desperation would he dream of squeezing beneath it!

There was no time to help them now. With Jackie driving the car, there followed a mad dash to the docks in the fervent hope she would be one of the lucky ones in that seething mass to scramble aboard a boat—any boat, no matter where it was going—to get out of that hellish mess.

The midday heat was appalling; the shouting and tears, the shoving and pushing. With a last embrace Jackie saw her safely aboard.

"Dorothy! Goodbye my darling!"

"Oh Jackie, take care. And Boxer. What about Boxer?"

"I'll take care of Boxer. Don't you worry about him. Goodbye my darling."

There was no time for more endearments, or for either to wonder when they would meet again, if ever. Jackie went back to the battle on shore, while my mother had one of her own—to find a cabin, and fortunately she managed to get a bunk. Six to a cabin for two; some slept on the floors, only too thankful for that small space, to be away from the chaos on shore. Oh, the appalling heat! The air system had broken down. She went on deck.

Heads bobbed in the tepid water as people swam towards ships anchored out in the harbor. Japanese planes flew low and the heads sank to avoid bullets that strafed the surface. My mother almost wept with anger "They were laughing Annette," she told me later—very much later, "Those Japanese pilots were actually laughing! We could see them clearly! They flew so low. They were laughing!" It was a scene she never forgot. Some heads surfaced as people swam frantically on towards the ships and relevant safety. Others did not. They were her friends—those who reached the ships and those who did not.

It was a terrible voyage to Australia. The heat in the cabins was appalling for want of air circulation, but at least a few were blessed with bunks, for space on deck was limited. Children screamed in terror when enemy planes attacked, some threw up. My mother hurled herself over a child whose own mother had been lost in the chaos. Many were seasick, all were afraid. But they got through eventually, and found people waiting to help at the docks. And now, having made contact with friends in Australia and friends in England, and finally her daughter, she arrived, home, at last! They say I am like my mother. If that were so, then all these memories would haunt her for the rest of her life.

London was a seething mass of humanity, both men and women, almost all in uniform, converging on the capital in readiness for what was to come in the days that lay ahead. But war brings out the best in people as well as the worst. Friends welcomed her with open arms and booked her into the only space they could find in London, the prestigious. Green Park Hotel—at their expense, where here she could relax in luxury, recoup and collect her scattered wits. The kindness and generosity shown to those from Australia and the Far East was overwhelming. And it was there at the Green Park Hotel in London, for a few wonderful days, when I was excused from school and able to join her and know that I had a mother again!

All the pent up anxiety and loneliness were now released as we relaxed in our comfortable room. There was so much to talk about, so much to hear—it would take days to express the feeling that was in both our hearts and minds. I was just lost in the joy of having my mother near.

But she, poor dear, had other, very pressing thoughts haunting her mind. She must get a job, and quickly, but must also find a place for us to live, a home for us both. A real home! That would be a new experience for me. I could barely remember a 'home' with my parents. I was six when we left Singapore with my sea-captain father, to enable him to receive the treatment he needed in a good London hospital, and to finally die in peace. Leukemia is a terrible disease. But a new home! When other girls at school would be packing in excitement for trips ' home for the holidays' I too would be 'going home' instead of 'staying with friends or relations.' Not that they were unhappy places; on the contrary, those were wonderful days, packed full of happy memories of weeks by the sea in the company of horses, dogs and other animals, and the sea.

Uppermost in my mother's mind at that moment was work. She must find work, and in some way fight back for all that she had lost, all that she had been through, for the sake of Jackie, now a prisoner in enemy hands. The sooner this awful war came to an end, the sooner he would be free to come home. She *must do her part* to help bring this about, and when my mother put her mind to something she always succeeded.

At that moment however, *my* mind was on other things. Cadbury's chocolate to be precise—the milky kind—the paler, sweeter creamy kind! I wallowed in a bath, filled to the brim with hot water, smelling of lilac and roses, and eyed the stack of chocolate—a gift of the British Red Cross for returning escapees—in their wrappings of blue on the edge of the tub. With dripping wet fingers I carefully unwrapped the slabs with pleasure as the thick, creamy fluid trickled down my throat. It seemed an age since such a treat had come my way. Although three sweets were allowed during naptime after lunch each day, unlike the other girls my 'relations' seldom sent such goodies back with me at the beginning of the term. It would never have entered their heads to do so, and I did not ask. So…these moments must be made to last.

My mother could be heard calling friends on the phone in the next room. "Annette, hurry darling," she called out, "Major Harris is taking us out to lunch at a wonderful restaurant, the Hungarian. You will love it."

Eyeing the stack of chocolate, now considerably reduced, I wondered if there was any room for lunch, but soon enveloped myself in an enormous towel, and was rapidly drying.

When the taxi dropped us at the Hungarian I fell silent, partially due to politeness but more in awe and bewilderment, as I gazed at the ornate red and gold décor and listened to the hub that filled the rooms. The voices were loud and excited, animated as if in anticipation of the unknown. There was a hidden urgency—a purpose, a job to be done to bring some order out of the chaos that had been brought upon the world by one man's maniacal, personal ambitions.

My mother followed my gaze to a pretty woman in navy uniform, "Don't stare, darling, she is part of the Navy, Annette. Women are fighting in the Navy now." I looked back at the girl who was joined by an Air Force officer, then escorted into lunch. "Will I ever be in uniform and have to 'go to war'?" I wondered.

My thoughts were interrupted by a slim, dark-haired officer in Army uniform who greeted my mother with joy and obvious relief. "Dorothy my dear! You are here! Thank God you are safe. We had better get our table. London is packed. Everybody arriving at once at once—all the 'goodbyes' before being sent overseas! Hello Annette! We'll talk at the table dear."

His dark eyes twinkled and I instinctively liked him, but could say nothing, for we were dodging and pushing our way to a table in the wake of the maitre 'd. A pity I never saw him again after that day. But this is the way things went in the war-torn days of the '40s when I was growing up.

We stood up as a couple joined us with hugs and kisses, and great excitement "You're here at last, Dorothy, at last! How is the room?" So! These were the people who had come to our aid and put us up at the Green Park Hotel.

"Oh Jan! How can I ever repay you?"

"No, no, don't say a thing. I am just glad we are able to help. This is Annette?"

I could not take my eyes off this picture of elegant beauty! Tall, slim, exquisitely dressed, a smart little hat, green to tone in with her suit, perched on her short brown hair. As she spoke she sank gracefully into her chair, removing her gloves finger by elegant finger, and placing them on the purse on her lap. Glancing up at her husband, Jan gave him a smile as he saw to her comfort before taking his place at her side.

Looking at Jan, I knew right there and then how I would dress and carry myself when I was free, and 'fledged the nest'. But at this moment however, wide-eyed, I gazed around as conversation flowed on over my head.

Bill Wily, Jan's husband, sported three gold rings of a Captain's rank on his sleeve.

"A big noise in the Navy, Annette" my mother confided, "very important job, darling—all very hush-hush," And with that I had to be content, for this was war and people did not talk about 'these things' in time of war. You never knew who might be standing next to you, who might overhear. That too was all part of my growing up. War and the secrets of war.

"Kitty should be here soon," said Bill.

"Has anyone heard of Tim?" Jan asked, glancing down at the menu.

"Not officially," her husband replied, "but we know he was killed in Singapore." Then softly, his voice full of compassion, "and here they come." A pretty girl, laughing at something her companion said, wound her way through the throng.

"Dorothy, say nothing," Bill said. "Let it come through the right channels. It is better that way my dear," for how do you tell a close friend that her husband did not surface when the Japanese strafed the water with bullets in Singapore harbor a few weeks before?

It was a cheerful reunion as all relaxed in these unusual circumstances, each with their own private thoughts. Jan, seemingly at ease, pondering on Bill's future in his 'high-up, hush-hush job,' for radar was in its infancy, and he was part of that enterprise.

Major Harris was taking a break before traveling north for 'special training.' With what I never knew.

Kitty chatted away to my mother. Yes, Jackie was alive, but in Japanese hands, and if *she* had news of Jackie, then news of Tim must be imminent any day now! She laughed and was happy with anticipation, never dreaming the worst. She turned to me with her lovely smile. "Annette. So! You go back to school tomorrow. Then what are you going to do?"

I opened my mouth to answer but before I could say a thing my mother did it for me. "Annette goes back to school tomorrow, then on to secretarial college," she said in matter-of-fact tones, then added "don't you, darling?" as if that last phrase mattered!

I gazed at her in silence. There seemed little point in trying to gainsay my mother, so I closed my mouth again, it was the only thing to do.

Kitty, playing with the stem of her glass, leaned back in her chair watching and grinning, her head a little on one side. She looked quizzically from me to my mother. "Dorothy?"

"Oh! She has some crazy idea about going onto the stage. Such nonsense! She has to get a decent job, and with a good secretarial training she can do anything and go anywhere."

Kitty looked back at me. "I don't know," she murmured. "I think Annette might make a very good little actress."

"Oh really Kitty!" My mother almost expressed exasperation. "How can you say such a thing? No daughter of mine is ever going onto the stage." As I happened to be her only daughter, my future looked pretty bleak as far as I could see. " Now don't put such ideas into her head." Her tone was final and she turned to speak to Major Harris.

Kitty transferred her gaze to me once more. Did I detect sympathy and understanding in the look she gave me before turning to see my mother's back erect and firm? Could she foresee the inevitable battle of wills looming ahead?

The party broke up after lunch, each one going their own separate way, and in the back of their minds, each one hoping—with a silent wish—a silent prayer they would all meet again in happier times. But it was all so uncertain.

I never saw Major Harris again. I wonder why ?

The following day we left the luxury of the Green Park Hotel. The taxi was waiting to take us on a round about route to Kings Cross Station. The blitz on London had transformed parts of the once beautiful city into rubble. One could see the devastation and sense the tragedy and fear now dominating people's lives. As we drove down deserted streets through a residential area, I was reminded of the dolls house from my early childhood days. The front opened on hinges, revealing the perfect interior of my dolls' habitation. Little rooms with miniature furniture, the tables set for meals, the sheets turned down on little beds in readiness for their tiny occupants.

But we were driving through something not only very real, but life size towering above us. The outer walls were not on hinges. Some lay in rubble in the streets, others had already been cleared away. But the floors were there, and the furniture strangely unscathed. Looking up as we passed we could see a kitchen table with its blue and white checked cloth, the edges of which waved gently in the morning breeze. The table set, probably for the mid-day meal. The other side of the passage was the bathroom, almost intact, with towels still on the racks, but the wash basin hanging precariously by its pipes over the edge of the floor, ready to plunge into the rubble below. The beds in another room had their spreads still on them and the dressing table was there with its chair undisturbed. It was as if a giant knife had sliced off the outer wall.

My mother looked at me in a way that told me she would have given anything to prevent my witnessing this scene. "Too young" she seemed to be thinking, "too young to see any of this. It will remain with her for years to come."

"And the animals?" I wondered to myself. My mind always hovered round the animals—the cats and the dogs, all innocent victims of man's destruction. What happened to them in the terror of the moment? As if reading my thoughts, my mother's hand reached for mine. Not a word was said, but our thoughts prevailed.

Then, passing through this deserted residential area we found ourselves suddenly plummeted, as it were, into another part of London almost unscathed.

I have always enjoyed the atmosphere and 'smells' of London stations which are unique unto themselves—the sound hissing of steam released in clouds from the engines into the air and onto the platform. My mother and I dodged the clouds as we searched for a suitable carriage and a corner seat by a window. The crash and clatter of metal on metal as those mighty engines shunted back and forth, causing carriages to collide one after the other in chain reaction. The great, gray pigeons that frequent London stations, waddled over the platforms, bobbing their pretty heads as they hurried out of the way of approaching feet, searching for crumbs and crusts of bread, or discarded sandwiches, showing no signs of fear. After all, they were the ones who lived there, away up in the rafters, high above the hustle and bustle of trains and humanity, their roosting place at night. One rose with a mighty flutter of wings as it carried its heavy body high up above, from whence its deep throated cooing joined in the chorus of its mates and others of its kind. What would London's stations be like without its beloved pigeons?

A feather floated down. I tried to catch it, but it dodged my outstretched hand. With a little laugh I bent down and picked it up to prevent it being crushed and ruined by a heavy foot.

"Annette, come on darling. You'll miss the train."

"Oh! I don't mind Mummy."

"Really, dear!" she exclaimed, then smiled. We were not used to each other's ways as yet.

I hung out of the window and waved to her as the train slowly made its way out of Kings Cross Station, picking up momentum as it cleared the suburbs as it began its run through the countryside. Then I settled back in a corner seat—the carriage all to myself. And through the open window came a rush of wind and sweet fragrance of God's good fresh air.

Clickity-clack, clickity-clack, clickity-clickity-clickity-clack. With the rhythm of the wheels on the rails and the swaying of the train I closed my eyes. A lot had taken place. There was much to think about, both the past and future. What drama to imprint itself on the mind of one so young. I must have dozed.

When I opened my eyes the fields, the trees and hedge groves of Hertfordshire, the sheep, the cows, the sparrows and crows, familiar things that could be seen and loved again, and all the while a soft, little gray feather lay in the palm, of my hand.

And so it was back to school, to work, to play and advance in preparation for final examinations.

*****

Was my mother's conscious bothering her when she gave me a gift of Shakespeare's plays and sonnets, or was she hoping the massive work might deter my enthusiasm for a stage career? No matter what, my love affair with his plays began as a child in boarding school and soon became one of my most cherished possessions. Many an hour was spent in the gardens of Princess Helena College, flipping through the pages edged with gold, gazing at the colored illustrations, not really appreciating at that time the names of the artists who spent days, weeks and months shaping their works of art.

I loved the feel of the leather cover—a soft burgundy color with Shakespeare's crest in gold in the center. The smell of the book mingled with the fragrance of the soft grass on which I lay, and the roses in the well-kept beds around me.

In those days young ladies at boarding school were none too careful with ink contained in small wells at the top, right hand corner of the desks. As I dipped the nib of my fountain pen into the fluid it splattered leaving a blue stain at the bottom of a few pages. Dismayed, I tried unsuccessfully to rub it out. Now I realize, it adds to the history of this book, my constant companion, which has accompanied me wherever I have traveled throughout my life.

There were to be many moves in the course of my life but the first impressive was to secretarial college in the early days of 1944. After endless confrontations with my mother, my desires for a stage career came to nothing—her excuse, 'the war'. I had to take a training that would get me a "sensible job" and help with the "war effort". However, in sending me to the Triangle Secretarial College, at that time evacuated to Gerrards Cross, courtesy of Hitler, she placed me in the one strategic spot that would mean so much to me in the future: close to the country home of Laurence Olivier.

But it was not a happy time for me. I hated shorthand and was not good at it. Bookkeeping was even worse. Typing, well that was more amusing. We typed to music, gramophone records, and as the tempo increased so did our speed and prowess on the typewriter. But what I found more interesting—the business side of the course—forming and composing business letters.

Another reason for my low spirits I was—in my opinion—horribly unattractive. My mother made no bones about it! The high protein diet to improve my sight had a devastating affect on my figure at that adolescent age when young girls seem to 'blow up'. She was forever warning me that if I did not diet I would never be able to wear the lovely clothes for which I yearned, and if I did not exercise seemingly morning, noon and night I would never look attractive. She impressed upon me that early morning walks would help to do the trick. So, as the sun got up, I dragged myself out of bed, donned walking shoes and suitable attire, walked tip-toe down deserted passages past closed doors behind which my fellow students slept in peace. I gritted my teeth as I crept down stairs that squeaked, through the deserted hall and heavy front door holding my breath, as the door had a tendency to slam, and so out onto the gravel drive to the road beyond.

The air was crisp and fresh those early mornings as the sun was rising. Mist hung about the hedge groves and country roads, down which I walked at a "good brisk pace" in accordance with my mother's instructions, past open gates leading to other country homes where, in my imagination, other people were folded in the comfort of sleep and happy oblivion, not on a crazy quest for a "decent figure" as I was.

My mind dwelled on one pair of gates that were always open. Beyond them a short curving drive led to an attractive house that lay back from the road, belonging to Laurence Olivier. The parents of a friend and fellow student were, in turn, friends of the famous actor who at that time was working on the movie of Shakespeare's *Henry V*. They kindly proffered an introduction, so it did not come as a complete surprise when I strolled in one early morning, book in hand. Indeed it was I who had the surprise and was thrown into complete confusion when the door opened revealing the great man himself! However his charm and friendliness soon put me at my ease. He seemed to understand a young girl's longing to go into a profession seemingly so hopelessly out of reach, namely to go on the stage. When I handed him the leather-bound book, he was impressed by my choice of reading material.

After glancing at some of the beautiful pictures and photographs of original Shakespeare scenes, Olivier signed his name on the back of a colored illustration of Anthony and Cleopatra.

I gladly refrained from partaking of breakfast that day. Indeed I was far too excited to think of food and could barely keep my attention focused on Pitman's shorthand. Olivier's words of wisdom kept running through my head. "Annette, take what you can get and then look round for what you want." The secretarial course, however dreary, took on new meaning for me, especially when short notes of encouragement from Olivier arrived in the mail.

The works of Shakespeare soon became one of my main sources of relaxation and remained so throughout my life. Pitman was banished to the far recesses of my mind—bookkeeping classes forgotten as the small print captured my imagination, I became lost in the adventures of Anthony and Cleopatra. I would turn the page opposite Olivier's name, pride of ownership swelling in my heart, and take possession. As I read on in peace, I knew that nothing and no one could take this sensation from me—my interest and fascination in the world of the theatre increased.

CHAPTER III
BLETCHLEY PARK

As abruptly as was my entry into college, so was the exit, for again my mother's wishes were to influence my life. She was working in the Foreign Office in those turbulent times, doing "her part" towards winning the war, and longing for her husband's release from Japanese POW camp. As deputy in charge of two hundred young women Women's Royal Navel Reserve (WRNS) in the Naval branch, her influential friends "pulled strings," so that I too found myself if not alongside, in close proximity as a civil servant working for the British Government. A far cry from the stage—but I had little choice—not yet of age, and what seemed a very long way from 21.

She had made up her mind that I was to be a codest, determined that her daughter would be in an equally as prestigious a part of the organization as she was herself. But at that time I had no idea what I was getting into or what this organization was all about.

Of course she was pleased. I was not only to be in Bletchley Park, but in one of the most sought-after places in the Park,—not as a cipher-breaker but as a Codest, wrapped in the secrecy of *Hut 10,* under the care of an elderly, but kindly matron, a certain Miss Montgomery. However I was not so thrilled. A codest? Why was my mother preening herself in such delight, bragging to her friends about "the wonderful job Annette was going to do?" What on earth *was* a codest anyway? And in the MI6 too! How was I to know I was going to work for the Secret Intelligence Service—a name one never dared mention aloud—nor ever whisper to oneself!

"Darling don't grumble" she'd say, "You don't know what a lucky little devil you are. Any other person would give their eyes to do what you are going to do. All in the service of your country too!"

I didn't feel at all like "a lucky little devil." In fact I felt thoroughly rebellious. This was *not* leading towards the bright lights of the theatre; and it was with nervous trepidation I headed towards the office of a very important individual called Mr. Nigel de Grey before entering

Bletchley Park for the very first time. Who was this Mr. Nigel de Grey? How was I to know that he was one of the great code breakers of the First World War?

I was horribly nervous—quite unnecessarily as it turned out. When his eyes fell on the painfully shy young girl standing in front of him, floundering in something about which she knew absolutely nothing, the security speech he normally gave was altered somewhat—it was firm of course, but kindly imparted. Never, but *never* was I to speak about my work to anyone outside the Park, but also *inside* the Park outside my *Hut!*

"How long for?" I asked shyly.

"Never—never in your life" came the surprising reply.

"Oh! All right." I said. And that was that! "Now sign this paper" he said and added "It is the Official Secrets Act—everyone who comes through the gates into Bletchley Park must sign this."

I picked up a pen, dipped it in the ink and signed away my vocal freedom presumably for life.

Aware of the gentle smile of Miss Montgomery standing by my side, I was delivered into the kindly hands of my very first *boss* to go in search of my billet.

After one or two disastrous and unsuccessful attempts at living together for the first time since my infancy, in excessively uncomfortable and dreary digs—where our elderly landlady peeked out at passers-by on the main street, through drab lace curtains from her rocking chair in a darkened sitting room—my mother unceremoniously installed me in the girls' hostel adjacent to the Bletchley Park estate. This was built to house the female staff in the organization not billeted out with the local population. *Nobody* lived in the Park; everybody was billeted out. The Army and Air Force had a huge encampment at the back, but all civilians and all Royal Naval personnel were billeted for miles and miles around.

Without a child hanging round her neck, my mother managed to find and move to, a more luxurious billet in the stately country home of two brothers, one of whom was a General, who had served in the First World War and now retired. General Blount's home stood in a spacious, well kept garden. He was fortunate to still have servants to look after the house and care for the beautiful garden, despite his complaints that the place was not kept up to its former standard. Cocktails were served on time, and a maid in a pretty little uniform waited at table. Changing for dinner once again, and living what she called a more civilized life, raised my mother's morale tremendously, but with one drawback. She was allotted the bedroom of a former maid, whilst her younger colleague from Bletchley luxuriated in the main guest bedchamber! This infuriated her and I had to keep a poker face to keep from laughing when she expostulated wrathfully on the subject on the few occasions when we met. Although somewhat bleak, it was not an ugly room, and I considered her extremely fortunate when comparing it to my own. Besides she was able to wine and dine with elegance in luxury.

On arrival at the hostel Miss Montgomery led me down the narrow passage until we came to an open door and she handed me a key. I stood on the threshold, eyeing with some misgiving the minute portion allotted to me for the duration. I discovered that whatever way I turned, twisted, cajoled my huge cabin trunk (a relic of the Singapore days) it was quite impossible to get it and myself into the free space of my bedroom—the room that was to become the only place I could call my own. I found that by dragging one end of the trunk into that room, then standing on my tiny bed, I could open the lid, but then it was impossible to open the wardrobe against which the lid rested, or for that matter any of the three drawers in the dressing table. Firstly I could not reach them from my precarious position on the bed, and secondly the trunk itself prevented them opening more than a couple of inches.

By now my antics had attracted the attention of my fellow occupants of this rather uncomfortable place and they good-naturedly offered some helping hands. Finely, in frustrated desperation with their help, we dragged the wretched thing out into the passage, where it fitted securely from wall to wall when opened. From there I proceeded to squeeze its contents into the minute hanging space and tiny drawers, happily oblivious of the fact my new friends found it necessary to step in the middle of the open trunk as they passed from one end of the passage to the other, on the way to their various destinations. This somewhat unique introduction to my fellow workers gained me new, if not life-long, then at least close friends for the duration of the war. By far the youngest person at Bletchley Park I was immediately taken under their wing, for I was desperately shy and grateful to anyone who threw me a kindly word or glance.

Once settled in my own domain, Miss Montgomery—a lady with the gentle eyes—again materialized and led me across the Park, dotted with several large Huts. We stopped at the door of one where she ruled over her band of girls. At each table, running down either side of a lengthy room sat, four young women bent over their work, concentrating on pages and pages of figures. No one spoke as they puzzled out their mathematical problems, turning figures into words from incoming messages and *visa versa* for outgoing replies. It was here what had jokingly become know as the cream of the park—"the Babes"—a friendly acknowledgement of respect by those outside *Hut 10*. Although they had no idea as to what we were doing, other inmates of Bletchley Park were anxious to get better acquainted with the charming, attractive, but strange young ladies. We were not in any way superior in our attitude, but definitely somewhat reserved, no doubt brought about by the very nature of our work. We were encoding to, and decoding messages from, what can only be described as exceptionally brave people—agents behind the enemy lines. Working with these unseen heroes—both men and women—during the following year, cast an indelible impression on my young mind. I longed to be with them out there in the field, gathering information, facing danger and excitement, and enacting brave deeds for my country. My imagination ran wild. Oh well! This I suppose was the next best thing.

Bletchley Park was folded in a cloak of secrecy with men and women breaking ciphers from anywhere where information could be obtained—German, Italian and Japanese (after 1941,) Swedish, Swiss, Vichy French, Portuguese, Spanish, Libyan, Iraqi, Turkey, Rumanian, Hungarian, Bulgarian—anywhere in the world. If in a place where information could be used to end this horrible war, ciphers were attacked. Imagine someone sitting there trying to break a Bulgarian cipher! It was a very busy hive of activity that I as yet knew nothing about, but was unwittingly drawn into, joining about eight thousand nine hundred people in 1944—just a tiny cog in an awe inspiring organization!

Equally unknown to me, Bletchley Park was only a part of a world wide allied international intelligence net. A triangle with Bletchley Park on one corner, Arlington on the other, with United States army and U.S navy code breakers on the other side, and in the base, Melbourne and Brisbane in Australia. Together we were the three main code-breaking and coding sites, manned by the end of the war by both British and Americans, working in each others countries, and in Australia manned by British, American, Australian, and Canadian. We were all coding and breaking ciphers. A worldwide effort together—a worldwide organization with probably half a million people working as interceptors, de-crypters and codests—and *not one of us* in Bletchley Park broke our vow of silence. We said we would say nothing about it, and nothing was ever said. Nothing. We kept our word. Instinctively, we knew we had to, if only to avoid annihilation by the enemy. The ultimate horrors of war were yet to surface, Belsen, Auschwitz, Dachau and other such ghastly places.

But for me, having made the first leap into Bletchley Park and across the threshold of *Hut 10* my war work was about to commence over countless heavy-duty white mugs. I was initiated by another girl of my age into the art of making tea. First, the water had to be boiled over a gas ring. The enormous enamel pot was then warmed with scalding water then emptied before ladling in heaped spoonfuls of black Indian tea, renowned to be the very best for drooping lids and weary eyes, warding of that blissful oblivion known as sleep. How we managed to avoid serious injure remains a mystery. When steam screamed its fury it was time to brace one's muscles, lift the hissing monster and pour the water onto the imposing mound covering the bottom of the pot. One waited three whole minutes, for apparently that was the *art* of preparing the perfect concoction. For then, and only then, would the liquid that flowed from the spout be firm enough for the proverbial spoon to stand upright in the delicious brew.

The cups now full to the brim, were carried carefully, so carefully as to not to spill one precious drop, together with a large bowl of sugar and a can of thick gooey condensed milk, into the room where silence reigned as ladies toiled, four to a table, with heads bent low over their work. We youngsters, who were virtually none-existent to those women in that silent hive of industry, left our works of art and returned to our own little niche in the pantry, there to chat quietly until it was time to creep once more into the holy of holies and retrieve the tray, now considerably lighter, for surprisingly every drop of the horrible brew had not only been consumed, but appreciated.

Needless to say it was not long before I decided that all those months of secretarial training, however dreary, were surely destined for something better than this. Besides, I longed to become one of the silent band of heads-bent-low and have the brew, however obnoxious, brought to me. I applied to the powers that be—in this case the elderly, gray-haired lady with the kindly face—and stated firmly that I wanted to join the band of silent ones. This was the moment for which she had been waiting—a word, a request from me, and behind the scenes a sigh of relief, a smile of delight from her friend, my mother!

Life now took on an exciting aspect. Poor and lazy at school as far as mathematics were concerned; I now had to pull myself together. Hours at a time, I began to work with figures—groups of figures—hundreds and hundreds of groups of figures coming over the teleprinter machine that thundered its importance in a room far from the silence of ours. Agents in other countries surreptitiously tapped their coded messages in Morse to our people who sent them by teleprinter to *Hut 10* to be transposed.

It was Churchill who kept us going through the darkest days of the war, forever inspiring us with his dynamic speeches over the radio "…I have nothing to offer you but blood, tears, toil and sweat" and it was Mr. Churchill who knew the importance of decrypted messages. He recalled an incident that took place in World War I when, as First Lord of the Admiralty, three German cruisers gave chase to the Russians up the Baltic when fog hampered their progress. They turned back, but in doing so one ran aground on rocks. At that moment more of the Russian fleet appeared. The two German ships bid a hasty retreat over horizon leaving the "Magduburg" to her fate! Before abandoning ship the communications staff put the German Imperial navy high-seas ciphers into a *weighted* canvas bag with eyelets to let in the water. One they threw over the side but, in their anxiety, left the other on the upper deck.

Retrieved by the boarding party, the Top Secret Cipher of the Imperial German Navy went to our allies at St Petersburg and from there it was brought to London, where it came into the possession of the British Admiralty and Mr. Winston Churchill! There a small group of code breaking personnel started using this book to break the cipher that enabled us—the British—to keep track of the enemy throughout that war!

Churchill remembered this when we declared war on Germany on September 3rd 1939. He was again First Lord of the Admiralty and within a week he contacted the First Sea Lord in command of the Royal Navy to the effect that he "hoped that they were making arrangements for German submarines sunk in shallow water to be investigated for the contents of their cryptographic material." He knew the value of decrypted messages and immediately became the spur that bought on the modern British system of cryptanalysis.

At the end of the First World War the Admiralty secret section was amalgamated with the Army, taken over by the Foreign Office that became the Government code and cipher school—the backbone until 1939.

Realizing that another war was eminent—not *if* but *when*—MI5 went on tour of the country looking for a suitable spot in which to continue their very successful code breaking activities. They chanced upon Bletchley Park and saw that sold to developers it was due to be demolished for a housing development, complete with all the beautiful gardens around it. So, they announced to the buyers that there were two problems. Problem number one—they no longer owned the property, the government did; and problem number two they could put the house back to its useable state, complete with the beautiful gardens!

In 1940 when the Government moved in, the top floor, once Lady Fanny's personal suite—became the Italian Naval decrypt. Two other rooms became the RAF intelligence where decrypting of the German day and night fighter ciphers took place. The enemy 'planes never took off from the same base twice in a row purposely to avoid attracting our own aircraft. They switched airfields. If the British were able to break the German cipher each and every day, they would know exactly from which field the fighters were operating and could therefore divert our bombers around them—hopefully reducing the number of our losses. Quite ingenious!

The *huts* that dotted the landscape when I arrived in 1944 looked somewhat out of place against the backdrop of the large country mansion. But it was the stable yard that held the greatest secret of all: in two cottages that at one time belonged to the former grooms—the corn store for the horses (now long gone) and the tack room, was housed a copy of Hitler's famous Top Secret Enigma Cipher Machine. This enciphered messages to and from his armed forces in the field—troop movements, the amount of ammunition, machinery and armaments on the move, and the exact locations to where they were being sent. And it was there on January 24th 1940, the twenty-seven year old British genius Alan Turing, with Gordon Welchman—a former mathematician don from Kings College Cambridge, worked on and broke the Enigma keys day by day.

This was vital for us at Dunkirk and during the Battle of Britain. By intercepting and decrypting these messages, we were able to see just how fast the German army was moving. By May 10th they were in France—by breaking the Enigma cipher we knew exactly where they were going. The movement of the German forces was sent up to London and with actual map references, those in command suddenly realized we had lost the battle of France and must evacuate the army. On May 17th, stationed at Dover, Vice Admiral Ramsey was ordered to start Operation Dynamo—the withdrawal of British troops via Dunkirk, Calais and Cherbourg. A call went over the radio for anyone who owned a boat to drop whatever they were doing and get over to France to save the men. And so they did. They came out in small boats, ships, little boats and big boats. The British army abandoned its stores on the beaches of Dunkirk—but three hundred and twenty thousand troops were brought back from France. That was the value of Bletchley Park—and that was what I was joining, totally oblivious of the importance of the place or the work that I was privileged to do! Although in a different part of the Park, I wished I had been just that little bit older to fully appreciate and understand what it was all about.

Then came the Battle of Britain. And they came! Waves of German planes in their hundreds—great clouds of heavy bombers lumbering under their loads with the light weight fighter escorts weaving in and out, darkening the English skies—and we British kept score as if it were a cricket match. A hundred and forty-six to twenty—we shot down a hundred and forty-six and they did away with twenty!

We kept it light, but Air Vice Marshal Hugh Dowding, Commander-in-Chief of fighter command had a problem—by the end of the Battle of France we had lost many Hurricanes and Spitfires to defend the United Kingdom against a thousand first line bombers, let alone the German Messerschmitts and FR109 night fighter squadrons. Although severely out numbered, Bletchley Park came in once again!

From *Hut 3* information concerning exact movements of German Army and Air force of the Battle of France—complete with map references—was sent to London, and it was that same hut that provided the information for Air Vice Marshal Hugh Dowding C. in C. Fighter Command, *and he was concerned.* Were we losing fighters faster than we were knocking down the German bombers? In other words, were we going to win the Battle of Britain? He turned to the people in Bletchley Park. Each night, before the following day's raid, each Luftwaffe squadron facing us in Holland, Belgium and France sent by radio to the Paris head quarters, the German battle orders encrypted in Enigma. The number of available aircraft, how many not available, the number of available crew members, how many were sick and the number lost; bomb loads, fuel loads, *everything* we wanted to know. In that way the Luftwaffe headquarters made their plans for the following day for the Battle of Britain. But every transmission that they made by radio was intercepted by stations high up on the Dunstable Downs in Bedfordshire, and around England and were sent to Bletchley Park to be decrypted!

By 8 o'clock and certainly by nine at the latest, from August 28th every single morning in the Battle of Britain, Dowding knew *exactly* how many German aircraft were to attack us that day. He knew precisely how many were available. So if he subtracted those available that day, from the ones available yesterday—as reported by Bletchley Park—he knew the number of their losses, and he could tell if their losses exceeded ours and if we were going to win the Battle of Britain. All this information from dedicated people in a *hut* tucked away in a corner of Bletchley Park, miles away from the action but absolutely pivotal in our battle for the world!

The one extraordinary fact was the Germans never bombed us! Security was so tight even devoid of camouflage—they were under the impression it was one of thousands of army and air force camps dotted around the British Isles. Why drop a few bombs on them? And we were left alone!

Until 1943 the Americans were not accepted into Bletchley Park. The lack of co-operation between the U.S Army and Navy intelligence in Arlington which—they insisted—was "full of security holes". So, if they couldn't trust each other, how on earth were we, the British expected to trust them with the greatest secret of all times—Hitler's Enigma Secret Code, used by the entire German forces? It only needed a single leak and we would be left completely in the dark. From the outset of the war, our success at Bletchley Park had literally been our lifeline and before joining us at the Park the Americans had to accept our high standards of security. It was very, very serious, but when eventually their security *was* brought up to British standards, an agreement was signed with Sir William Travis, head of Bletchley Park, on May 1st in 1943 and two hundred Americans were working side by side with the British very successfully in 1944. That was when I stepped somewhat nervously over the threshold—and they scared me half to death!

Hardly aware of the importance of the opposite sex, my sheltered childhood into woman-hood had not prepared me for the sudden jolt into the world of reality and all its implications…

CHAPTER IV
COMRADES IN ARMS THE AMERICANS!

We were invaded yes, but not by the Germans. It was the Americans who descended upon us, which was much more to our liking. Our island seemed to be one seething mass of khakied masculine humanity, all speaking an unfamiliar language which, surprisingly, we more or less understood. Having resided in a girl's boarding school since the age of eight, then thrust into a young ladies college, followed by a department almost entirely manned by women, this latest development was quite mind-boggling. Why, I could never understand, but it was out here in the country during the World War II that the Americans first made an indelible impression on my mind.

They were here to prepare for the invasion of Europe. As soon as their security was brought up to standard—our standard—two hundred of them crossed the sacred threshold to work with us at Bletchley Park. They decoded with us—nothing was barred from them. We shared the information and they were the ones who decided what the President would see in America, not withstanding the fact that we were facing the Japanese as well!

But life was not all work. War maybe, but relaxation was eminently necessary—so realized the powers that be. Out there in the country peace and quiet was in abundance. On the estate we had our lake, the lawns on which to lie, weather permitting, and trees that spread their branches, offering shade. In peacetime, life progressed at a slow and lazy pace in that part of England. Villages and isolated cottages graced its beauty. But in the Forties all were jolted out of their dreamy existence. Every empty room that did not boast a living being in each an every house and cottage now had someone 'billeted' upon them. It *was* the happy invasion of the Americans!

During working hours, everyone at Bletchley Park became engrossed in whatever job they were doing. My mother was in charge of two hundred girls, but I knew nothing of that. It never occurred to me to ask on what it was that she was working. Sadly we seldom met, and when we did our meetings were brief, surrounded by a throng of people who gathered in the main reception hall or recreation room before or during lunch breaks. People from every department or *hut* mingled and talked as if their very existence depended on these breaks from the life saving work they all performed. Middle aged and young alike, men and women in uniform and civilian clothes, all talking at the double—all, that is except for me! What *did I* have to talk about? This was my first experience of the outside world so nervous and out of place.

Yet some of my colleagues made life worthwhile. There were two Jeans—Jean Gibson the Jean Walters. They were best friends in their twenties. Both tall, one light the other a dark brunette, kind hearted with a delightful sense of humor. If there was a drawback with the similarity of their names it did not disturb the Jeans. Although *they* called each other and got a reply with perfect ease, should anyone else address them by name, a dual response would be received, sometimes both in agreement—sometimes not. This could lead to all sorts of complications. In exasperated desperation they eventually were known as Jean One and Two—not very imaginative, but affective!

The Jeans sat at the same table working in *hut 10,* and I sat with them. We invariably had meals together, and made a threesome for the dances in the assembly hall. One or two of Jean Gibson's evening dresses came my way. They had to be cut down to size, but why not? Where coupons were involved, anything was acceptable.

Then there were Liz and Phillip, both who wore army officer uniform. Of course, I never enquired nor cared *where* they worked. This was war and the secrets of war continued to dominate my life. Away from the office, the mind switched and relaxed—that was all there was to it. Liz was an exquisite blond—slender with blue eyes and soft gentle voice—a perfect match beside her handsome man. They were engaged to be married. Why they befriended such an unattractive little bundle seemed a mystery, but their hearts were as great as their appearance. When first they took me back to their humble billet and asked what I would like to for lunch, I replied, without a moments hesitation,

"Scrambled eggs on a piece of toast," relishing the thought, unaware that this would mean there delving into a into their precious ration of eggs. The anxious glance that flashed between them brought me to my senses and, horribly embarrassed at my thoughtlessness, I turned a firry red! With my composure finally restored by their understanding, we sat around a cozy kitchen fire to devour the most delicious scrambled eggs on toast, the memory of which remains with me to this day. Like so many poignant moments, I often wonder what happened to that wonderful couple.

Normally, I joined the others for sustenance in the cafeteria where both Americans and British passed through in a never-ending stream. The food, if not exciting, was nourishing and many, like me relied on it for meals three times a day. Even now, so many years later, when I see a dish of shredded cabbage, invariably I recall the cafeteria of the Forties with some amusement. Between us we consumed mountains of shredded cabbage at Bletchley Park. I wonder if I sometimes rubbed shoulders with Alan Turing over a dish of shredded cabbage. What a privilege that would have been!

Bletchley Park was a hive of industry with hundreds of minds working together—a vitally important part within the general scheme of things—joining the allied forces to bring about the invasion of Europe. From the very top to the lowest rank, each person had a vital job to perform—even down to making a cup of tea to bring relief to tired and weary minds. It was now my turn to be grateful for the strengthening brew.

Our allies—the Americans—relaxed with us. On summer days, the sound of their laughter and strange accent mingled with that of our British voices as we initiated them into the art of "rounders" as apposed to their national game of Baseball—or was it visa versa? Sometimes they just lazed on the grass in the shade of the trees before returning to their various huts and work. And on occasions when, unbeknown to us, the great man himself visited Bletchley Park, Churchill would stand at his favorite window at the top of the building, quietly watching the events of the Park. Unimaginable responsibilities lay on the shoulders of that incredible man. Did he smile as the allies became acquainted or was his mind on other things—possibly the origins of the Enigma?

In the evenings, American officers from surrounding camps would laughingly descend upon us. Arriving literally in truckloads, to fill our recreational hall to overflowing and dance away the night hours in frenzied exuberance to bands brought with them from America, the like of which we had never seen. I found it difficult to take my eyes away from Glenn Miller and his band, high up on the stage. The brilliant lights reflected in their brass instruments, from which strange sounds emanated as they tested and warmed up for a mighty burst of music. At a signal from the leader, their music flooded the enormous hall and uniformed men took ladies in their arms, and swept them onto the floor. Loud talk and happy laughter, together with the music, belied what was subconsciously at the back of everybody's mind—War and what in the immediate future lay ahead?

Glenn Miller led his band as they blasted away on their glittering instruments. The more energetic of the couples danced up a frenzied storm, as if to grasp whatever enjoyment they could, before coming down to earth, in anticipation of what lay ahead miles away, across a narrow strip of water, on whatever beaches they were due to meet their destiny, where soon all hell would break loose. Now was the time to grasp life to the full, because for many there would be no other dance.

Momentarily out of breath, I relaxed and stood to one side by the wall and watched it going on around me, so near and yet so far away. It was as if my body was separated from my hovering soul—absorbed, yet not living in these moments. So many of these men, handsome in their uniforms, alive and carefree, enjoying every moment with British girls, would soon be lying dead, face down on France's hostile sandy shore.

As if realizing that everyone was by now quite be out of breath, the leader and his band played to a different beat—soft and slow, the lights dimmed and uniformed men drew their partners close. Shadows moved gently on the floor as long gowns floated round the room. Now dancing cheek-to-cheek emotions ran high. Some thought of wives and sweethearts left behind them in America, realizing that they may never meet again. And the others? Well, others seemingly had different ideas! Hearts were lost and won in the excitement of the moment.

Once again, I found myself drawn to the present by a pair of arms belonging to a slim young officer, but now our movements were short-lived, for when the drums rolled and went on rolling, dancing ceased. My partner turned to his friend near by, an officer dancing with my friend Joan.

"Gundy! Have you heard this man on the drums?" There was excitement in his voice, his blue eyes shone with anticipation. When his buddy shook his head he continued. "It's incredible! Just listen. No one can play the drums the like him!" Then, with a little laugh, "No one moves when this man plays!"

Sure enough, the couples were gravitating expectantly towards the stage, and we moved with them, to watch and listen to the magic of the drums, as a very young, good-looking Buddy Rich, first coaxed, then drew out those magical sounds as only he knew how, into an ever increasing, mighty crescendo. His colleagues put down their glittering instruments and paused for a while, as he took center stage. The baton came to rest and Buddy had his way, disappointing none. On he played, and on the floor no one danced, but listened and watched enthralled. Eventually, one by one, the other members of the band picked up their instruments as their leader joined the tempo with his arm. And once again all were drawn together by the rhythm of the drums. Music played as spontaneous applause broke out with shouts of joy and admiration we began to dance, and dance the night away.

By the end of the evening Joan concluded she was in love, and after another two weeks my tall, slim, beautiful friend accepted Gundy's proposal of marriage. I blinked rapidly a couple of times, but other than that showed no surprise as we went about our daily work, Joan now floating on air, and I plodding along behind, like a happy little puppy dog. However, sparks flew when her equally tall and beautiful but very much wiser elder sister, Connie, got wind of these developments.

"What in heaven's name do you think you're doing? He's an *American* Joan. What makes you think he is going to *marry* you?" Her voice rose in agitation over concern for her younger sister. "These men are going to fight a war. He's not serious. Besides he may be dead in a couple of weeks. Anything can happen." Joan tried unsuccessfully to interrupt the tirade, but Connie was unrelenting.

Listening, wide-eyed I watched the sisters battled it out, polite but firm on either side. Forever loyal to my faltering friend, I trotted after her as she made her way to the main building, passing through the hall and sitting room, where people were relaxing after lunch. Ultimately we arrived at the telephone room, and for lack of a shoulder on which to weep, Joan was bent on calling her fiancée for consolation. Unfortunately all the booths were occupied—breaks and lunch hours were popular times for people to snatch a few moments away from their desks to talk to loved ones at home.

A lovely dark haired WRNS in navy uniform smiled as she waited ahead of us and took her place in the booth that opened first. Stepping inside, she picked up the receiver, slipped the coins into the machine and dialed the number she wanted but forgot to close the door to give her the privacy normally desired. At that moment the door to the booth beside her opened and a man stepped out, leaving it vacant for Joan. Built for one—too much of a squeeze for two—our door was also open, allowing me to hand Joan the necessary coins and hold her purse, whilst she searched for Gundy's number which she began to dial. By the time we had juggled ourselves into the space and a relatively comfortable position, the pretty WRNS next door was speaking audibly to someone at the other end of the line.

"Hush!" Joan silenced my queries as to what coin she needed next. I looked up at her face, as it changed colour at a most alarming rate—first red, then green, then an ashen shade of grey. I followed her gaze through the glass to the next booth, and listened.

"Please will you leave him a message? Tell him his fiancée called. Yes. For Captain Gundison. Captain Gundison," she repeated, "and tell him I will be free this evening, after six." There was a pause, then "Thank you very much." She put down the receiver, turned and on seeing me staring at her, little realizing the horror she was causing to my friend, she threw a happy, innocent smile in my direction and left the room.

I turned to look at Joan. Visibly shaking, her knees had given way and she was sitting on the chair inside the booth. Slowly she replaced the receiver, the number undialed. I pressed the button and the coins came clattering out, bringing her back to a despondent reality.

Captain Gundison appeared to be a very busy man. It transpired that he had acquired three fiancées during his short stay in our land—all lovely, all at the same time but unfortunately for him, not far enough apart!

"I told you so!" Connie was ruthless in her wrath towards her younger sister. Her black eyes blazed with anger at the mention of the Captain's name that would never appear coupled with Joan's on the register of the nine hundred year old Norman church just over the fence from us! Nevertheless, the list of marriages between British girls and American men is quite impressive. Cooperation really went beyond normal bounds!

As for me, "Hmm…Men!" I muttered to myself. Having had a strict upbringing, my opinion of men at that stage was pretty low. It would change later, but at that moment, "Hmm…Men!" would suffice.

*****

Clothing coupons were the bane of my life. There were never enough with which to buy even the bare necessities, let alone any little extras that happened to catch the eye. With Princess Helena College now a thing of the past, a whole new wardrobe had to somehow materialize, to replace the uniform that had been my lot for the past few years. A silver-gray green tweed coat and skirt with overcoat to match—it was charming. It made me feel like I "belonged" giving me a feeling of security—I was reluctant to let it go.

Money was a problem too, but in those days the main headache were those wretched coupons—and they stretched nowhere at all! Jealously guarded by everyone, they were few and far between. I used one pair of my mothers' hand-me-down shoes to work, until eventually they split across the top, but out of sheer necessity I continued to wear them, feeling horribly self-conscious and certain that every pair of eyes were automatically drawn towards my feet.

On one of my days off, I boarded the train for London. It was for me a very great occasion and one to be treated as something special—to go in search of a pair of shoes—possibly *two* pairs of shoes! One for every day wear and, who knows, the coupons might just stretch to a second pair—pretty ones for party wear.

The train chugged its way to London where I caught the underground to Piccadilly, and from there I wound my way to Bond Street, feeling very conscious that I seemed to be the only person in civilian clothes. I found the elegant shop my mother wanted my to visit—like myself she had great difficulty in finding shoes small enough to fit.

The place was almost deserted. I felt self-conscious in my split hand-me-downs, my feet sinking into the thick carpet as I crossed the room. But a young assistant soon put me at my ease. She produced one or two boxes containing good serviceable shoes that I tried on and finally chose a pretty wine-colored pair. Then I enquired about gold ones for evening-wear. After a while the girl returned with another box. Seemingly, the only other shoes they had in my size, which, to my annoyance, were silver. I pointed out that I had specifically requested gold, whereupon, without a moment's hesitation she looked me straight in the face and without the blink of an eye said: "Madam, these are white gold." I gazed at her in blank amazement—what audacity—but left London proudly bearing a second pair of brand new shoes, white gold or not, they were suitable for dancing the night away with our new friends—the Americans! Those shoes were to be put to very good use sooner than I thought.

CHAPTER V
GROWING UP?

Leaving London armed with new shoes suitable for the office was one thing,, but now it was time to think of something other than figures thundering out of the teleprinter and landing on my desk in the form of five-figure groups, to be transposed into messages. It was time to take stock of the immediate future—in other words—tonight!

Ours was not the only hall to host the Americans. We were invited en bloc by the British officer's to dance—if not the night away, a good portion of it to be spent as visitors of the army, in one of the surrounding messes, however a certain amount of sleep was not only advisable, but an absolute necessity—those figures still loomed ahead the following day.

What to wear was the immediate problem necessitating a certain amount of thought, but not too much. It was a choice between two—a long, demure, cream color lace gown with a brown taffeta sash, deemed by my mother as both suitable and enchanting for one of my tender years. The other, and more to my liking, a swirling, black lace and net skirt with a bright colored top, a cut-me-down of Jean number two. Both Jeans thought it time for their young friend to step out and have some fun. As both girls were tall and able to talk with ease to each other well over my head, the cut me down was of course, what we considered, an extensive work of art involving the three of us.

We set to work with scissors, needle and black thread, a great deal of excited chatter and the result? It was definitely the more exciting of the two evening dresses and bound to have a devastating affect on the men. Although much too shy to join in the jitterbug—the American dance of the day, the quick waltz would be ideal to show of the swirling black skirt and I changed in readiness for that evening with excited anticipation.

It was now our turn to load into the bus and drive a few miles away from B.P. the office, the girls hostel and above all the onetime pad of figures—those never ending figures which we, who worked on them, were fully aware meant so much towards the lives of the agents in occupied countries, not to mention that of ending the war.

We joined the other girls—all codests, some from other huts and departments—climbed onto the bus amidst a great deal of chatter, left Bletchley Park and drove to our destination five or six miles away, there to tumble out into the arms of our waiting hosts amidst laughter from either side. We were led to a hall where a band struck up with the music of the day.

In those days before the invasion it was amazing how short a time it took to get acquainted after a drink at the bar—there was an urgency to grasp and enjoy life to the full. A kind young officer, a British army Captain, took me under his wing despite the fact I declined all his attempts to persuade me to have a "decent" drink—that is other than water. However, *everyone* wanted to dance. Drifting onto the floor in each other's arms as lights dimmed and the band played, immediate friendships formed, some long lasting but all were fully aware they would probably be short lived. Nothing was certain those days of the war.

At the end of the evening with the young officer walking quietly by my side I followed the Jeans and their newfound friends slowly across the drive and the open area onto the grass where the busses were parked under the trees. The drivers leaned against the busses or stood, talking quietly together waiting for their female cargo wandering towards them, each with an army officer escort, whom no doubt they would never see again.

One officer, an American at that, had balanced himself it seemed to me, on the edge of an tall upright stump of a tree, his cap tilted on the back of his head, with very long legs stretched out before him. My Captain and I waited, talking quietly together to allow the Jeans to bid their farewells with all the time and emotions the call of day demanded—when suddenly a strong pair of hands clutched me firmly round the waist and pulled me, tumbling between the legs of the long legged officer still propped up on the stump of the tree. Practically breaking my back as he pulled me towards him he planted a kiss firmly upon my bewildered lips.

It didn't take long for the wretched creature to raise his face, look down at me then throw back his head, mocking me with a mighty laugh. "She's never been kissed!" he roared to the world at large at the top of his voice. "This girl has never been kissed!" Covered in confusion, cheeks aflame I gazed up at him in bewilderment Oh! The humiliation of it! What was I supposed to do? There was no feeling in me. Not the feeling I was bound to learn, to experience in the not too distant future. But now, oh dear!

"Let her be Joe" the young Captain was facing him at his side, very softly but with danger in his voice, "Leave her Joe! Let her go!"

The strong hands slowly loosed the grasp on my waist, to be replaced by a grip from the back on my arms. I was dragged backwards by one of the Jeans, a heel got caught in the grass, I lost my balance, Jean caught me, propped me up and pulled me backwards towards the bus where her friend was waiting at the top of the steps to haul me up. They thrust me into a seat by the window for safekeeping where I gazed out blindly into the darkness of the night, overcome by humiliation and disgrace.

CHAPTER VI
THE ENIGMA

It was decided that *all* intelligence for D-Day should be handled at Bletchley Park. As it started pouring in and as D-day approached, it was to Bletchley Park they turned for information given out by Hitler, and of course, that from his Enigma machine. So few people knew of its existence in our midst.

Concerned that the Germans were overly interested in the movements of the Royal Netherlands Navy, the Enigma rotor cycle machine was first invented in 1915 by two Dutch Naval officers serving in a ship just off Java—now called Indonesia. The Germans had broken the current Dutch navel cipher and were using the information about ships from Holland patrolling the area. This enabled the Germans to slip between the vessels to gain access to the Pacific Ocean, where they could attack allied shipping. Unfortunately, the Dutch Navy omitted to patent their brainchild—their invention—a fact not lost on the Germans. In 1919, a German engineer and businessman Alexander Koch, working together with Arthur Scherbius, took over the idea and patented it for themselves and subsequently built the first Enigma machine.

It was a simple device—just a commercial typewriter with three rotors between the keyboard and the print basket. It *acted* like a normal typewrite to print a letter on a piece of paper, but at that stage the machine held hardly any security at all. For those initiated in the art, the cipher was easy to break—possibly in a matter of about forty-eight hours. One of a whole family of machines made round about the same period, from 1915 to 1925, Enigma was, in fact, only a trade name.

By 1928, the German army was looking for a cipher machine to use as a secure cipher for the whole of their armed forces and went on to develop the Enigma, which took them about four years, between 1928 to 1932. They continued to modify the Enigma so that the first machine, which resembled a typewriter, looked nothing like the one that went into the final operation.

They made several changes before starting test transmissions with the enciphered message being sent in Morse Code from North East Germany down towards the Austrian border. There it was received by an operator, who passed it to the Enigma operative to be deciphered, who then encoded a reply, again sent in Morse Code. They generated a great deal of traffic in Morse that was not unnoticed by the Poles, who were becoming increasingly interested. They intercepted and copied down these five letter transmissions.

At the end of the First World War, as reparations the Poles were given part of Germany—the Danzig Corridor separating Prussia from Bavaria—and they realized that the Germans would do their utmost to get it back. In order to keep abreast of German intentions they formed a small cryptographic team of three young mathematicians and trained them in the basic art of code breaking. Once trained, they handed them a bundle of cipher messages and told them to try and break them! And that was all they told them—nothing else, not even the fact that they were from a cipher machine! Marion Rejewski and his two companions Henryk Zygalski and Jerzy Rozycki were extraordinarily brilliant mathematicians and between them in 1932 they broke the Enigma machine cipher.

At the same time, the Germans were in for another problem. A German working in the ministry of information started to sell these secrets to certain people in the French Government. The French Government showed little interest and offered them to the British. But we declined the offer because at that time we couldn't intercept the German transmissions from so great a distance. Then, believe it or not, the French offered it to the Poles!

The Poles refrained from enlightening the French that they already knew the basic secrets of the Enigma cipher and put on a reluctant face, but did accept it under the pretext it *might* come in useful in the future! Consequently, the Poles, with their own skills and armed with the information the Germans gave to the French, who obligingly passed it on, were breaking the Enigma non-stop right up to 1938. A secret they kept entirely to themselves. Why? Quite simply, they did not trust us!

German-speaking Czechoslovakia was ceded to Hitler to appease his appetite for territorial expansion. But then he annexed the rest of the country. The Poles assumed that they would be next sacrificial lamb. It was only when Britain and France gave an ultimatum to Germany that *any* attack on Poland would result in a declaration of war, did the Poles approach the British in the form of Dilywn Knox and Alistair Dennison—heads of Bletchley Park! They told them they were aware that both men had been attempting to break Enigma cipher since 1932, and that they themselves had broken it about four months after it came into use, and were now prepared to share their secrets with us.

At that suggestion both men, together with their French counterparts, went to Poland in July and were shown what the Poles had achieved up to that point. But then they had a problem. Since 1938, the Germans had increased the number of rotors available for selection from three to five, which in turn increased their mathematical problems. The Poles admitted they were unable to break since they did not have sufficiently trained staff to cope. It was just too great a mathematical strain. But they did offer to show it all to Dennison and Knox in its present form and the way it worked. If they could find out mathematically how the whole thing came together they were welcome to it! And they also had a copy of the original Enigma machine to boot! They would be only too delighted if the British men and the French could decipher the German Enigma incase war was declared.

As far as we know, someone from the Ministry of Information in Germany sent an unclassified diplomatic pouch to Warsaw. It arrived late on a Friday afternoon and because of its unclassified status was locked up by the Poles in the customs warehouse. About ten minutes later, a dispatch rider from the German Embassy was sent in hot pursuit to request possession of their property, but the guard on duty pointed out that everyone had left for the weekend. The more persistent the dispatch rider became in his request for the bag, the more adamant was the guard on duty that he should turn round and go home. Monday morning was the time for him to return and he would be most welcome to collect the Germans property then.

The more the talk continued in this vane, the more suspicious the Polish guard became and as soon as the dispatch rider left—in a bit of a niff—the Pole telephoned security. They arrived at once and carefully undid the pouch, pulled out the Enigma Machine and took it apart, photographed it and put it back together again. They then locked up the pouch and gave it to the German dispatch rider on Monday morning upon his return!

In July 1939 the Poles gave Dennison, Knox, and the French copies of the machine, and on 1st September that same year the Germans invaded Poland. True to our promise, the British and French declared war on Germany two days later, sending the Polish team post haste from Warsaw for France, to team up with their French counterparts in the Chateau de Vignolles, just outside Paris. In England that December, John Jeffieys, when attacking the five rotor problem with Gordon Welchman and Alan Turing, startled the British team when he said: "I think I know how we get around the problem of *five* rotors"!

Alan Turing, just twenty-seven and being the youngest of the team, was sent to France with Jeffieys idea, to talk to the French at the Chateau, thereby missing his Christmas in England. On the morning of January 4th 1940, the combined Polish, French and British cryptanalysts broke the first German key of the war. On 20th January 1940, Turing returned to Bletchley Park with the information and the first Enigma key of the war was broken.

They now knew how to select which three of the five rotors had been chosen for that particular day's key, their sequence in the machine, and their start position. Some two weeks later, in the room at Bletchley Park, the same German key was broken for the first time in the war and we knew how to attack the German universal cipher machine. However, the procedure was slow and *very* tedious!

It was by sheer coincidence Bletchley Park attacked the one key that was needed to give us the information that helped us at Dunkirk and the Battle of Britain. Out of eight-three daily keys they could have attacked, they hit upon that one, purely because the German operators were sloppy and making mistakes!

The Enigma also helped us with the war at sea, where German U-boats were making life extremely difficult for us at home. Eventually President Roosevelt's Lend Lease Act enabled the Americans to send us much-needed food and supplies—thank goodness—and our rations went up, which was a great relief to us all. But the convoys were sorely hampered by the German Wolf-packs, as they were called, that lay in wait to cause havoc to the convoys. That is until professor Hugh O'Donnell Allexander, nicknamed "the pro" (a chess grand master and a brilliant man) together with Alan Turing, got inside the 'Atlantic key' used by the German U boats. And Enigma saved us again!

Before the war, we had intercept stations in the Middle East—one in Baghdad when we were in charge of Iraq, another in Sarafand in Egypt, and one in Cairo, and of course we had the Naval intercept stations in Malta and Gibraltar, so when Mussolini attacked Albania in 1935, we were already intercepting messages in the Middle East. He declared war on Britain on June 10th 1940 and moved his Italian troops not only down into Greece, but also through Libya into Egypt, where he captured the Suez Canal.

The problem *we* now had was to avoid letting the enemy know that we—the Allies—were interrupting their radio messages and bringing the information back to Bletchley Park! In England, we had the Cable and Wireless station—headquarters of that wonderful great undersea cable network—tucked away in Cornwall at a little place called Porth Curno; its counterpart in America was the Westinghouse Cable Network. From then on, information came from the overseas stations along these cables into Bletchley Park, to be deciphered and sent back down the cables to Malta for the Navy, and to Cairo for the Army and the Air Force. All their messages were whistling around beneath the keels of their submarines and ships and nobody on the enemy's side had the remotest idea as to what was going on.

And as D-Day drew near at last, all the information—in the form of Morse Code—came pouring in, was intercepted and forwarded to Bletchley Park to be deciphered, then sent on to the Allies, and to the Army, Navy, the Air Force and, of course to London and 10 Downing Street.

CHAPTER VII
VICTORY IN EUROPE

As suddenly as they had arrived the Americans departed, much to the relief of many English mothers who were forever repeating the phrase that our American allies, although delightful, "were overpaid, oversexed and over here."

The invasion of Europe was on! An eerie silence descended on our land. Their cheerful voices, the laughter and their bands was replaced by the ever increasing rumble of tanks and trucks making their way towards the southern coast and surrounding airfields, and with them went our own countrymen and women. No more laughter came from the men we grew to know so well in so short a space of time; little sound came from between their tightly compressed lips. For a while they had played with enthusiastic, lighthearted, exuberant energy but now they focused on what lay ahead. They arrived at their takeoff zones and waited. Thousands upon thousands of them gathered together—waiting. Just waiting for the weather. But our English weather, always unpredictable—even on an occasion such as this—maintained its reputation and let us down! For three frustrating days and nights they waited for a break in winds, the rain and the clouds, until eventually it came, and with it, the inevitable word from General Eisenhower: "We go." It was June 6th 1944—D Day!

The night skies were suddenly filled with dark shapes overhead—the steady roar of planes coming together from airfields all over the country—the deafening drone of one mighty Armada. We on the ground gazed in awe as the giant American Flying Fortress bombers lumbered on their way with their heavy load of bombs. Wave after wave outlined against the darkened skies. I thought of Coventry and London—the terrible bombings those people had endured, and thanked God that I was not on the receiving end of this! Was revenge in the minds of those men overhead?

With the exodus from our land and the mighty surge of men into France, our work increased in volume and intensity. In our hut, at tables of four, we worked with heads bent low deep in concentration. In front of each girl lay pages of figures—hundreds of figures in five-figure groups—that were quietly transformed into letters, then into sentences and finally into messages. Where these were sent we did not know; our only concern was to get them transposed as rapidly and accurately as possible. A man's life could depend upon the result. Some incoming messages stamped IMMEDIATE or MOST IMMEDIATE in bold big red letters were turned into legible reading matter with urgent replies to be transposed into figures—oh those interminable five-figure groups! One had to keep a clear head! If glasses were worn, it was imperative to keep them clean, for with or without them, there were times at the end of a shift we felt positively cross-eyed. Oh yes! How thankful we now were for those wonderful cups of good strong tea!

From radios we heard news of the fighting on the continent and from our department we gleaned more. What went on in other huts we neither knew nor cared, *our* main concern was to get our own job done to help our men fighting over seas. We never dreamt that in "the cottage" so close and yet surrounded in a vail of secrecy, brilliant minds had already broken the Enigma, Hitler's top-secret military code, enabling the allies to track enemy movements, and help them in their bloody advance in Europe. Had I come face to face with Alan Turing in the cafeteria, or in the sitting rooms at Bletchley Park, or by the lake, or walking on the grass, I never knew. My mother knew him and was not impressed with "that untidy man". Had she appreciated the impact of his brilliant mind, his work to break the code, her opinion of him might have changed. Looking back after all these years it is strange to think that Turing appeared as—just one of us.

But at this time our own work increased. Men and women working behind the enemy lines, reporting movements by road and rail, in towns and villages throughout the countryside, were risking their lives to get messages sent through, enabling our planes to track down and destroy weapons to be used against us. How I admired the courage of these people! *They* were my heroes, working out of uniform, those whom Churchill called his Fifth Column. How apt a name! They ones I longed to emulate.

One day, on glancing up from a difficult problem to take a drink from my steaming mug, I noticed that two strangers had entered the room and were greeted by our supervisor Miss Montgomery. That lady, we all respected and admired so much for the quiet dignity and charm with which she kept control! Sitting together at her table, their backs to me, I was unable to see either of their faces, and indeed there was little time to study them as I quickly bent over my work once more. But they were dressed—differently. Both wore dark coats—unobtrusive clothing that would blend in with a crowd or the shadows of the night. They listened to what our leader said, talked in undertones together, accepted their books, their "one time" coding pads, glanced through them and put them in a bag. Then they left just as quietly as they had appeared.

Alone that night, tossing on my uncomfortable little bed, I wondered about those two. Who were they? Were they members of the fearless SOE ready to drop behind the lines. Why had the entered so secretly, indeed why had they come in at all? Where were they now? Movies at that time were usually about the war—the air force, the army, the navy, all long arms of battle and destruction together with amazing feats of heroism from the people of the resistance that held and thrilled their audiences, inspiring them to stretch to the greatest of their ability, and increase in their own "war efforts" in whatever work they were performing. Had I not been pitched into the Bletchley Park at my mother's urging, I might have found myself doing "war work" in some factory, which would have been very much against her wishes. "Darling, I don't want you working in a factory"! So there, lying in my bed, instead of dreaming of nuts and bolts and planes, I dreamed of live men and women in an enemy occupied continent, finding and helping our men shot down, sending us their messages. Now in this I too had a part—decoding their messages, encoding the replies. At last I felt that I belonged, that I was part of them, doing my little bit in helping to fight this war, even if it *was* just working at a table out there in the country, safe and snug in my own land—England. Where were those two people now, and for them what dangers lay ahead? Were they in comparative safety, still in England, or were they walking together in a crowd in France? If so, how did they get there and why? Slowly my daydreaming took effect and in time I dozed off into a deep and heavy sleep.

*****

Paris was liberated in August 1944, two months after D-Day, with overwhelming relief and jubilation from the people of France who had suffered so much under the Nazi occupation. However there was never a pause in the work for us at Bletchley Park, or of the other coding stations. On the contrary—it increased and the air was filled with the sound of Morse Code flooding the wires, taking our messages at lightening speed to our friends fighting in their own way, harassing and hindering their tormenters in whatever way they could and helping our men, shot down.

Soon we moved from the peace of the country back to our offices in London, and found ourselves living in one of the more beautiful parts of the town that had escaped the bombing—Eaton Place. From the look of it, in former times this lovely building had housed one of England's wealthier, more elegant families. But now the romantic past was put on hold, serving as temporary quarters for a number of women engaged in helping to bring the war to a speedy end. We arrived by bus, entered the building and went up a flight of wide, majestic marble stairs leading to a spacious landing from which doors opened into what was obviously once a large and beautiful sitting room. Now what I saw made my heart sink. Two rows of beds, neatly made and ready for use. Back to school again! This room was to be in continual use; for those who worked at night, slept throughout the day and visa versa. Would this war never end?!

Now, as I dressed for work in the dormitory, I wondered what my favorite blonde, blue-eyed cousin Betty was doing. My mother told me she had taken a course in agriculture and was working on a farm. The land army would suit her well. I envied her as her love of animals and the countryside matched my own. When, if ever, would we meet again? I made my bed, and went down to breakfast, and in search of my two friends.

Six years of war, it was almost over at last! Mind you, we still had the Japanese to contend with. At this moment in time I couldn't imagine life without a war. My very existence revolved around it—or so it seemed. Now the whole thing came to a resounding halt in Europe, and everyone without exception, went wild with joy. We shouted, we *yelled* in jubilation, we laughed until tears filled our eyes in overwhelming relief. We hugged and slapped each other on the back, jumping up and down, leaning precariously from windows shouting our joy to the world, as did everyone else in London. Then one and all we stumbled downstairs to overflow onto the streets and joined the jubilant mass of humanity surging down every road in town gravitating towards Whitehall or Pall Mall, and ultimately to—but where else? Buckingham Palace! And that is exactly where we three headed—the Jeans and me.

Being short of stature—all of 4ft 11inches tall—no matter where I went crowds did tend to overwhelm me, even on the dance floor! I found it rather alarming to be confronted by a bodily mass of backs or chests, especially when they were all on the move. However on this occasion things were different. The very mood was enough to uplift the spirit, if not the body, to higher elevations. Once we found our way to the Queen Victoria Memorial fountain, not far from the railings in front of the palace, we found gaps in the crowd where, not only could we wander with comparative ease, but gaze up at the famous balcony in anticipation of the appearance of our King and Queen. Having shared so much with us throughout the war; their presence instilled the love and affection we felt for them and it was very real. Both had tirelessly visited the worst of the bombed out areas, stepping over and through the debris as they consoled the victims of each night's raids. Indeed their own home had been bombed—a wing of Buckingham Palace!

We did not have long to wait before the King escorted his radiant Queen onto the balcony, to be greeted by the shouts and cheers of their jubilant people! Relief mingled with joy resounded in our cries, and when both princesses joined them on the balcony our appreciation increased. Princess Elizabeth had donned the khaki uniform of the

Auxiliary Territorial Service, (the ATS), had trained and lent her support to the war effort. But the sound of the crowd was nothing to the mighty roar that filled the air as Mr. Churchill stepped through the open window and joined the Royal family on the balcony, beaming down with his great smile. He raised his hand with the famous 'V for Victory' sign and the crowds went wild. Oh *what* a day! With tears of joy streaming down our faces, we shouted and waved to that mighty man who had led us through such dark and terrible times. Had it not been for him, his leadership, and the rendering of so many of his now famous speeches of encouragement, heaven only knows what would have taken place. The Germans were but twenty-one miles away, across a narrow strip of water, within swimming distance of a strong and able person! It does not bear thinking about. Even now, recalling this, I shudder. He had told us he "had nothing to offer but blood, tears, toil and sweat." The world heard his powerful, resolute voice by radio many a time, leading us on: "…we shall not flag nor fail. We shall go on to the end. We shall fight them on the beaches, we shall fight them on the landing grounds, we shall fight in the fields and in the streets, we shall fight them in the hills; we shall never surrender." Emotions ran so high with the feelings we had for this great man who led us to hell and back. Looking around me, I saw tears streaming unashamedly down faces of people in the crowd as they cheered and shouted their appreciation and love for him.

We stayed there for the best part of the day and I was glad to be between the Jeans. Occasionally one or other of them grabbed hold of me as we jostled this way and that amongst the crowd. Finally physically and mentally exhausted we returned to Eaton Place—to sleep!

Our jubilant ride on the crest of the wave was short-lived. From the height of wild hilarity, our spirits plummeted to rock bottom a few days later when every page in each and every newspaper was plastered with photos of the allies arriving at the enemy concentration camps.

Photographers in uniform were men endowed with enormous courage throughout the war. Although they carried arms, their main concern were their precious cameras, to record *exactly* what was taking place. And they did their work with total disregard to their own personal safety. But now, what should have been an event of relief and joy turned out to be the opposite. The liberation of the concentration camps was heart searing. One picture in particular lies indelibly imprinted on my mind—that of a grim faced General Eisenhower, erect and silent with an officer on either side, gazing across a sea of living corpses stretched out before them. Human beings reduced to skin-covered skeletons, barely able to move. These were the images that would haunt people for years—a heart-rending reminder of the horrors of war.

During the era of steam engines, railway stations boasted small news theatres designed solely to bring interest and entertainment to people who had an hour or so to wile away, whilst waiting for their trains. Members of the public could slip into these small theatres, watch a cartoon and catch up on the news, without the frustration of pacing the platform for hours at a time. Here, of course, the images seen in the papers came to life. The skin clad skeleton on the ground, sitting at the General's feet, moved. Slowly it raised an arm. Eisenhower bent down to speak to him, then straightened, anger mingled with compassion written on his face. He turned to the officer at his side who in turn issued orders to others, and help was on its way. So much agony, so much horror, so many lives lost—and so many living dead.

That night I called my mother on the phone. She too had seen the papers and read the news but her thoughts took a different twist. If this was taking place in Europe, what should we expect from the fury of the Japanese? It was a frightening thought for anyone who had loved ones in the Far East.

Although *my* work continued, it was time for her to prepare for her husband's anticipated return. She resigned from her position in the Foreign Office. I still have her letters of credit and appreciation for work well done during her years of service. Not knowing what to expect, her dilemma was in the extreme. Would Jackie be a physical wreck? His mind was bound to be affected by the ordeal of his four-year sojourn in Japanese hands, but to what extent she had no idea. The brutality that was coming to light in Nazi Europe might well be an indication of what to expect in South East Asia.

My mother's anxiety soon gave rise to feelings of nausea and eating became a chore. She would turn from a beautiful little soft-boiled egg, complaining that she was "really not very hungry," but still insisting that I eat mine. "*You* have to do a day's work, Annette. I am—just—not—very—hungry," she would say and turn her head away, her eyes filling with tears. She was destined to wait until September 1st 1945, when devastation of gargantuan proportion—wrought by the dropping of the atomic bomb on Hiroshima and Nagasaki, finally brought the Japanese to their knees. A little flat, or house hunting, would keep her mind occupied and steer it in a happier direction.

CHAPTER VIII
JACKIE WAINWRIGHT'S PERSONAL ACCOUNT OF THE FIGHTING AND FALL OF SINGAPORE AND HIS SUBSEQUENT LIFE AS A JAPANESE PRISONER OF WAR

15/2/42 to 22/3/42

We have now been prisoners of war for over a month. Taking everything into account our treatment to date cannot be complained of—needless to say, there are many drawbacks chief amongst which is the lack of running water and modern sanitation to which must also be added the almost negligible supplies of vegetables and fruit. On a main diet of rice, of which there is plenty, it is essential in the interest of health that some steps be taken to augment the supply of vegetables and fruit. Gardens have been started by each unit, but with something like 60,000 to 80,000 prisoners to provide for, the magnitude of the task can be appreciated. Seed and cuttings we must have!!! We have only ourselves to thank for the absence of running water and electric power as the plant was blown up during the last days of the war.

Wounded cases in the hospital amount to something like a thousand to which must be added over 900 cases of dysentery. Open latrines and consequent breeding of flies, which are exceedingly numerous, has caused this disease to spread. It is certainly an eye opener in a country where flies were, comparatively speaking unknown. The problem is being energetically tackled, but absence of disinfectant does not help matters. Another obstacle is the disinclination of troops to cooperate which can be attributed to sheer ignorance. Mosquitoes are, so far, practically nonexistent which is tribute to the strict control exercised during peacetime.

The camp extends from Changi Jail, to Changi Point (2 miles frontage on each side of the main road), a part of which overlooks the Changi Straits—the location is ideal giving Coy (RASC Command) is in two. Warrant Officer's married quarters overlooking the Straits.

Accommodation is cramped, 20 officers to a small house—N.G. and I share a small verandah at the back of the house; generally speaking there are 6 officers to a room which gives some idea of the lack of space. The only furniture is that which we have been able to scrounge. N.G. and I have got camp beds and an almeirah so we have the photos of our wives well to the fore. The Japanese have brought in Tokyo time which is 1-1/2 hours ahead of the Malayan time. In some respects this is an advantage, as it does not get dark until 8:30. We are generally in bed by 9:30 and as reveille is not sounded until 7:45, we put in nearly 11 hours sleep each night—we find this quite easy on the diet we are getting, Nobody has any energy and everyone is getting very thin, faces sunken in, etc. We also sleep in the afternoons. For the purpose of these notes Malayan time will be adhered to. Meals are as follows: Reveille 6:15 A.M. (Japanese time, 7:45 A.M.), breakfast 7:30 A.M. (Japanese time 9:00 A.M.), Tiffin 11:00 P.M. (Japanese time 1:00 P.M.), tea 2:30 P.M. (Japanese time 4:00 P.M.), dinner 5:30 P.M. (Japanese time 7:00 P.M.), lights out 9:15 P.M. (Japanese time 10:45 P.M.)

There is a batman for every two officers but even so I prefer to do my own washing every three days.

N.G. = Northcott Green

We are given 15 cigarettes a week, no pipe tobacco worst luck. I am now down to my last few ounces.

Life would be much more tolerable if we had electric light and running water, as it is water has to be carted in tins from the wells. Everything gets so infernally dirty and soap is very scarce. All motor conveyances have been taken from us. Another thing, which is extremely trying, is the complete absence of news from the outside world-listening-in sets are strictly forbidden. We are only allowed to bathe in the sea once a week. The enormous camp area is split up into areas which are wired in; at present we have our own M.P.'s on the gates but we hear that these are shortly to be replaced by Japanese guards. Also, for the time being, we are under the Malayan Command for discipline, but there is a Japanese Colonel with HQ at Changi Prison who is Camp Commandant. The "screw" is gradually being put on by various ways and means but even so, I repeat that so far the Japanese have been quite considerate, after all we are prisoners of war and such a large number of men must be a distinct embarrassment to them.

The food question worries us no end, similarly health. We hear that medical stores are running short. Our childish appreciation of any fruit or other little luxury which we are able to obtain outside is rather pathetic. We always go to bed talking of what the food we would like to have, "Wouldn't it be nice to go to Raffles for a grill! Boy pengil Attias". The lovely dishes we concoct gives us great pleasure. Nobody seems to worry about alcohol now and I fancy it will be the same when cigarettes run out. One thing this experience has taught me is the unnecessary expenditure one indulged in civilian life. I wonder if we shall go back to the old ways when it is all over.

We have lots of leisure time on our hands so it is essential to try and get a job. N.G. and I are local Purchasing Officers and armed with Japanese passes, we set out into the Kampong[1]s outside our own area, but within the main area which extends roughly from Ayer Manis—Changi Prison to a line running across Tampenis Road. We take a party of men with us to carry this stuff back which nearly all goes to the hospital. We bring fruit, vegetables, poultry, pigs, etc., and pay cash in Straits currency. The money comes from the Command Imprisoned Account. These jaunts involve us in 6/8 miles foot slogging; we go out every other day. Every afternoon there is a conference at 4:30 where to our delight we are given an extra cup of tea and a biscuit for our labors. These trips although trying in the heat, are really enjoyable as they take us away from the camp. It certainly brought back happy memories to me when I saw Ayer Manis where Dorothy and I used to go for picnics on Sundays.

There is not a day which passes when I do not dwell on our little home at "The Cottage" and the happy married life we have had together over the last five years. It is sad to think we have lost all we loved, all I now want is my Dorothy!!!

1 Kampong = small area containing a few Malay dwellings

I don't know how long we shall be able to continue L.P.[2] not indefinitely, as we shall have no shoes left. My watch has let me down and I fear the main spring has gone. There are a good number of books to read and I have now started Contract Bridge again. Norhcottt Green is one of the very best. I am extremely lucky to have made such a friend (he is a Kedah planter married to an extremely pretty girl who is in Australia with her kiddy). We have now mucked in together for about two months. We get occasional news from Singapore which has been renamed Syonan by the Japanese. Apparently the place is "dead" and there is nothing doing. It is amusing to note the number of houses (Asiatic) with Japanese flags hanging outside.

By the way, in order for us to bring in our Local Purchases stuff we are using motor chassis which have been stripped of everything with the exception of the steering wheel and front brakes. These queer looking objects are hauled and pushed up the hills and "coast" when the going permits. It all causes great amusement, some 15 troops holding on like grim death when going down the hills—the "Changi Special" is the last word in speed. All the Volunteers (SSVF and FMS) are quartered in this wired sector—Southern Area—in consequence of which not a day passes when I do not run into people I know. Of my more intimate friends Withers Payne, I have seen heaps of times; his

great moan is no pipe tobacco—poor old Withers, how he loves his pipe—he and Hoyan (lawyer from Penang) have built themselves a kind of room out of odd bits of wood underneath the bungalow, a bit of a contrast to Holland Hill where a shell completely demolished his study.

Tom Calaham is busy at dental work; he has made his own dental chair, he was allowed to go into Singapore to fetch his equipment. He went up to the house and found everything in shambles. Jack Harvey, Kinahan, Kinder, Gulliford, Holt I see pretty frequently and I have also had talks with Gilbert, John Grant, Pennefathey. Steve Sidford is an elusive young devil and I have yet to contact him. From all accounts he practically lives on his unit's (J.V.E.) vegetable plot some distance away, and has even built himself a shack. I hear he looks very thin, and it has been suggested he is overdoing it.

2 L.P. = leg plugging (walking)

Four young gunners were court martialled by the Japanese the other day and shot for attempting to escape. They were caught in Singapore in civilian clothes. The Japanese have now issued orders that if anyone attempting to escape will meet the same fate whether in uniform or not. Of civilians in Changi Jail I have seen Doc Bain, Seymour Williams (Malacca), the latter driving G & Co. liquor van which I happened to purchase in 1939 from Borneo Motors—this amused me no end—Davis, Dawson, Shepherd (M.C.S.) and Hyde (P & S) all of which were stripped to the waist carting and felling wood for the cook house.

The last few days in Singapore were very dramatic:

10/2/42:

In the afternoon whilst I was attending the Civil Liability Tribunal the Base Supply Depot was heavily bombed. I returned to Joo Sena about 5:30 and found this place completely empty of staff including the Jagas[3] and guard—all the godowns were quite intact. I then proceeded to the B.S.D. and found the depot bombed out—happily there were no casualties, everybody having evacuated to the racecourse. Col. Fox and a few other officers and men were endeavoring to assist the P.A.D. Staff to put out a number of fires. On the way back to the house N.G. and I thought it would be a good idea to have a drink at Tanglin. We found a few of the old brigade—Harold Godwin, Cupid Horsley and John McLeod and I eventually went home with the latter to his house for a drink. On our way back we noticed formations of Australians taking up positions in the Tanglin district. Little did we imagine it was to be our last night at the "Cottage." I think it must have been about 11/2/42 2:00 A.M. when I was awakened by more than usual heavy gunfire, particularly in the direction of Holland Village. At times the burst of machine guns appeared so close that after a hurried consultation with N.G. and Noakes, it was decided to clear out. We eventually left the "Cottage" at 4:00 A.M. taking as much kit as possible (in my case a suitcase and kit bag). We dropped the "boy" and his "barang[4]" at the

3Jagas = Indian warehouse security guards
4 barang = luggage, belongings

end of the road. Boxer[5] (poor dear) traveled with me. N.G. and Noakes [6]Amah following behind. I might add, that the house staff had found the strain too much for them. and a ketchil[7] boy left a few days previously without a word and the "boy" was in a complete "flap." The only one who did not appear to worry was the Kebun—we left him in charge and that I would keep in touch by telephone if possible.

Before we left I phoned Col. Fox whom instructed us to report at Farrer Park at 8.15 as they were evacuating the "Race Course." We went down as far as Cyranos in Orchard Road and slept in the cars until 6:00 A.M.—parties of troops coming past who had lost touch with their units in the front line. I was not very impressed with some Australians who said they were making for the docks. As soon as it was light we pushed on to the Adelphi for a cup of tea but none of the "boys" were helpful and we had to go and help ourselves from the kitchen.

Before reporting to Farrer Park I took poor Boxer to the dog's infirmary and had him painlessly destroyed—"Pushty" was left at home as a cat is able to forage for himself—dear old Boxer was in an awful state with all the din, and we nearly lost him at the Dog's Home as the Japanese were shelling the district. It was a sad moment when I parted with him.

Our quarters at Farrer Park were in the old grandstand underneath the clock tower, which had been an old M.A.C. post. From the time of our arrival shells were passing continually overhead and low flying Japanese aircraft were dive bombing Thomson Road, Bukit Timah, and Adam Road districts—we could easily see all this going on from Farrer Park. It was decided to try and reestablish the B.S.D. at Farrer Park and to try and get as much supplies as possible out of the race course—at this time the Japanese were somewhere in the region of Ford Motor Works at about 8 miles Bukit Timah—to do this we sent up relays of convoy drawn from 47 M.T. Coy commencing in the morning and carrying on throughout the day and night. I was in charge of a convoy which went up to the Course just before dark. Everything went well until we were

5 Boxer = Jackie's bull-terrier

6 Ketchil "boy" = small boy, child

7 "boy" male servant

heavily shelled for 10 minutes—shells actually falling in the car park where we were working. The only thing to do was to hide amongst the stacks and hope for the best; it was a nasty experience hearing the swish of shells as they fell near and I must confess it was the first time I had experienced real fear. The Indian labor did not stand up to it at all well and were positively shaking in their boots. I was glad to find a bottle of gin handy. Jimmy Forbes' house was well in the line of fire. When we departed about 7:30 several of the stables were well ablaze. The Chinese drivers behaved very well but understood little Malay and did not know Singapore; apparently they had been recruited from Penang and Perak. The night was very noisy and Noakes and I got little sleep.

12/2/42:

Batteries of R.A. arrived at Farrer Park and went into action from the Serangoon Road side—the din was pretty hectic and it was not long before we got a pasting with shells and bombs from aircraft; this went on at frequent intervals. Singapore town was also getting it's share. I tried to get up to the "Cottage" to see how things were going but only got as far as Napier Road and was ordered to turn back. The Indian Hospital at Tyersal Park had been bombed and was burning furiously. On the way back I tried to get a drink for the two troops who were with me, but the best I could do was a glass of water handed personally to me by Wassey—all his "boys" had done a bunk. I saw poor little Mrs. Skinner still waiting for a boat. I hear she got away in the end but how far she got is another matter. Singapore was completely deserted with fires all over the place; it was a rotten sight. The Memorial Hall, Cricket Club, Municipal Offices and Cathedral had been turned into Military Hospitals—graves were being dug all round the Cathedral grounds. In the afternoon I took a convoy out to Chickabu Food Dump (11-1/4 milestone Thomson Road) to try and get in stores; all along the road transport was returning towards Singapore; our troops were also preparing to leave. One could not help but think this was the beginning of the end. Having completed our job without incident, we were held up at the junction of Lornie Road where an ammunition truck had been set on fire by dive-bombing and was expected to blow up at any moment. I decided to get round the difficulty by going down Lornie Road and turning up Caldicott Hill Estate Road into Thomson Road further up. It was impossible to make Bukit Timah via Lornie Road as the golf course and Adam Road were under Japanese machine gunfire.

When I got back to Farrer Park I had the sad task of burying a dispatch rider who had been killed by a shell just a few yards from our quarters. In the evening Col. Fox and a party left us hurriedly for Java (it is problematical whether they actually arrived there) we were very sorry indeed to lose him as he had set a splendid example under very trying conditions, especially to some of the younger men fresh out from home who were beginning to feel the strain. His departure was a great loss and everybody felt very flat that night.

13/2/42:

In the morning I volunteered to make a reconnaissance up Thomson Road to see if it were possible to get any more supplies out of Chickabu dump. For this purpose I took my Austin"10" (S7798) and two B.O.R.s P.15 Laughton and Gilbey—to spot for low flying aircraft. We were compelled to take cover in drains quite a few times on the way out, and were only able to get as far as the 6th M.S.—just by the turning into the Island Golf Club—we were turned back by the troops who were just on the point of blowing up the bridge. Our troops had, therefore, retired 5 miles overnight. On the way back two Japanese planes singled us out for attention by diving and machine gunning but luckily we spotted them coming up behind and hid under a culvert by the roadside—we suffered no damage, neither did the car. Japanese planes seemed to do exactly as they liked as all our aircraft had left the island days ago. However, they got pretty warm receptions from our artillery who acquitted themselves very well. I also noticed at this time that the shelling of Singapore proper was becoming more intense; further there was now no question of air raid warnings being sounded—enemy planes kept up more or less continuous bombing all the town.

In the afternoon the batteries on Farrer Park were bombed and put out of action; it was a ghastly sight with men being horribly mutilated. The ammunition wagons were all set alight and the flames and reports were still going off well into the night—we had a grandstand view of it all being on the other side of the park. That night the pace got so hot it was decided to evacuate to a safer spot if this could be found.

In the early hours of the morning, with trench mortars dropping all round us and the rattle of machine guns uncomfortably near, we moved off to Spottiswode Park near Tanjong Pagar. I drove the Austin with two Privates in the back. It was not easy going on account of debris and shell holes across the roads.

The Padang[7] was chuck full of vehicles, guns, and troops (very bad sign) and just by Fullerton Building was stopped by two Signals men who asked where the Singapore Club was. Apparently they had an urgent message for the Governor from Fort Canning (another ominous sign from my point of view). H.E. had moved his quarters from Government House. I had the utmost difficulty in getting sense out of the Asiatic staff at the door which was only unlocked after I had used my hand to some good effect. Eventually after a lot of trouble and confusion I found H.E.'s room and got the message through. Poor Lady Thomas[8] was lying ill on a bed attended by a nurse. A hurried reply was given and the signals rode off on their bikes to Fort Canning.

Robinson and Anson Roads were in an awful mess, and it was only with the greatest of difficulty we got to the Railway Station. Here we were told that there was no room at Spottiswode Park so the whole unit was stranded by the roadside just by Gate 3 in Tanjong Pagar. It was just beginning to get light and shells were whining overhead onto the wharves, many of the godown[9]s being on fire. I suggested that the best thing to do would be to get all the vehicles up to the center of the town and to park by the Victoria Hall—this we did and after a hurried meal out of tins—we had not had our clothes off for 3 days—and precious little sleep—we were ordered by Fort Canning to report to Godown 55 (Gate 8) which is just by the St. James Power Station. Here we endeavored to operate as a Base Supply Depot having been more

7 Padang = large open grass area, field for exercises, games or parades, etc.
8 Lady Thomas = H.E.'s the Governor's wife
9godown = warehouse for storage of merchandise

or less in the front line and not far from it at Keppel for that matter. We now came in for some most hectic bombing (14/2/42) which was concentrated on Mount Faber but a number of the bombs fell on our area by Keppel Road. Our conditions were wretched in the extreme and we seemed to spend the whole time in the S.H.B. shelters. Bombs fell so close at times that the blast could be felt through our clothes.

In the afternoon of 14th Gilley and I went down to the main wharf to take notes of food stuffs in the godowns which were in an awful state—looting had commenced and so far as I could see all the public services had broken down—however, the European members of the Police Force were trying to cope with the situation and continued to do sterling work until the end.

Gilley's wife was doing work at the blood transfusion center at the General Hospital so we decided to pay her a visit. I was greatly impressed with all I saw, especially with the women who appeared to be in charge of Mrs. Dickinson, the wife of the I.G.P. By this time Singapore was being heavily shelled and fire could be seen all over the place.

15/2/442:

We continued to carry on but it was quite obvious the situation was hopeless. We got a direct hit from a bomb in the morning but luckily there were no casualties, everybody very sensibly taking cover amongst the rice stacks; however, we had to put out a fire on a loaded lorry of tinned stuff right alongside the godown. Godown 55 was right in line of the shells, which were being put over on Poeloe Brani and Blakong Mati. In the afternoon there were all sorts of rumors about cars having been seen going up Bukit Timah Road with white flags—later on there as a lull in firing and all sorts of chit chat at 2030 Hrs. (8:30 P.M.), an armistice was signed and we had capitulated. That evening I drove Gater up to the Pavilion Theater which we had taken over for a food dump; parts of the town were in an awful mess and reminded me of the pictures we had seen of Warsaw. I don't know whether it was relief it was all over or what it was, but we had a bit of a party in the restaurant that night and then I drove back amongst the debris to the B.S.D.-Telok Ayer and Clifford Pier districts were well alight.

16/2/42:

At daybreak the Japanese made their entry into Singapore via Keppel Harbor Roads and the main Bukit Timah Road. Incidentally the armistice was signed in the new Ford Works just by Hume Pipe's new works. The east coast area of the island had come lightly, the Japanese having landed on the west coast and Krangi districts. I don't think they even came through the Naval Base or down Thomson Road. I must say they looked a pretty scruffy lot, of their efficiency there could be little doubt. The first lot I saw stopped outside Godown 55 and an officer sauntered in and said "have you the English cigarette "Pall Mall" (good advert for Rothmans I thought) but their troops were demanding wristwatches from some Australians so I quickly put mine in my pocket. The Japanese made for the center of the city occupying all the main buildings; it was not long before their poached egg flag was flying from the Cathay Building—sentries were posted all over the chief points but there were no demonstrations.

I lost the Austin "10" in the morning in Raffles Place. I was searching for some Indian Corps labor which had got lost in the general confusion; and when my back was turned the car was stolen by Chinese—apparently they were making a practice of this as well as looting all the European godowns and shops. It was a rotten sight and the Japanese lost no time in using the Tommy gun. Anyhow, the car had to go so perhaps it was best that way. I had intended to drive it to Keppel Harbor, and "drown it." As I had 5 miles to get back to Godown 55, I cadged a lift on a lorry, but not before calling into the Anglo Thai Office in the Mercantile Bank Building where I had curry Tiffin[10] with Holisday, Fristy, New and his wife, preceded by two Gin Pahits. All this time the Japanese were swarming into Singapore and opposite the Post Office they were assembling for a triumphant march with cine cameras in attendance. All very strange as I was free to move about as I liked. In the afternoon we had (Mike Silley, Holley Hims)

10 Tiffin = lunch

the loan of a car, as I wanted to go and see what I could get out of the "Cottage" in the way of food. The house itself was untouched but of the inside the less said the better. Our little house was nothing but a shambles. Everything littered all over the place, and "D's" clothes everywhere. Pushty was nowhere to be seen but the Siamese cat next door was in its usual place in the suntrap. The Australians had done their "best to clean up" the house which had been followed up by the Chinese squatters in the district. It really made me feel quite ill (our lovely decanters all smashed on the floor, the canteen completely stripped) and I was glad to get away. We took away with us a few beer mugs and fish knives, and forks.

17/2/42;

We had to march out to the prisoner of war camp at Changi in the afternoon—19 miles—luckily we got a lift after walking about half the distance.

17/5/42:

We have been P.O.W. exactly three months today. On the whole the time has passed very quickly I suppose. I've been fortunate in doing local purchase work which has taken me away from the camp.

We are hoping to be kept here but the air is full of rumors and large numbers of troops have already been moved to camps in Singapore—some to spots overseas. We simply live for the day of release, nobody with any sense, I think, expects to get out in under 12 months from the time in which we came in. We have acute phases of depression and optimism according to the particular frame of mind we are in. We have had some sticky periods in here particularly in regard to health and food. Although things have improved at the hospital it is a place to be avoided like the plague. The trouble so far as I can see is the lack of equipment and proper food for nursing patients back to health—such stuff as Marmite for instance—with the result numbers of them "go under" whereas had we been at home or any other place for that matter, proper care would be given. As it is we have to put up with the best that can be done. As things go on the food problem will tend to get worse. There is an acute shortage in Singapore and we hear that the position is really serious up-country. Another point about the hospital is that they ought to have a staff of qualified nurses and a matron in charge. There is too much filth and dirt and there have been some nasty stories floating about concerning leakage of food, such as extras as we on "local purchase" bring in the way of fish, eggs, fruit and vegetables.

Patients say they "never see anything," which no doubt is exaggerated, but the fact remains the position needs checking up. This is where a matron would be invaluable. The Japanese are curious in many ways and I can see no objection to a female nursing staff being installed; there are many sisters interned at the jail. The expected outbreak of beriberi put the wind up everybody, so much so that the Japanese have been supplying vegetables from Johore and Sumatra.

11/12/42:

I am 43 today, and on the 15th will have been a POW for 10 months. The time has passed very quickly indeed. The main thing is to keep your mind occupied. Being on Local Purchase as I am keeps me very occupied both mentally and physically. We have little opportunity for bemoaning over our position. Health is the great asset and what we do not know about vitamins isn't worth knowing. We are practically living off the land—food that we would not have looked at in peacetime. We still get a ration of meat twice a week—Australian mutton. When that is finished there will be no more I imagine. What gets us down is this infernal rice. If we could only have bread and a plentiful supply of potatoes; it would not be so bad. We have our vegetable gardens and I must say our own particular plot has done very well. As usual, there's not nearly enough of anything. However, Ceylon spinach, sweet potatoes, and kang kong[11] seem to thrive very well. We get vegetables supplied by the Japanese. What we need badly now is a Red Cross supply from South Africa. We have had two lots of food from S.A., which were very welcome, but we are now out of everything.

My pay as a 2nd Lieutenant is $10.83 [Malay dollars] per month all other officers above this rank get $20.[Malay dollars] The difference

11 Kang kong = type of local vegetable

in my opinion is far too marked. Health is better I am glad to say, but owing chiefly to food deficiency there have been a great many deaths—well over 500 by now (i.e. since we came in) the cemetery is well cared for and one day I imagine the lay out with flowerbeds will be most impressive. My chief recreations are bridge and reading. I have got very keen on the former. I have never read so much in all my life. Cecil Roberts, Negley Farson, and Beverley Nichols are my favorite authors. It is a great comfort to read about the flowers and countryside at home; also of birds. The bird life in Changi is simply great and they are all so tame. Sparrows come into the house and hop all around us taking no notice. Most of the flowers which we had at the "Cottage" are to be seen here, especially the flowering trees and shrubs. It all helps to make life easier, but I suppose there are heaps of people who never see anything. What a lot they miss. But they doubtless lack imagination.

My glasses are a great comfort. My eyes went back on me owing to food deficiency. We were very sorry to see the last of the Malayan crowd of volunteers who left us in Oct. I am glad to say Northcott Green and I are still together. He has been a wonderful friend to me. We still share a back verandah at the back of this house. One feels very sorry for the prisoners shut up in the Changi Prison, particularly the women and children. They never get out at all except when doing their own fatigues when they are strictly guarded by Sikh Police (armed with rifles) and they are not allowed to speak to us. We are allowed much more freedom. The camp is run by our own officers and there are canteens, concerts, lectures and any amount of games for the troops. It must be terribly hard for women and children who only have their prison walls to look at. They all sleep in cells. At least the Japanese could have put the civilians somewhere else—there are many places in Singapore. I have not once been into the town, and from what we hear everything is more or less at a standstill. There is no business worth speaking about. Prices of food are soaring up to absurd heights and most articles cannot be obtained at the requested prices but only on the "black market" who ask what they want.

A few personal notes: I have been most fortunate over kit. When I came "in" I had a camp bed, kit bag, and my large suitcase. I was able to get away all my army clothes, a pair of Grey flannel bags, sweater, waterproof coat (no longer as such) 3 pairs of pajamas (my nice ones) dressing gown (Austin Reed one which Dorothy game me) my rolls razor and my blades also a Gillette, hair brushes, etc. I scrimmaged 4 pairs of short underpants and vests brand new from one of the S.H.B. godowns and have just after 10 months started to use them as my old aertex (4 sets) have done me proud. For shoes I took from the house 2 good pairs, my walking shoes, plus army boots and red indoor slippers. I brought also 2 of my nice beer mugs (recently broken by the batman) and one cut glass tumbler just as a reminder of good days, which I still have. But best of all I have with me my darling Dorothy's nice photo, signet ring and the lucky ivory charms. These are a constant joy to me. When you think that for 10 months I have only used 3 shirts, 3 sets of underwear, and two pairs of slacks; and 3 pairs of shorts it cannot be said I have done badly. They are still in use with the exception of the underwear which has been thrown away this week. By the way, for my bed I have a most awful mattress, a blanket and sheet. What I am short on is towels, handkerchiefs, socks, toothbrush and the usual toilet stuff, which is most difficult to get. I repeat I have been most fortunate over kit for if we are moved it is quite certain a lot of my stuff will have to be left behind. What wouldn't I give for a Xmas letter and a small parcel? Perhaps it may even come.

April, 1943:

Some very interesting talks have been taking place between the Japanese General in charge of POW camps and selected individuals (Officers from various areas within the Changi Camp. The talks have been conducted with the utmost cordiality and refreshments were dispensed by the Japanese—beer, soft drinks and smokes. The General is widely traveled having been to England and America and speaks fair English. All sorts of questions were asked and news invited for improving conditions such as food, health, and hospital supplies. Personally I think these interviews may be the cause of improving conditions—they can do no harm. One very interesting sideline has been brought out at each meeting. The General said he could not understand why we all surrendered; in his country the men would have fought to the death or as he put it "cut belly" (hari kari). It was pointed out that in our army we obeyed orders, and that the act of "cut belly" would be an act of cowardice and quite against our religion. I gather the matter was dropped by stating that countries all have their own codes and customs. I also gather that it is generally felt the war will be long and that events are not turning out as expected—Germany appears to be a bit of a complex. I felt that I had to jot down this "cut belly" business as it is of particular interest: apparently in Japan it is quite common to commit *"hari kari'*, in fact if you sacked the office boy you might find him on your doorstep with "cut belly" which in our country is, of course, a crime and suicide. All in difference of ideas and custom.

Aiken
Charles Ambler
David Anderson
Joe Anderson
Assitery
Aitkinson (Harpers)
Bagot
Doc Bain
Ball
Jim Barrion
Shelton Agar
Battiscombe
Beavis
Jack Bennett
Beverley
Bidlake
Bingham
Buroney Boid
Binnie
W.L. Blythe
Borneman
Bousefield

Bowerman
Brandon
Brett
Brisk
Buchman
Burnham
Burns
Bryson
Byrde
Eleen Pearson
Edith Rathray
Bess Rogers
Ailson West
Mrs. Graham White
Marion Aitken
Elizabeth Burnham
Margaret Burns
Mary Burstall
Anne Griffiths Jones
Lady Thomas
Helen Wills
Rose Donnell
Alma Williams (nee Toby)
Lucy Fletcher (N.S.)
Mavis Seth
Dr. Elinor Hopkins
Mrs. Renton
Mrs. Bateman

[The reason for the above list of names is not known.]

The following are the only surviving letters written by Jackie Wainwright as a POWEngland.

EX.PW.MAIL

Mrs. D. WAINWRIGHT,
c/o Hongkong & Shanghai Bank,
9 Gracechurch Street,
London E.C.3.
1 St. Andrews Mansion,
Old Church Lane,
Kingsbury N.W.9
Sender(Written in English
(No.——-
(
(Rank.Lieut. S.S.V.F.
((Name.J.N. WAINWRIGHT.
Changi,
Singapore.
7/9/45

My Darling Dorothy,

At long last the day which we have been waiting for has arrived—you can imagine our feelings. How excited I am and how much you have been in my thoughts. Just fancy all these years of separation and waste of time; and what a "party" it has been.

The Authorities are now in the process of making arrangements for our evacuation, and we are hoping to be away from here in a few days time. You will have heard on the wireless all about the events taking place here so there is no need to go into details. I feel too excited to even eat. There is talk my sweet of our probably putting in at India on the way home—'tho I'm fairly fit a good overhauling is badly needed. I never want to see any rice or spinach again. We have been living on 1500 calories per days since Feb., so you can see we did not have much energy.

What a grim show it has been. My weight is not bad 9—6 [12] and I should put on a bit now that good food is coming again. Won't it be

12 9st. 6lbs = 120lbs

grand to sleep between clean sheets and have a hot bath. There is so much to tell you. You have always been in my thoughts. I wonder if you have felt me thinking of you. I've always kept your photo by me, the one taken on leave in 1940.

Poor old Boxer. I had to have him destroyed near the end—poor dear he was so frightened with all the din. Bless him, he left the "Cottage" with me and the "boy" in the early hours of Wed. 11/2/42. Amah did a bunk a few days before.

I've had letters from Eileen Pearson and Wardie from the Civilian Internment Camp at Sime Road. There may be a chance of getting in to see them before we leave. Lady Thomas has been simply magnificent so I hear.

My darling give my very fondest love to Mother and give her a good account of me. I do pray she is well—next all the family Margery, Dorothy, and Uncle Will; Aunt Betty, Aunt Florril and Uncle Haylett (Horners Fel stone). Then my darling write a nice letter to Sir John and MacEwan. I do hope that Guthries have been doing their stuff—

My love to Jan and Bill—What wonderful friends they've been to you. I don't know how to thank them enough. How is the old TOP? I wonder if he will be coming out here again.

Tom Calham and Withers send their love; also Freddie Edwards. Great fun we are getting all the wireless programs from London—jolly good race the St. Leger[13] I thought.

Darling I will keep you posted of my movements. We must go away somewhere nice in the country my darling. A nice little Inn.

My fondest love to you and Annette, and bless you both.

Your loving husband,

Jackie.

St. Leger = horse race

Changi Gaol P.O.W.

9/9/45

My Darling Dorothy,

13

One of the lucky ones is leaving here by plane tomorrow, so I'm hoping you will get this early. The position is we are waiting for a boat to take us off! And it may be any day now. Don't worry darling, I'll get to you as soon as possible. This waiting is nearly sending me crazy!!! It may well be that we shall have to stop in India for Medical examination but that is not at all certain. Anyhow I wish they would get a move on as it is just about a month since Japan packed in. It is the limit!!! Keep in touch with the Bank my sweet and leave an address for me.

What a reunion it will be—we must go away darling to a nice little Inn or Hotel in the country somewhere. Saw Eileen and Arnold a few days ago—the women have been simply magnificent.

Much love, Jackie.

EX. PW
1 St Andrews Mansions
Old Church Lane,
Kingsbury\
NW 9
Mrs. D. Wainwright,
c/o THE HONGKONG & SHANGHAI BANK,
9, GRACECHURCH STREET,
LONDON E.C.3.
ENGLAND
Sender J.N. Wainwright Lieut.
S.S.V.F.

Certification:
This "privilege" Air Letter will not be censored
in units but will be impressed with the unit censor stamp.
The contents are liable to examination at the Base.
The following certificate must be signed by the writer:
I certify on my honor that the contents of this "privilege"
Air letter refer to nothing but private and family matters.
Signature) J.N. Wainwright/Lieut. S.S.V.F.
Name only)

Changi P.O.W. Camp,
Singapore 13.9.45
My Darling Dorothy,

Well we are still here in Changi with no definite news of getting away. We now hear there is a possibility of going on Sat. I was on a draft which left here last Tuesday but unfortunately got taken off at the last moment. Are we impatient? You can imagine our feelings. We are all completely fed-up, especially as there is so much talk of getting P.O.W. away, I'm afraid my darling it's the same old story which you and I know so much of—the difficulty of course is "shipping"!!!

My word I am longing to get to you—what a meeting it will be Dorothy. We must plan a lovely little holiday on our own—somewhere nice and snug in the country. What a lot we shall have to say to each other.

We are now on the usual army rations plus all sorts of comforts—the stuff keeps on rolling in, everything imaginable. I must say everybody has been tremendously kind—too much so. I am just getting over a beastly bilious attack—change in diet. Once I'm on the ship I shall really feel things are happening—until then——.

I've been into Singapore three times. The first occasion I went and saw Wardie, Eileen and Arnold Pearson at the civilian internment camp at Sime Road near the Golf Club. We talked so much of you and had a great laugh. Arnold made scrambled eggs. Everyone looked so thin and pale but are picking up rapidly. Heaps of inquiries for you. Edith Ratts kissed me. Quite impossible to see everyone. V.J. is now down to 107 lbs. Wardie just the same, Lucy Fletcher and Sister Brom of General Hosp.

Next time I went in I looked round the town, and called on a few Chinese dealers. There is no business doing and the Japanese have looted everything. The town is quite dead—what a relief it is all over—just one nasty nightmare. Do you remember the old sugar towkay[14] who used to give Chinese dinners, and you hated going. He inquired very kindly after you; also M.S. Ally and the paper man. Wassimulli were very pleased to see me. All shops empty of course, but at the latter I got you a rather nice dress length and an indifferent pair of stockings.

14Towkay = merchant

Yesterday I saw the formal surrender of the Japanese. Marvelous parade on the padang. I don't see any object in your writing to me here but please note the official address is:

c/o No. 2 R.A.P.W.I. H.Q., S.E.A.C. Singapore. I expect you can feel how impatient I am when reading this.

All my fondest love darling.

Your loving husband,

Jackie

———

Addressed to:Mrs. D. Wainwright

1 St. Andrews Mansions

Old Church Lane, Kingsbury Mog

London Ec3England

EX POW

Mrs. D. WAINWRIGHT,

1 St. ANDREWS MANSIONS,

OLD CHURCH LANE,

KINGSBURY,

LONDON N.W.9.

ENGLAND

OPENED BY EXAMINER

THIS LETTER ID FOR THE USE OF H.M. FORCES ONLY

Written in:ENGLISH

No._______

Senders Rank: LIEUT.

Name:J.N. WAINWRIGHT

S/s/Alanzora

R.M.S.P

Thurs. 20/9/45

My Darling Dorothy,

I was simply thrilled to get your letter of 24th August; also one from Annette; it was sweet of her to write. I can see that I am really to be spoilt when I get home. The description of the flat sounds most attractive. I don't suppose by any chance you will want me to de-bug the cannas will you! Do you remember those days? You're letter arrived just at the moment of leaving Changi Prison where I have been since May 1944. Sounds awful doesn't it? Before that I was 14 months at Changi Point and the rest of the time in the old Gordons Barracks. How lucky I was darling not to be sent on some of those awful parties up-country[15] and to Japan. Our lot was bad enough as they were slowly starving us to death; another six months and I really don't know. The terrible stories now being relayed to you by wireless are in no way exaggerated.

I was most fortunate to be in a permanent job for 3 yrs. and so did not have much spare time on my hands. I purchased supplies of food for the Camp and for six months ran a canteen for the officers.

I shall need a really first class overhaul and intend to get all I can in way of treatment from the authorities. Just fancy my sweet, my weight is only 120 lbs. Much too thin even on your standards. I haven't any behind at all!!! Flat as a board as you would say, and most scraggy around the neck.

This ship is a trooper, and in addition to us, there are a few hundreds of civilian internees. Lots of friends of yours and heaps of inquiries for you. Eileen and Arnold are with me, the Wests (APC) and Toby and her husband. What a motley crowd we look. Eileen sends her love to you and is looking forward to a meeting.

I was very sorry to hear about Uncle Haylett. I think you liked him. Needless to say I was more than pleased to hear Mother is O.K. I was quite prepared for other news. Isn't it terrible to think one has been shut away from the world so long. Will you tell Mother I'll write her as soon as I can but at the moment we can only send one card and you naturally have first call.

I say darling do you think you could get some good, but inexpensive pictorial record of the war. I am also itching to see some news films.

We expect to reach Colombo Sunday and then proceed straight home. I'll keep in touch with you and I would suggest you get Bill to advise you where and when this ship berths. There is nothing secret and all censorship has been removed.

---

15 "up-country" = north up the Malay peninsular, i.e. towards Kuala Lumpur

What a meeting we will have—just like another honeymoon. Now don't you be silly and get all shy; it will be just as if I am returning from a trip up-country. It will be lovely to feel you near me again. You have never been out of my thoughts once. Gosh am I excited? My tummy is all upset and I'm completely off food and smokes. The last 6 weeks have been too much for me, I thought we were never getting away.My fondest love to Annette and heaps and heaps for yourself.

Your loving husband,
Jackie

H.M.T. Almanzora,
Indian Ocean.
Wed. 26/9/45

Darling Dorothy,

We left Colombo yesterday after a stay of two days one day of which was taken up for repairs. Although comfortable this ship is an awful old tub and was due for scrapping in 1939. We have had nothing but delays—2 days aboard in Singapore and should think that there at least five POW ships ahead of us. We had a tremendous reception at Colombo and the din made by the ships on the harbor was really deafening, the navy very much to the fore—at the same time—bands aboard naval ships played as we moved to our anchorage and the cheering was terrific. You can well imagine the scene—quite took the stuffing out of us. I don't think I've ever seen anything so moving. The organization ashore was a masterpiece.

As we came alongside the jetty we were met by Wrens—very smart girls and terribly sweet and fresh looking and in the main young. I was very impressed and tried to picture Annette in that kind of kit. Don't laugh the first person I ran into was Eve Palmer, in Wren uniform—quite in her element of course. She could not do enough for my little party of Officers—piloting us here and there. Everywhere we went military bands were playing—Red X presents of all kinds heaped onto us—Government House to the fore, information bureaus, baths, new clothes—but nothing to fit me. I'm glad to say I've gone up 6 lbs. and am now 126 lbs.

Eve said she had seen you 18 months ago—looking as smart as ever. Good girl, give me a little kiss. L.V. Taylor, the Wests and yours truly had tiffen with A.P.C. friends. First time in a bungalow after nearly 4 years—quite a thrill. Eve startled me when she said she thought I had been bumped off by the Japanese. She questioned me about her brother George who has lost his life, his ship being torpedoed.

I say darling have you heard Shrubbie died suddenly in India. I gather sometime last year. Kenneth Irie (also in the ship) got the news in Colombo; and also that Clarke died of cancer at home. All very distressing—poor old Shrubbie. Did you know of this? I sent a cable to you at Colombo and luckily Nestles sent off one for me to Guthries.

I ran into John Pickering in naval kit waiting to return to Malaya; he has been in Australia all the while.

There was literally nothing to buy in the shops at Colombo. We hear most disquieting news of restrictions at home. Don't worry darling I'm used to living on nothing. What a lesson it has all been. This ship is T.T. but are given a bottle of beer a day and 100 cigs a week—+ L2 a week. The civilians only get a L1.

My tummy is still all to blazes—I've taken all sorts of dope[16] but nothing "happens." I suppose it is the change in diet. I've no appetite and a beastly taste in my mouth.

This is only a short note—you'll get more from Suez.

Fondest love to you both,

Jackie.

Enroute Colombo.

P.S. Try and see if you can get a letter to me. We may stop at Suez or Port Said. Bill Wiley might wangle you a signal—we come under the Admiralty.

P.P.S. You had better advise Sir John and Mac Ewan of my movements. I sincerely hope the Firm have done their stuff.

16

CHAPTER IX
GERMANY

When my stepfather was finally released from Singapore the excitement was both moving and intense. As the tide turned at last, with the war nearing its end, and my department now reinstated in what remained of London, I joined my mother who, in anticipation of Jackie's return, left her job to find and prepare a home for the man she loved but had not seen for so many years. She worked both hard and well for the Foreign Office, determined to do her best, receiving praise, appreciation and gratitude from her superiors, together with thanks and affection from those who worked under her direction. She found a duplex flat at Wembley, just outside London. It was furnished, comparatively comfortable if not up to her standard of the attractive! However, her artistic mind soon went to work and with yards of Hessian, a sack-like material for a which clothing coupons were not required, numerous packets of do-it-yourself pink dye, and gallons of water in the kitchen sink. She even fashioned a darling little curtain-draped bedroom for me. Needless to say, various parts of the kitchen were, for a while, mysterious shades of pink, but that too was beneficial for her nerves—she used excess energy scrubbing the offending areas.

Mentally, she was prepared for almost anything on the day of his return, although she did confide in me that she felt "sick with excitement". We both stood in the sitting room, gazing at each other, not daring to speak, waiting for the unknown and wondering what to expect. Although numerous horror stories had reached our ears concerning Japanese POW—details of torture, disease and starvation—Jackie's letters seemed cheerful, filled with excitement and longing. His main gripe—the agony of waiting and the seemingly senseless delay in returning home. How she managed to contain her emotion, anticipating the sound of his steps on the gravel path I shall never know, after hose interminable years of waiting and wondering, pushing herself to the limit with her work. Would he make it or would he not? And now, at last, footsteps outside! The front door opened, then he swept her into his arms, enfolding her in a wondrous, long embrace. Strangely, although excited, I felt a little forlorn as I watched, as if I didn't belong in their special moment. Should I leave them to wander in the garden alone with my thoughts? But to my joy, I was not forgotten; with one arm still around my mother, Jackie opened the other as I went towards them. He drew me to him. A small family reunited at last. A moving little scene re-enacted by families all over the country.

Jackie looked sun-burnt, which detracted somewhat from his hollow cheeks, but he was pathetically thin. His clothes hung on him just waiting to be filled, but he would never again don the uniform of the reserves to fight. He could now begin a well earned rest, to recover both physically and mentally from the ordeal of the last four years. Jackie was now destined for a very much happier life beside the woman he loved, for whom he had longed all those wretched years of imprisonment. My stepfather would like to have had a family of his own, but without one, welcomed me with open arms. Circumstance kept us apart, however. As much as I would love to have stayed, it was only natural for the two of them to want to be alone. Much to my disappointment, off I went again to spend some time with friends before rejoining them, even then it was only for a few delightful weeks. Realizing they needed time alone to recapture their broken lives together, as she helped him back to health, both in mind and body, I volunteered to go abroad—to Germany—and do my small part in 'clearing up the mess'. Still too young to act upon my own desires, I obtained permission from my mother, but on one condition , I would be accompanied by an elderly, close friend of hers, Elizabeth Shea who worked with me in the London office. Together we set about the exciting task of gathering suitable cloths for hot and cold weather for the next two years, complete with fittings for the necessary khaki uniforms mandatory for civilians working in Germany at that time. I was told to take my riding habit,—stables were within easy reach of our quarters; and it was with some trepidation both Lizzie and I armed ourselves with skis, as skiing was on the agenda for our amusement. This looked more promising!

Feeling rather like a round little butterball all wrapped up in khaki—the Officer's uniform of the Control Commission—I was ready to be on my way to Germany. It was 1946—the year following the cease-fire, that of the Nuremberg Trials.

However, one thing remained to be done. The night before our departure, on the invitation of a friend in the cast, I went to see a Shakespeare play in London. Following a thrilling performance, my friend Stephen, still in the costume of a soldier in the king's army, took me backstage to meet the actress, Sybil Thorndike. I held my breath as this revered lady signed my own precious volume of *Shakespeare,* with Joyce Redman and Margaret Leighton looking on with interest. Deep in thought, one of them took the pen from Miss Thorndike's hand and wrote her own name, whereupon the other followed suit! Then two men—not to be outdone—laughed, turned the pages and finding empty ones, added theirs. The signatures of Michael Warre and Nicholas Hannon, both friends of Laurence Olivier and acting in his film of *Henry V*, now graced the pages of my lovely book. With the sound of their voices wishing me God speed I took my leave in readiness for whatever lay ahead.

Stephen followed as I clattered down the back-stage stairs in my new heavy walking shoes. I reached the pathment and turned to see him framed in the doorway, against the light—a uniformed soldier of King Henry's force! He watched me cross the street to disappear into the London night.

On a dark foggy day, with *Shakespeare* tucked safely at the bottom of my enormous zip-up canvas bag, Lizzie and I arrived at the airport, Liz as skinny as a rake in her brand new khaki uniform, and mine? Well, it didn't quite have the affect I would have liked on my round, plump little figure.

An army plane was standing on the runway, revved up and ready to go, as if akin to the ghost of some impatient demon, anxious to be off and lost from view in the mist above. We drove up to this noisy beast, where Lizzie was courteously helped and handed up the steps as befitted her age, by a tall, heavily mustached army officer. Having made sure she was more or less comfortably settled on one of the cold metal seats running down one side of the plane, he turned to me. Looking down from his great height, he grinned and said, "Well, you're a little one" whereupon he unceremoniously picked me up and tossed me into the belly of the plane. My huge canvas bag and I landed together in an undignified, sprawling heap upside down upon a cold metal floor at my chaperone's feet.

"Annette, my dear girl!" she laughed, as she kindly helped me up to sit beside her on an equally cold metal seat. From under my lopsided army beret, now covering one eye, I glared at the officer. However the would-be knight in shining armoure was now engaged in carefully assisting a blonde, long-legged WAAC into the plane. Oh well!

No time was lost in sorting ourselves out in readiness for a none too comfortable ride. The door slammed the impatient pilot, anxious to be off, signaled his farewell to those still standing on the ground as we began a short spurt down the runway and rising to be enfolded in the dark clouds overhead, and England was lost from view. It was a foggy winter's afternoon when we landed at Bucheburg, in the British zone of Germany, were met and whipped away in a staff car to the officers quarters at Bad Salzufflen, not far from Bad Oynhausen. With our luggage deposited on the doorstep, we were spirited away to another part of the compound, to meet the Commanding Officer of our unit.

Col. Julian Soames was standing behind a large oak desk, in a spacious comfortably furnished office overlooking the valley. From the windows he had a splendid view of a marble statue of Aphrodite—the goddess of love—in the valley below.

Julian was not the elderly soldier with weatherworn features and large mustache that I had expected! A young man, blond with laughing blue eyes and a warm, happy smile advanced towards Liz with outstretched hand of welcome, before turning to me with a grin. "Hello, Annette"! I felt my hand taken in a strong firm grasp, and wondered why Lizzie was smiling so broadly as she introduced us. Julian Soames was stunningly handsome, not what I had expected at all. After the initial pleasantries I was in for another shock. He immediately suggested that we go in search of Phoebe Preston, the daughter of my mother's former supervisor, (a beautiful dark haired, sweet mannered girl, a little older than myself) then invited us all to the officer's club for tea and pastries. Of this, he was sure we were in dire need after our trip; besides it would make us feel more relaxed and at home. By now I was beginning to realize that this was not exactly the sort of place I had expected to work. Actually, I wasn't sure what I had expected, but it became increasingly obvious with each passing moment that life was about to take an abrupt and wonderful turn.

The officers' club was a large building, which, like so many others in the area, overlooked the valley. Throughout, the striking black and white interior was designed to impress. A vast dining area with tables already set for dinner surrounded a spacious, well-polished dance floor, with a stage at one end for the band. The opposite end where we now stood opened onto a solarium. Here squat, glass-top tables stood low to accommodate armchairs for relaxed comfort, and this is where we enjoyed our first taste of fluffy cream pastries, the like of which Lizzie and I had not experienced for years. Mouthwatering slithers accompanied by cups of hot English tea, together with cream—stuffed chocolate eclairs served by white-clad German waiters. After the drama of the last few weeks, the hectic flight, not withstanding the shortage of food and rationing over the years, it was small wonder the initial introduction to what appeared to be unheard-of luxury rendered us almost speechless. It was difficult to comprehend how so much in the way of food could be produced in a country just defeated in war. But of course, until the previous year *they* had been the conquerors. Even more surprising, there appeared to be no animosity on the part of the German waiters; on the contrary—the service was implacable, and I realized that they considered themselves fortunate to be able to partake of any leftovers after their customers departed! With all this running through my head I felt like poor company at my first of many afternoon tea at the officers' club. I allowed an amazed and stuttering Liz to be the sole voice in answering enquiries regarding our flight.

The compound at Bad Salzufflen was encompassed by barbed wire—not designed to keep us in but rather to keep the Germans out. Although damage from the war was not at first sight visibly extensive in the area, food was scarce and many people deeply resented the presence of the conquering forces; the effects of war had taken their toll. Not that anyone would have done us bodily harm; but theft? Oh yes! On more than one occasion, the agitated voices of the German maids reached us from the kitchens below. Arriving early in the morning to perform their duties, their anxious cries reached us as we donned our uniforms in readiness for the day's work. We came to recognize the cause of their dilemma: intruders had again broken in during the night, forced the padlock on the pantry door, and made off with some of the food.

The women's mess was not uncomfortable. The windows of my spacious bedroom opened onto what would be in the spring, a picturesque garden, but it was now ready for a heavy fall of snow. And how it snowed in Germany! I loved every moment, watching the soft flakes floating down, casting a blanket of white as far as the eye could see. The trees with their stark beauty against the sky now cushioned in snow, soft white snow! I felt that it was a place which, under different circumstances, I could grow to love, a feeling that increased during the course of the next sixteen months I was stationed there.

Once again my secretarial training eased my way into the work, and many an evening as I made my way home, sometimes plunging thigh-deep through the snow, I thought of my volume of *Shakespeare* as it lay on the table by my bed, ready to be perused in the snug warmth of my room, over a glass of sherry from our rations. This was my first experience of the glowing warmth of alcohol creeping down my insides when emerging from extreme cold.

There were but few women in our area those early days following the war. Because of this, we were destined to be very much in demand after working hours to wile away the hours on the dance floor of the officers' club, or further afield on horseback, or racing dawn the mountains on skis. It was not long before life became too hectic for much Shakespeare reading. Dinner and dancing at the officers' club became almost a nightly occurrence. Skiing excursions high in the magnificent Hertzberg mountains and Goslar were arranged for many a weekend. The exercise did wonders for my figure, and the majestic beauty of the landscape brought peace to the mind.

For some people—those hardy ones well practiced in the art—this racing down the mountain on skis was their idea of heaven. With frozen noses, icy fingers and toes, their features took on a rapt expression, their voices softened in ecstasy as they expounded on the delights of battling the searing winds battering the body. With ice forming on chins and brows, the agony of stiffened limbs toiling on the uphill climb, they finalized in the ecstatic rush of relief as they hurled themselves downwards from the top in the final descent.

Liz and I were loath to show reluctance. After all, if everyone else could do it, so could we—but I wondered how. In all those clothes I could hardly move, let alone show my prowess on the skis, wielding a pair of poles with ugly looking points on the ends. I wondered if these might possibly pierce my boots and thence my foot in sheer malignance. Bundled in all the warmest clothes—vests, sweaters, two or three pairs of woolly socks and gloves, topped by a khaki battle dress with the thickest of balaclavas on our heads and round our necks, we staggered out to the 15 tonne truck parked outside our quarters where excitement abounded. It seemed that almost everyone in the unit had been smitten by the ski-bug. I ploughed my way up to the truck, head bent low under the burden of a rolled-up sleeping bag and a pair of skis complete with poles.

"Here, give me those, Annette!" I looked in the direction of what must have been the voice of an angel, and saw a large pair of black army boots on the icy road at my side. My eyes filled with gratitude as they traveled up the longest pair of legs that I had ever seen, eventually reaching a slender body. Long arms enveloped my gear which was on its way into the truck. I looked up into the smiling face and laughing eyes of one of the most handsome men that I had ever seen and forthwith lost my heart, a large portion of which remains lost to him to this day. Oh yes! I promptly fell head over heels in love for the very first time! The lean, clean-cut features, laughing brown eyes and light brown wavy hair together with an infectious laugh, completely captured my imagination. Like everyone else this young 'Greek God' wore battle-dress, and the gold crowns sported on his lapels clearly indicated that he bore the rank of Major. Major Perry Mark-Johnson.

In no time at all my kit was handed up with ease to his friend, Captain Roy Mitchell, and stored away as excited voices and happy laughter of men and women bent on fun, filled the air. It was contagious and impossible not to be drawn into the excitement of anticipation as we climbed aboard the covered truck, and settled down. Bundled up with rugs across our knees, our feet in woolly boots, all with balaclavas on our heads, we must have been a strange looking party heading for the Goslar Mountains The weather was expected to be rough. We did not realize just how rough, but accommodation had been arranged and we were expected.

CHAPTER X
WHO SAID SKIING WAS FUN?

We left the village behind with Perry at the wheel and Julian at his side to give assistance on the long and difficult drive from Bad Salzufflen to the mountains. The drivers in charge of our luggage in the second truck had a rough time in keeping up as they swayed and skidded on the icy roads. Despite the occasional thought of the cozy warmth of beds we left behind, the mood throughout was one of fun and relaxation—although one or two of us would gladly have snatched a few extra moments of sleep. Attempts at drinking hot tea from a thermos were useless, an army truck is neither smooth nor the most comfortable form of transport and Perry pushed it hard, anxious to reach our destination high up in the mountains before dark. We finally arrived at an isolated little German chalet snuggled amongst the trees on the outskirts of a forest.

No time was lost admiring the picturesque beauty of the place. We were anxious to reach the slopes before increasing winds and rough weather made it impossible to ski. Already snow was falling in whirls as strong winds buffeted our bodies, and judging by the gathering gloom, a great deal more was on the way. Even before the sleeping bags had been unloaded each of us had recognized and claimed our skis. Mine looked quite absurd standing upright in the snow between Perry and Ian Richards: both men well over 6ft tall, with skis the regular length—their height plus an extended arm—conforming to the fashion of the 40s and early 50s. I pulled mine out of the snow, laid them flat, stepped onto them and promptly landed on the ground as one ski instantly became mobile. I tried to regain my balance—and composure—with the help of the poles, and found myself flanked by Roy and Ian both laughing at my antics as they bent over my boots to adjust the bindings.

"Now you're alright! Just push off with your poles and go."

Liz and I had never been on skis, and soon both realized they seemed to have minds of their own. As far as I was concerned their intention did *not* coincide with mine at all. However, the first tentative steps were on flat ground. We had a fifteen-minute 'walk' to reach the slopes, or so it seemed to me. And to the others? Oh, they reached them in no time at all, but when *I* arrived at the top there was no one in sight! The weather deteriorating so rapidly made it impossible to see much in any direction. The wind rose to a blizzard, huge white flakes cavorted round my body and face from every direction. A human shape sped by, hurling itself downward oblivious to the elements, probably half-blinded by the blizzard, for blizzard it was, no doubt about that. Another shadow passed, this time more slowly on the upward climb, on reaching the top, the ghostly form flew by and passed me with a swish and disappeared into the howling wind in a flurry of flakes.

"Alright, Annette?" the voice that came from somewhere in the fury did not wait for an answer: "down you go."

I gritted my teeth, set my jaw, and thrust the points of my poles into the snow, gave a mighty thrust and a jump and sat back with eyes tight closed, and away I went. Whew! How cold it was—it took my breath away. I sped down hill, gathering speed and after a while relaxed. This was really rather fun. I opened my eyes but still could not see a yard in any direction. Another ghostly, gray form went whizzing by, but it was impossible to distinguish whom. My nose was getting numb, despite the balaclava helmet on my head and woolly scarf wound around my neck and half my face. All these clothes!

Suddenly I realized that no one had told me how to stop. Oh well! Eventually I would reach the bottom and presumably come to an automatic halt. A familiar form went by once more, but on the upward course—good heavens, that was the same one on its way down a moment ago. It was large—it must have been Ian! Certainly not skinny Liz! No time to ponder on her fate; I seemed to be slowing down and must have reached the end of the run. Yes! To my relief and with no effort on my part the skis slowly came to a final halt. Well, in spite of everything, it was really rather fun! Now, I had to turn around and climb back up, but that was easier said than done. I turned half-left with the inside ski, toppled, caught my balance, then tried to raise the right—it would not budge. The back of the left ski crossed over the back of the right, and pinned it firmly to the ground. I promptly fell. It took some time to sort myself out, pick myself up, brush the snow from the back of my pants, and plant myself in what I hoped was the right direction. The blizzard did not let up! No longer at my back and thrusting me down, I turned to what seemed to be an endless climb. The mighty blasts blew against me, howling around my cumbersome form, battering my body, endeavoring to do battle with every move I made, supposedly towards the top. A ghostly figure passed in the same direction with surprising agility and speed. It plunged its poles into the snow to give its body a boost—ski followed ski *sideways*—no sliding back for them! I turned my right side to the hill and tried my luck in similar gait—first the right ski to make the move up, then the left to join it. I made a small, a very small advance. Slow going! Slow and painful going! Lift the right foot encumbered by a ski, and place it sideways up hill, then the left to join it. First one ski and then the next...first one ski and then the next...Slow and painful—just a few feet at a time, sideways supporting what seemed to be great shafts of wood—onwards and up, just on and up. The steep ascent, the ever-increasing muscle-weary legs assured me of the right direction. I struggled on in the encroaching darkness.

The shadowy forms no longer passed, either way: not up, nor down. To be alone in unfamiliar surroundings was not my main concern—I must reach the top come what may. I had to keep up with my peers, and not disgrace myself in asking for assistance.

Meanwhile back at the chalet, the others gathered in the dusk. Liz told me later with Phoebe's help, how they grappled with bindings to release the skis, their fingers stiff from the cold, then stamped their feet—their boots crunched through the top icy layer as they sank in the snow. The sound of the crisp crack of wood against wood rang out in the gathering gloom, as ski met ski in an upright position to be carried to shelter for the night. They told of cheeks that glowed as they came in from the cold to the warm, dimly lit room, of candles that cast their shadows on cabin walls and logs that hissed in a fire that blazed one end of the room. The fragrance of burning wood and warmth acted as a magnet as people emerged from the cold mingled with a tantalizing aroma wafting through the door of an adjacent room where the inn-keeper's buxom wife served up bowls of steaming hot stew with warm crusts of bread, all provided by ourselves. Food was too scarce for the local population in these parts to be imposed upon by a mob of hungry skiers. How rewarding is a good hot meal after the exertion of battling the elements! Everybody relaxed for a while, little was said as they savored the first few moments of the delicious hot brew. Then, with their appetites momentarily assuaged, the conversation started slowly as they compared the excitement of the day's activities to those of more climatic times.

"Your first time on skis, Lizzie? How did you like it?" Julian joined the older woman.

"My dear," Lizzie laughed apologetically "but thanks to the patience of Ryan I would never have managed at all. As it was I cheated and came in early. I expect Annette did very much better."

Julian laughed and turned towards the others. "Annette!" he glanced around, and there was a poignant silence, "where is Annette?"

Lizzie's face fell. "Oh, my God. Where is Annette?" Phoebe laughed as she told me this part of the tale, poor old Liz went as white as a ghost!

"I passed her going down. She was doing quite well, from what I could see, but the wind is still pretty strong and the snow was…" Cynthia, Julian's secretary looked from Lizzie to Julian, then at Perry and Ian before sinking down beside Phoebe, her voice trailing off. All three men made for the door, but Ian beat them to it, and by the time they got outside, his tall figure already on skis, enveloped by whirling snow, had disappeared into the storm in the direction of the slopes.

As he reached the top, so did I, tired, aching in every limb, out of breath and exhausted. Through flaked covered lashes, I looked up at the large figure hovered above, and reluctantly grabbed hold of the pole stretched out to assist me up the last few steps.

"You alright?" If looks could kill, this young giant might have dropped dead in his tracks. I glared up at him and said nothing. His lips twitched and it was not caused by the icy wind, he tried not to grin. Perhaps it was just as well I was not to know he was suddenly taken by what he considered to be this spunky young girl.

"Follow me," he yelled, to make himself heard above the howling wind: "Put your skis into my tracks."

Now on flat ground I was not about to admit defeat. Methodically placing one ski after the other, I followed Ian who turned and went ahead, blazing the trail. Putting my skis into his tracks as instructed, I found that in spite of weary limbs and aching muscles the going was very much easier. His body acted as a barrier from the elements and I had to admit, if reluctantly, his very presence was encouraging. But my ego had received a blow.

After what seemed an eternity, welcoming lights from the little windows of the chalet appeared through the blizzard. Perry's tall figure loomed in the doorway, a mug of ale in his hand. He put it down in the snow and soon helping hands were propping me up and unsnapping the bindings of my skis. The men stooped to get through the door and the warmth from the room hit us in the face as we entered. A steaming bowl of delicious hot stew was placed in front of me—I sank down on a chair by the fire; the aroma alone was enough to keep me awake until it all had been consumed. The tables, already cleared, were pushed back against the walls to make way for sleeping bags, pulled from their stack in the corner and laid out down the center of the room. We prepared to rest and restore our energy in sleep, arranged alternately head to feet, men and women, we settled down on the floor.

Two of the officers stood by the fire talking quietly, Perry leant against the wall—a burning log fell at his feet, sending sparks flying with little snapping sounds. He laughed at something Roy said and kicked the log back into place; bending, he chose another from the pile close by and threw it in is place. The two friends talked in undertones, mulling over the day's activities. It was a peaceful group of men and women; all friends at ease in each other's company.

Exhausted, I zipped myself into my bag and almost before my head touched the floor was asleep, lulled by the murmur of voices, as friends recalled the day's experiences with those closest to them in the line. Liz's feet, snug and warm in her sleeping bag were by my side; to whom the others belonged the other side, I neither knew nor cared. The hot comforting meal, and soft voices of men and women settling down for the night, the flickering light from the fire all had their affect—I was lulled into happy oblivion.

The sun rose on a perfectly glorious day, the vista transformed overnight. There was no sign of the previous day's storm. The air was crisp and still—the snow packed and sparkling in the sun—perfect conditions for a good day on the slopes.

One by one the bundles in the center of the room stirred, the contents of the sleeping bags withdrew in turn to the rest room, to brush up and prepare for a day's excursion. They gathered round a table at one end of the room where toast, butter and marmalade, accompanied by mugs of hot tea acted as a magnet to the enthusiastic.

"Skiing, Liz?" Phoebe, putting on her gloves on her way to the door, turned to the older woman with a smile.

"You know, my dear, I think I'll give it a miss." Lizzie said with a sheepish grin. "I can hardly move!" Phoebe laughed and went outside to find her skis amongst those lined up against the log wall of the chalet. There was a bustle of activity; everyone collecting their equipment, strapping on bindings, blowing warm air into their gloves before putting them on.

I must admit I was reluctant to relinquish the warmth of my cocoon for the winter cold outside, and in no time at all realized that there were muscles I never knew existed. Winding an agonized course across the room and through the door to the great outdoors, I looked askance at Perry, as he assured me with a grin, that these would soon 'loosen up and be back to normal' the moment I started 'ploughing down the slopes.'

Ploughing down the slopes! I looked across in Lizzie's direction and saw her sheepish grin as she purposely avoided my gaze.

"Lizzie?"

"Well! I'm not sure my dear." It was obviously rather difficult for her to move at all.

"Lizzie if you do, I'll have another go at it!"

After some protesting she capitulated and we both steered a painful and ungainly course towards our skies propped up with the others, as if challenging us to try our luck once more with the excitement of the sport.

It was indeed a glorious day. As we followed the others down the lane towards the slopes, we absorbed the beauty of the countryside in the depths of winter under a deep blanket of snow. Even as we passed, the trees on our right, their boughs laden, one or other would dip under the weight and deposit their load with a plop onto layer beneath and then to the white covered ground. The air was still, but bitterly cold, although the sun shone bright enhancing the brilliant beauty of the day, reflecting on delicately laced icicles balanced precariously on needles of green, on the tips of branches of some of the trees. A winter wonderland into which one longs to tread and listen to the silence! Stretch out an ungloved finger and gently touch the shimmering wisps of icicles, but is afraid to do so, for fear of marring the exquisite beauty of nature's masterpiece.

Perry was right—he certainly knew what he was talking about. In no time at all, muscles that had seemed to creek before, loosened their stranglehold on movement. We reached the top where the others were cavorting with the season, and away we sped, our breath hitting the cold air in clouds as we laughed with the sheer joy of living. If *only* I had a camera to capture the beauty of the place, the antics of my friends and companions, photos at which to laugh amongst ourselves and share with my mother and Jackie back in England.

Later, riding home in the truck, content, weary but happy, I voiced my longing. Ian looked at me thoughtfully through thick-lensed glasses. "Have a word with Corporal Andrews. See what he can do for you."

"Corporal Andrews? Who is he?" I asked.

"Our photographer." he replied, then after a pause "you'll find him in the dark room."

It was late as we rumbled into Bad Salzufflen, tired, happy and for many of us women, with aching limbs! Although the men were tired after the exertions of the weekends activities, they did not admit to any discomfort, all being in prime condition. However, everyone was ready for a good night's sleep!

CHAPTER XI
CHRISTMAS IN THE MOUNTAINS

I lost no time in seeking out Corporal Andrew's dark room, only to find him securely locked behind closed doors. No amount of rattling or knocking made any effect on the quiet little man, just a gently voice from within assured me he would emmerge eventually. I subsequently learned that this was often the case with dark rooms; film was either in the developing stage or in the fixing solution, the only light permissible—the soft, almost indistinguishable glow from a single red bulb to prevent one bumping into the immediate soundings. Consequently, the door was almost always locked. My inquisitive mind immediately became fascinated with all this paraphernalia inside once I had gained access, but it never occurred to me to question why we had a dark room in the first place, or what negatives lay floating in the solutions or hanging up to dry. It was just a matter of course that these activities took place, and not for me to question the why or wherefores in the aftermath of war. Eventually, I persuaded him to initiate me into the art of developing and printing my own films. But for the moment the subject uppermost on my mind was the purchase of a camera, at a cost that would not keep me in debt ad infinitum.

Corporal Andrews had obviously been forewarned of my impending visit. It was I who was somewhat startled when this soft-spoken little man—strangely out of place in his pale blue airforce uniform amongst so much khaki—asked with a twinkle in his eye if I smoked. Taken aback I assured him I did not, whereupon what appeared to be another seemingly irrelevant question came my way—had I kept any of my cigarette rations? Yes, actually I had! I can't think why, but there were cartons of cigarettes tucked away in the bottom of my wardrobe.

"Good! In that case bring me five hundred cigarettes and I'll be able to get you an excellent camera." The German black-market—I should have known!

Although there were about eight female secretaries in our unit all sporting the oversized green and gold flashes of an officer of the Control

Commission, the opposite sex outnumbered us by far. Our group of four, all girls, was led by Lizzie. Alone in a room reserved for codests, each was able to concentrate quietly on her work, with an occasional impromptu chat with one or another in the unit, anyone who happened to drop by to pass the time of day. As for the secretaries, each was assigned an officer.

This was my first experience of working with the opposite sex en mass. Initially I found them somewhat intimidating, no doubt due to their awesome appearance in uniform, but thanks to their charm and fun-loving ways I soon relaxed and lost my shy demeanor. They became personal friends, and over the months there grew in me a tremendous respect for each and every one of them. As far as work was concerned, not once did I question their respective jobs. A strict code of secrecy instilled in me at so early an age, it never entered my head to question the whys and wherefores. In one form or other, all the occupying forces in Germany were working towards the trials to be held in Nuremberg. We were there to bring order out of tragedy and that was all there was to it, no questions asked. We worked and when it was time to relax, we played.

Being young and under age, however, did set me apart. These endearing, patient people tolerated and indulged my innocence and youth. While Liz watched over her young charge with a motherly but eagle eye, Julian took on an even greater task—his officers! It was not until we all met at a cocktail party in London a few years later, that he jokingly confessed to me as far as I was concerned, he 'had more trouble keeping his officers in check' than all his other problems in Germany put together!

Surprised, I gazed at him blankly. "I beg your pardon? Julian, what do you mean?" His eyes still crinkled at the edges when he laughed!

"You had better ask Ian" he grinned, nodding in the direction of the tall, quiet man gazing at us from behind thick lens from across the room. But it *was* for me, a unique experience to be in Germany. Had it not been for the war, I would not of had the chance of so much foreign travel, visiting places made all the more interesting under such extraordinary circumstances, with history taking place before my eyes. Nor would I have witnessed the majestic beauty of a deserted magnificent countryside, unspoiled by human population.

*****

A Zeiss lens for 500 cigarettes—unthinkable in this day and age! The new camera, a Zeiss Ikon, gave me both interest and tremendous pleasure. With practice, not only beautiful pictures of the little town of Bad Zallsufflen and surrounding scenery began to emerge, but excellent and amusing photos of my friends and colleagues taken indoors with a flash and other, more relaxed images, at leisure, playing in the snow. Fascinated with my new toy, not to mention amazement at the remarkable results, I shot reel upon reel of every conceivable person and scene I could find, and with practice derived much amusement and interest in the dark room under Corporal Andrew's tuition.

Although in time cameras changed and I lost access to the developing stage, my passion for photography lasted all my life, with some excellent results. Of course copies of the present photographic efforts in Germany, were soon winging their way home to England, much to the delight of my parents—but not all of them. I began to take personal shots, what I fondly imagined—and quite rightly so—were excellent pictures of my companions with whom I worked in Germany. They were happy moments captured in the innocence of youth.

"Annette!" it was Julian watching and laughing with Perry, at my efforts to focus and "catch" a good still-shot, "give those rolls to Sergeant Thomas. He can send them away to be developed."

Perry, feeling that I needed some sort of explanation interjected "Corporal Andrews is too busy to do them at the moment."

Back at the office I sought out the tall imposing figure of the sergeant, and handed him my precious rolls of negatives. He assured me they would go to the right place, and the probably did—but I never saw them again! Security! All this endless security! I was far to shy to tackle the sergeant and demand the return of my precious photos.

But one I did manage to save! It was taken on a scenic collection. A splendid photo of Julian smiling at me across the snow—a photo I have and cherish to this day. A strong reminder of times gone by!

*****

As ships, filled with former captives, sailed slowly into port in 1945, Jackie witnessed the emotional welcome with other ex-POW from one of the decks. He watched the WRENs in their smart Navy uniform, parading on the docks of Colombo in Ceylon, as it was called in those days before being granted independence by the British. After years of degradation and despondency, not to mention the humiliation of a Japanese prison camp, the sight of these lovely young girls greeting them with joy and overwhelming jubilation proved too much for the emotions for many of the men. Jackie's beloved wife and the girl he thought of as his daughter were very much on his mind, and he pictured me in that self-same navy outfit serving in the forces. Now, although the uniform was khaki and the service of a civilian nature, he was not disappointed and continually asked for more photographs. He took enormous interest in all my activities. It was clear in letters from them both that his health was improving, although his mind would never be completely free of the experiences in Singapore. It was also mental anguish for my mother to witness him recalling the nightmare years of incarceration. During the early days of newfound freedom, Jackie read his diary aloud over and over again, elaborating upon incidents in camp. My mother listened, hoping that by reading it he would be released from the horror he had witnessed and undergone. She encouraged me to write more often and with ever lengthening letters, as these provided them both with much interest and amusement.

As the weeks and months progressed Jackie's more somber, wistful moments became less frequent. His natural sense of humor reappeared and the infectious laughter was more often heard. The inevitable visits to the doctors, which at first had taken up so much time, became less frequent, then finally ceased. Now he was anxious to return to work. Jackie wanted to resume his position in Singapore with Guthries, and the powers that be were only too delighted to send someone with experience and knowledge of the local contacts back to their Far Eastern office. So, with excited anticipation, the two of them spent time preparing to return to a place they both loved—to set up their new home sometime in the following year. In the meantime my mother asked me to send home a "really good" enlargement of a photo of myself as a Christmas gift.

A really good enlargement—this was a teaser! I brought the subject up over tea and pastries at the officer's club one cold, winter's afternoon. The oncoming Christmas season was under discussion—where to hold our festivities, what gifts to send home from the Army store in the nearby town of Bad Oynhausen, where other units were stationed. We had already made several friends and enjoyed the invitations of their officers, some of whom remain close friends to this day. With Christmas looming on the horizon, I wanted something unique, not the usual perfumes and toiletries. An enlargement of a photograph would be ideal, but it had to be good!

Once again, Corporal Andrews helped me on my way. This time his directions took me to the village after work on a dull, overcast day. Deep snow lay on the streets and the going was slow as I made my way down a narrow path beside a row of tall houses. Windows that opened out onto the path in summer were tightly closed to keep out the bitter cold. The winter of 1947 was the worst on record.

In answer to my knock, a door like any other on the street was opened by a tall, slim woman. Her bearing and quiet charm donated that she was of the upper middle class, hit by the effects of war. Neatly dressed in a blouse and skirt of somber colors that had obviously seen better days, her dark sleek hair pulled back from her smiling face, giving her a look of extraordinary peace, putting me at ease. Her elegant sister, who might well have been a twin, hovered at her shoulder as they bade me come in, with a warning "mind the puddles" seeping over the doorstep!

Once furnished with taste, the place was now somewhat the worse for wear—shabby and bitterly cold without heating (apart from an oil stove in the center of the room), and damp stains appearing on the walls. I began to realize what these people were experiencing in the aftermath of the war. It opened my eyes to appreciate the benefits of our mess and the lifestyle that we were fortunate to enjoy within the confines of our military enclosure.

My knowledge of the German language was poor although improving, and their knowledge of English, absolutely nil. However, their brother spoke fluent English, and it was he I went to see. No longer in a German uniform, but living with his sisters, a photographer of his caliber would find it difficult earning a living in his profession in those early days after the defeat of his country, unless of course he could prove useful to members of the conquering forces. But, in my sweet innocence, I thought nothing of this! After all, his friendship with our own photographer *might* just have been a coincidence. This was the person I was seeking not only for his expertise with a camera, but also with a brush! I thought how sad it was that talent such as his should be wasted in time of war. Or was it wasted?

As I write this, I turn to look over my shoulder at the extraordinary, unsigned portrait hanging on my wall. Gazing at the wide, deep set eyes and searching for any imperfection in the picture, but find no mark from his brush in the light oil wash. There is peace in that portrait, and the coloring near perfection. The only thing indicating that it is not just an enlarged color photograph are the pearls lying softly on the turquoise blouse, almost a match of the material. I have never seen pure pearls reflecting the color of a blouse before!

I look at the picture now and think to myself "What manner of man painted you my friend?" There is no signature! What other pictures did he produce to keep his hand so well in touch all through those years of war? How did he become a friend of our photographer? What mystery lay behind his skill? What stories could he tell? As for that what mystery lay behind *ourselves!* I realized that more lay to our unit—that "No. One Planning and Evaluation" was just a cover, that our officers were a band of very special people—but if anyone knew what we were supposed to be planning and evaluating, they certainly forgot to tell me! But at the time my mind was *not* set a wondering! A few days following the sitting during the visit, I returned to choose one from three small shots. My heart sank. How could a "decent photo" come into being as a result of one of these miserable looking, tiny little black and white things? A disappointment lay in store for my parent's back in England, or so I thought. Too shy to question or express my feelings, having chosen what had the potential for the best result, I departed with a sinking feeling, his instructions to return in two weeks time ringing in my ears.

During the time leading up to Christmas Day we worked hard at the office and afterwards trudged back through the snow to our mess. Some evenings I spent reading *Shakespeare* or relaxed with friends. But more often I dined and danced at the Officers Club, or with newfound friends further afield in Bad Oeynhausen.

Julian took a party of us to a ballet in Hanover, which, in the absence of a theatre, due to the efforts of the allied bombers, took place in large and spacious stables. The rightful occupants no longer in residence, their place was taken by a company of excellent German performers, dancing to the accompaniment of a fair sized orchestra made up for lack of numbers by their standard of performance. Members of the local population were making efforts to resume their former way of life. Despite the absence of comfort of normal theatre seating, it was an enjoyable evening for they were good. We were impressed, and later went on to the officers club to mull over the evenings activities before returning to the mess. Here hunger pains took over. We searched out the larder key from its regular hidden niche, undid the padlock and in our exuberance of secret searching amongst the edibles for a suitable snack, I slipped it into Julian's pocket for momentary convenience. Unfortunately our minds now completely focused on the goodies never gave the key a second thought. That is, not until the early hours of the following day when all-hell broke loose from the nether regions. Pandemoniun from the maids—no key, the padlock firmly closed. Even worse when the offending object was finally retrieved from the inner depths of the C.O.'s pocket!

"Really Julian!" disapproval was belied by the unmistakable grin, which spread across Lizzie's face.

Time flew by as it always does when one is occupied and in good spirits. Two weeks nearer Christmas and once again I made my way to the village. This time both sisters greeted me at the door in a twitter of excitement and, without further ado, ushered me into the inner sanctuary of their brother's studio. His back was turned towards us as he contemplated his latest work resting on an easel in the center of the room, and from the smile on his face as he turned our way, it was clear that he was pleased—and well might he be! It was perfect. The pastel shade of the turquoise blouse, blending with the pink tones of the skin, enhanced the deeper shadow around the eyes that gazed into space. I could not believe the transformation from the small, passport image of the previous visit, to the sixteen by ten-inch oil painting now confronting me. It was several minutes before I could speak. And when I did, what I said seemed totally inadequate. But aware that three pairs of eyes were intently watching my reaction, spontaneously allowed my features to express my feelings and the artist and his sisters were delighted.

Congratulations poured out from one and all and I departed with the delightful, lighthearted feeling of exuberance, clutching the precious gift safely encased in wrapping paper and sheets of fine wood for final packing and mailing overseas. Together with the satisfaction of having made new friends, but that two women were able and anxious to make new cloths for me, in anticipation of the time in the very near future when we would change our uniform for more glamorous evening attire.

Because I knew my parent's telephone would be constantly busy with calls from friends from Malaya in similar circumstances and friends in England with Christmas greetings, I telephoned them two days before Christmas Day. Although the lines were congested as the occupying forces called family and friends during the Christmas season, eventually Jackie's voice came through quite loud and clear.

"Hello Jackie." I called "Happy Christmas!

"Annette! Hello! Lovely to hear you. I say, you really did it this time! Your mother is thrilled with your present! You couldn't have given us anything better.

"You opened it." I said in mock dismay, " It's not Christmas yet."

Jackie laughed. "She couldn't wait. But don't worry—I wrapped it up again and put it under the tree for Christmas Day…But mind you I don't know how many times it will be opened as people drop by before the great day… Dorothy, come quickly. It's Annette."

He sounded well and *very* happy. It is hard to fathom what was going through his mind that year—the first Christmas at home, away from the sights and sounds of that wretched camp, recalling former efforts of a pathetic 'festive' meal to celebrate the birth of Christ. His own home at last, decorated for the Christmas season, complete with a magnificent tree, the house filled with love as the never ending stream of friends and well-wishers dropped by to welcome him home. The aroma of Christmas fare wafted through the kitchen door as it always did in my mother's house that time of year, the like of which had not tickled his senses for so long! I could detect in his voice the emotion of the whole experience, which must have brought tears to his eyes and I imagined him gently sinking into his very own armchair by the fire, sipping a drink from a crystal glass with my exquisite beautiful mother—bedecked in black velvet—free from anxiety, relaxed and divinely happy at last. It was a joy to hear her voice, light hearted and happier than at any time that I could recall.

"Darling, what are you doing for Christmas?" she asked. "I expect you will have fun with your friends?"

"We're all going up into the Harts mountains," I replied "There's castle up there, a German schloss. I hear it is a terrific place for a party."

Jackie must have been standing by the telephone. "Phew, she is going to have a wonderful time!" I heard him say. For a while we talked excitedly and in doing so found myself swept up into the spirit of Christmas, enfolded in love from home.

I did send back the toiletries—perfumes that my mother adored, with fragrant soaps and lotions, little luxuries Jackie had so sadly missed for years. But the piece de resistance was the picture and this gave me a feeling of satisfaction and well being, knowing that I had brought a surprise with so much joy.

*****

Excitement increased over the next couple of days in anticipation of the trip. This time, work and skis were left behind. It was to be a late afternoon to evening Christmas party and with this in mind, we donned our formal coats and skirts—instead of the usual battle-dress. Using more comfortable cars in place of trucks, we rode in convoy, which enabled us to gaze out and appreciate the dramatic winter scenery as we climbed slippery roads banked in snow, high up into the magnificent Herz Mountains. Oh yes it was cold but squeezed together with rugs over our knees, we kept each other warm.

Phoebe, Liz and I sat in the back, while Jean, Ian's ultra efficient secretary, rode in front with the driver. With dark hair, wearing glasses, Jean was of a more serious disposition than most of us. Deep by nature she seldom spoke unnecessarily, yet instinctively one felt that in an emergency she would be invaluable, the first to take over in any unforeseen situation. But at the moment, cares of work put aside, all of us were looking forward to some fun in celebration of our Lord's birth. On and up the winding mountain road, sliding and slipping many times in spite of chains wrapped around the wheels, the cars eventually reached the summit and our destination. Driving out onto a vast, flat area white with snow, I caught my breath. It was as if we had been transported back in time, to a fairytale setting of the Brothers Grimm. I could hardly believe my eyes. Snow fell gently easing out a watery sun, which in turn invited dusk to take over prematurely.

Across the open area, to our left, a small castle complete with pinnacles, perched on the edge of the mountain overlooking a deep ravine and wide valley, its outline silhouetted against a darkening sky, with little windows filled with light shining through the falling snow. One could almost expect hobgoblins to come tumbling out! In the distance to our right, stretched a large, silent forest into which the denizens of this fairy wonderland had retreated quietly, to curl up into cozy nooks and crannies for the night. Would Rumplestiltskin appear at the edge of the snow-laden trees, chanting witchcraft? The sound of happy voices and laughter, already in the spirit of Christmas, came from within the schloss. The cars pulled up to the door and somewhat reluctantly we unfolded ourselves, loath to relinquish the warmth of the rugs, to plunge through the mists formed by our breath as we hit the cold.

"Come on girls." Jean's practical voice broke into our spellbound gaze as our eyes became accustomed to the bright lights.

"Oh, my dears!" gasped Liz as she was drawn into the happy throng of officers each trying to outdo the other in volume, glasses in hand, wishing one and all the greetings of the season. After a while, the meaning of Christmas very much on my mind seeking solitude, I left the revelers and slipped outside. Snow fell gently as darkness slowly stole the light from day. Pausing only for a moment, I made my way towards the forest, through the snow. It was cold against my stockinged legs, but the reward of peace was too good to miss, and soon the sounds from the revelers faded and the castle left behind. All was quiet and apart from the falling snow, very still.

Looking in the direction of the trees ahead, I smiled, almost expecting to see the fire around which the wizened form of Rumplestiltskin would ghoulish dance. Suddenly I froze in my tracks—no fiery flame or crackling wood or little gnome—but a real, more wondrous sight pulled me up short. Round the edge of the forest to my left against the backdrop of the trees came two wild horses galloping with tails and mains flying free stretched out in the wind unencumbered by saddle or reigns. One was gray the other of a darker hue, faint but distinct through the falling snow. They made no sound as, with necks stretched out, they raced full length of the copse and upon reaching the end of the trees to my right, turned left around the corner disappearing from my sight.

I held my breath as this was taking place. Although no figment of the imagination, others might doubt its authenticity and I was not about to share it with them. Wonderful, but private, this was mine to keep and savor to myself, without inviting doubts as to my sanity. Many times throughout my life I have relived the whole scene in my mind, particularly when in need of peace. Reluctantly, I turned back towards the schloss and trudged back across the snow, loath to break the spell.

The sound of happy voices resonated through the halls of the schloss as the festivities continued until late into the night.

*****

The ski enthusiasts took full advantage of the holiday season, 'swanning' to the mountains near and far, visiting Goslar, Bad Harzberg and Winterberg. But for Mary, one of our beautiful blond secretaries, and her boyfriend Ryan, nothing but the Bavarian slopes would do. They made a wonderful looking couple, for he was as dark as she was fair—a stunningly handsome Swiss officer, stationed in Hanover. Their expertise on skis made me almost green with envy. They spent the weekends racing down the mountains, their senses thrilling with the sport and at the same time reveling in the glorious scenic countryside.

As for me, I had had my fill of skiing for a while and sampled instead the nightlife of Brussels. Having had no previous experience of nightclubs, I was fortunate in my choice of beau. Handsome, debonair and wealthy to boot, hailing from a prominent Scottish family, Captain Andrew Pettigrew was stationed with a unit in Bad Oeynhousen. He proved to be an exciting escort!

The hotel in Brussels was luxurious, but as instructed by the ever-attentive Liz, the adjoining door between our separate rooms kept locked—the key my side! The rooms were spacious and ornate, and oh, so very comfortable. The nightclubs were filled with exuberant people in uniform as well as civvies, all seemingly with a frantic desire to grasp life to the full, determined to make up for time lost to the war. I watched the Belgium girls, dancing close in the arms of their escorts, their long evening gowns floating across the floor. Although losing weight toward a more sylph-like figure, I felt cumbersome in my heavy khaki uniform with low-heeled walking shoes and longed for more glamorous evening attire to give the local beauties just a little competition!

In Andrew I had the perfect escort, attentive to my every whim. He was man who carefully scrutinized the menu before ordering an excellent meal accompanied by wine suitable for the palate and the occasion, and to my joy, an expert dancer on the floor. I recall with nostalgia that enchanting evening, and took as normal consideration the charm with which he escorted me, standing as I rejoined him at the table, concerned with elegant ease to my every comfort, not only opening the car door but closing it when I was seated. Now, as we enter the 21st century, I look around and watch and wonder—where, oh, where has chivalry disappeared in this day and age.

On our return I lost no time in visiting the two German sisters with lengths of beautiful material from England sent by my mother, to be transformed into evening dresses in preparation for the time in the very near future as the demand for uniforms after dark would be abolished.

CHAPTER XII
'SWANNING'

Early in the New Year Perry was called to the Berlin office, which temporarily disrupted a very pleasant relationship for a rather unusual trio. Close friends, both he and Roy had taken me under their wing. I had a tremendous crush on Perry whilest Roy complicated matters by having one on me.

On my arrival in Germany, we three met and soon became accustomed to each other's company, enjoying easy banter with plenty of laughter. They called me Roo, after Kanga's 'Roo' from A.A. Milne's Winnie the Pooh because, as Perry laughingly put it, "Roo was such a very little thing"! I missed Perry and was therefore, delightfully surprised when Julian suggested that I visit him. Although unable to go himself, he was sending his car east through the Russian zone to Berlin with his driver, a slight individual with an expressionless face. I did not question the reason for his car to be travelling empty to the war-torn capital, but certainly jumped at the chance of a ride through some glorious countryside, in the comfort of the C.O's personal transport.

Leaving Julian to tackle Liz, I gathered a few things together to throw into an overnight bag, and with her words ringing in my ears, "Only one night, Annette," coupled with Julian's laughing voice, "If you are stopped by the Russians and Harry shakes a bit, don't worry—he's trigger happy, but it's alright." Then, as an afterthought, "experiences during the war you know." His blue eyes were filled with laughter—a stark contrast to Liz's anxious ones as she clucked like a broody hen.

"Now remember, Annette, you *must* be back on time. We need you in the office. One night only!" I wondered if she worried more about the Russians or the fact that I was visiting Perry! But realizing she was more agitated each passing moment, assured her that I definitely understood this proviso then sat back in the comfort of the CO's car to watch the vast expanse of scenery passing swiftly by. Everything in Germany seemed oversized—fields and woods stretched for miles into the distant horizon, with magnificent views as the sun shone on a cold but glorious day. Out in the open country there seemed no physical trace of war; just deserted, open fields and beauty everywhere one looked as we sped along the autobahn.

Gazing out of the window my thoughts began to wander and the scenery now passed unnoticed. The very fact that I was in a foreign country at that time was extraordinary to say the least, but leading the type of life that had fallen to my lot, almost unbelievable. The allies had at last won a devastating war that, in one way or another affected every single person on the planet. But now that hostilities were at an end we found ourselves right in the middle of another war, if not as devastating, an equally dramatic fight against oppression—the Cold War.

With Germany divided into sectors between the four great powers, mopping-up operations were carried out in the zones of the occupying forces. The Americans were in the South, reaching up to the British zone and doing pretty well as much the same as we were doing in the North—living presumably as we were living, and carrying out their job to the best of their ability, co-operating when our paths crossed, endeavoring not to step on each others toes. As for the French, they were in the West and if our paths did cross, as far as I can remember, no news of it came my way. Then there was the Russian zone about which I knew absolutely nothing, apart from the fact that it was drawing closer each moment we drove east.

As we slowed to round a corner, there before us was a barrier barring our way, patrolled by armed, dark clad soldiers in a strange uniform. Black trench coats reaching mid way down their high black boots and caps pulled low over unsmiling faces made for a formidable scene. As if to lend emphasis to the situation, an enfolding blanket of darkness from the trees of the great Black Forest stretched from immediately behind the barrier as far as the eye could see, and seemingly ready and almost eager to sweep us into its clutches like some greedy spirit. Only the thin gray thread of the empty road ahead—the autobahn—gave hope and relief of possible light at the end of the day.

The driver brought the car to a standstill as the Russian soldiers approached, bent down and peered through the open window. Harry appeared not to understand one iota of Russian, and in return their knowledge of the English language seemed absolutely nil. Luckily it was not difficult for them to understand the word 'Berlin,' and without much ado the barrier was raised and as we moved slowly forward, I for one drew a huge sigh of relief.

Almost immediately a blanket of gloom enfolded us as we entered the forest. The stark contrast between the British and the Russian zone was like night from day and could not have been more pronounced. The magnificent giant evergreens closed in upon us. I peered into the forbidding darkness, from left to right, first one side then the other and got the eerie feeling that we were not alone, that unseen eyes followed our every move. Harry showed definite signs of nervousness and I wondered why. What was he afraid of? Was something hidden in the car to be delivered to the office in Berlin, and if so where? Or was there something about his person that acted like a magnet, on view for everyone to see? It was an uncomfortable position to be in and one only for the intrepid! His foot clamped down on the accelerator and we lunged forward sending me plunging back against the soft upholstery. The car kept on going as if all the devils in hell were on our tail, slowing only when a lone, uniformed figure loomed as a speck in the distance in the middle of the road, gradually increasing in size as we closed the gap between us. More unnervingly, he proceeded to wave us down. Just one soldier—no sentry box and no companions—in sight! Just one guard in the middle of nowhere!

He sauntered to the driver's open window, bent down and peered inside, allowing me an excellent view of his round, expressionless face and an opportunity to study his features. His heavily-lidded eyes, gazed through narrow slits. He would have looked more at home riding a small, rugged horse on the wind-swept steppes of Mongolia, where riders and sure-footed, swift little steeds blend into one, rather than pacing the autobahn alone in the middle of Germany. All was quiet and very still. I wondered how many pairs of unseen eyes were peering at us from the darkness of the trees. What would happen if he took a dislike to us on sight and raised the alarm?

Trigger-happy, is that what Julian had said? I looked at the back of my driver's motionless head. He sat rigid—not a muscle moved.

It was with a feeling of relief I saw the guard at this strange random checkpoint finally straighten up and saunter round to my open window. He bent down and looked inside for what seemed an eternity. Eventually I followed his gaze down to my hands lying loosely in my lap, and to my horror realized what held his attention so acutely. Over the years I had collected small charms now attached to a fine gold chain around my wrist. One that had been given to me as a child was a replica of Rudyard Kipling's good luck emblem—the swastika in reverse. This lay resplendent on the top of my hand in full view! It was a moment fraught with tension but, after what seemed an eternity, his narrow eyes rose to my face and gave me a searching look, then traveled again to the back of the driver, who remained rigged and motionless. Eventually turning back to look at me and realizing that I was nothing more than a harmless, innocent young girl, he sighed then smiled and his face was transformed. He stood back to let us pass.

Harry's right foot slammed down on the accelerator and away we went, not pausing until the outskirts of Berlin came into sight. As we drew near, the most prominent feature loomed ahead—a monument to the victorious Allies, built by the jubilant Russians. Mounted on a giant concrete block high over our heads, aloof and alone, stood the first Russian tank to enter Berlin, that fought its way into the fury of the battle. Now, with its painted coat of gold gleaming in a watery sun, no one could mistake the fact that it was the first tank to bear the brunt of the last Nazi resistance. As we passed I looked up, craning my neck to see this strange memento. It was truly an awesome sight for anyone entering Berlin, especially for the very first time.

We made our way to the outskirts of the city and the British zone. To my surprise not a building was standing in our sector, the damage had been cleared and everything was flat—quite neat—but totally flat as far as the eye could see. I wondered where the local population lived. However, on the perimeter a number of buildings stood undamaged and habitable, and it was there in the British sector of Berlin that we had established our offices.

Perry was on hand to greet us with Captain Johnny Johnson in his wake, but with a hurried "Hello! Be with you in a moment Annette" he led Harry down a corridor and through a door to his inner sanctuary, where they remained for a good fifteen minutes. This came as a bit of a shock and I began to realize that there was more indeed to this trip than met the eye.

Although it was freezing outside and getting colder by the minute, as evening drew in, the building felt pleasantly warm and comfortable, thanks to a generator producing electricity and light. The local people were not so fortunate. Supposedly one of the coldest winters on record, they were getting a taste of what they had doled out to millions of people over the last six years.

I saw little of Berlin. Perry was very protective of his young friend. He still had work to do, but made sure that I remained indoors and settled down with a book to read until he and Johnny were free. It was a paperback—a thriller that held my interest; good, not stupid and dull like so many love stories of the day. My tentative suggestion that we visit the Russian sector of the city was received with marked disapproval. Perry's handsome face lost its normal laughing stance; a slight frown marked the forehead, the dark eyes hardened.

"No!" came the short but firm response. I left it at that for the moment, fully aware that because he knew me well—as someone special, he hated to let me down. However, I would find out soon enough, exactly why he was so reluctant to agree to my request.

When he and Johnny were free to relax we spent a delightful afternoon playing cards. In those days I was good at cards, and we were all well matched. The German maids brought tea and biscuits, and occasionally Perry unwound his tall frame to reach over and throw a log on the fire that burned cheerfully in the grate. I was fascinated by the way his long, slender fingers handled the cards and his merry laughter was contagious. Time passed all too swiftly, only to be rudely interrupted by the jangling of the phone from the office. Perry went towards the door leaving Johnny and I to pause and stretch our legs. I went over to the window and looked out; it was getting dark and cold outside. Where were all the local people? On his return, Perry glanced at his fellow officer who raised an inquiring eyebrow.

"Julian?" Johnny asked. Perry smiled and nodded, but said no more and soon we sat down to dinner.

Thanks to our generator the house was pleasantly warm. After a good night's sleep I collected together the few things that I had brought with me, in readiness for the return trip, went downstairs and joined the two men at breakfast. After a cheerful greeting Perry happily announced that he had sent Harry back to Bad Salzuflen with Julian's car, but would keep me in Berlin one more night to drive back with Johnny the following day.

I was horrified! "Perry! Liz will kill me. Why did you do that?"

Perry grinned "Don't worry, Roo, Johnny will handle Liz. He'll drive you back tomorrow." I glanced at Captain Johnny Johnson and very much doubted his ability to handle Miss Elizabeth Shea and from the look on his face he did not relish this idea at all! I giggled at the thought of the two of them battling it out, but Perry was firm. Having discussed it with Julian on the phone, they both agreed that an "extra day away from the office would do me the world of good."

"What a line!" I thought, but kept it to myself. "Harry must have something in that car, even if it's locked inside his head!"

I was very young to be in occupied Europe, especially in that situation, and Julian wanted me to enjoy myself and not take life too seriously. The figure work in coding was concentrated and hard on the eyes, but in his opinion I had proved myself as conscientious and doing well. As for my craving for a visit to the Russian sector?

"Em! Oh dear…" Julian had made no further comment except "For God's sake take care of her Perry," then added with a laugh "otherwise you'll be facing Liz!"

I was told about this years later at the reunion given by Julian in London, and was touched by their genuine feelings of warmth and concern for my safety. But at the time, no matter how hard I tried, it was impossible get a reasonable answer out of either Perry or Johnny. All I could do was to try and forget Liz's instructions and hope that Johnny was staunch enough to withstand her inevitable wrath.

Both men had business to attend to during the day and being anxious to finish my book before leaving Berlin I settled down to read. Sometime during the morning, reaching the end of a chapter I put the book aside and wandered into Perry's office. He was working at a metal object in his hand as I entered the room, but glanced up and smiled, "Come in, Roo," he said and continued scratching the silver piece with a sharp pointed needle. He opened a drawer of the desk, and taking a cloth, rubbed it until it shone. Curious, I bent over to see the shining object. It was a pretty thing, two inches in diameter—a poppy—a beautiful silver poppy!

"Perry! How perfectly lovely! Where did you get it?" I asked.

He replied quite simply "From a Russian agent. He made it for me," and taking my hand in one of his placed the pretty thing in mine. As the strong fingers closed over mine he said with a light, happy laugh "It's yours sweetheart!" I turned it over and saw a pin—it was a broach! On the back, scratched so laboriously the words "Roo, yours ever Perry." It had been made for Perry, with me in mind, by his Russian agent—what strange times we lived in! I walked on air for the rest of the day, as happy as a sand lark. I love that broach and treasure it to this day—my one connection with the man I truly adored.

That evening Johnny suggested another game of cards.

"Cards? Here in Berlin!" and turning to Perry I opened my eyes with what I hoped was an imploring look: "Perry, I want to explore. Why can't we go into the Russian sector?" I might as well have asked for the moon.

"Roo, we cannot. It is strictly out of bounds." He was adamant. Even Johnny was making anxious murmurs in the background, normally so placid, he too showed definite signs of agitation. Stretching whatever wiles I could muster, it took quite a bit of feminine persuasion to achieve the desired effect. Reluctantly they both relented and sure enough, after the sun had disappeared, I waited in the hall to meet them in expectant anticipation.

Eventually there were voices and the sound of heavy army boots on the landing above. Looking up I could hardly believe my eyes. In battledress armed to the teeth with pistols, sheathed knives in their belts, and heaven knows how many rounds of ammunition round their waists, they came clattering down the stairs.

“What on earth…?” I burst out laughing, “The war is over Terry!”

“Annette! We are not allowed to go into the Russian sector! If we are caught we are in dire trouble.”

Without further ado, they ushered me through the front door and out into the night. It was pitch black—no friendly moon shone above and not a star to be seen in the sky. The clouds were heavy and filled with moisture. All was perfect for our escapade! Holding the back door open Perry said, “Get in the car, and if anything happens, lie low.”

“What on earth could happen?” I thought to myself but said nothing and followed his instructions. The door slammed and my two ‘gallant heroes’ somehow folded themselves and all their paraphernalia into the front seats of the little car. Perry switched on the lights and started the engine, put her into gear and we were on our way heading for, what one day would be a solid wall dividing east from west. At the moment however, gaps dotted the structure, just large enough to allow a small car through and maneuver its way to the other side. It was through one of these more narrow sections we followed the beam from our lights and surged into the forbidden sector of our Russian allies and into unknown territory.

Perched on the edge of my seat I strained to peer into the darkness, as we followed the lights of the car plunging through potholes filled with water and ice, bumping our way along narrow tracks banked with rubble and littered with debris. Great planks of wood protruded from high mounds of earth and bricks, which made our progress not only difficult, but also positively dangerous. Suddenly, as we wound our way round a curve, the front wheels of the gallant little car rose over a bump, forcing the headlights to rise to the top of a great giant mound of earth, bricks and rubble ahead. Silhouetted in the beams of light, high above us, were two young men, Germans, pistols aimed each at the other.

“Look!” exclaimed Johnny, “over a loaf of bread!” The loaf was lying to one side, clearly visible.

“That’s it! We go!” Perry hauled on the wheel with screeching breaks, the car almost tipped over, the right side climbing the mound as we turned to the left in the frantic effort to retrace our steps.

"Perry, what are we doing? We haven't been anywhere yet." Trying to keep upright, hanging on to the seat in front, I voiced my protest as best I could.

"We've seen enough," he replied. "Now let's get out of here."

"Hold on, Annette," Johnny's hands were on the dashboard trying to steady himself.

The car gave an awful jolt as we lurched over a plank of wood in the so-called road, and charged towards the gap in the wall. We missed it in the dark but found another further along, skidding and sliding in puddles in a frenzy to get away from all that was Russian, barely slowing down as we plunged through the gap, back to the comforting sanctuary of our own sector.

"Why? Why are we going back? We haven't seen a thing yet!" I was trying with all my might to remain upright, gripping the back of the seat in front and talking in gasps.

Perry gradually brought the car to a stop grinned at me over his shoulder as he tried to explain. "Roo, if just one of those boys fired a shot, the place would be swarming with Russian police and we would be in the thick of it. We were out of bounds!" then added, "Don't worry sweetheart, you can say with all truth you have been through the Wall and into the Russian sector!"

A Brandy was in order for both men when we reached 'home' and I went to bed with a mug of delicious hot chocolate. But I was shocked. My eyes were opened to the reality of what had to take place in order to achieve the peace the world so desperately needed. I began to realize the importance of the justice we were determined to meter out to those responsible for the horror of the past six years. There was an awful lot to fully comprehend. However, I was right in the center of it now and unwittingly, whether I liked it or not, I would remember it all for the rest of my days.

Julian opened my eyes to a number of things at the party he gave for me in London, and his own blue eyes filled with mirth as he recalled those times. Together with Liz they had a problem, being duty bound to return me to my mother whole and intact after my two year posting in Germany. Laughing, he joked that as far as I was concerned, he had more trouble holding his officers at bay than any other problem he had with the Germans, Russians or anyone else amongst his other duties. How naive I was. Had I realized what powers I held, I would have used them to far greater effect!

CHAPTER XIII
THE AFTERMATH OF WAR

Johnny did *not* handle Liz—she handled him.

A stark contrast to the original ride to Berlin, the pleasant drive back to Bad Salzufflen was uninterrupted by Russian guards who were, no doubt, camped in the forest but out of sight. We were neither stopped nor troubled. However it was a different thing when we walked into my own office where the atmosphere was brittle! Phoebe glanced up for a moment, but quickly returned to her work as Liz vented her wrath on the poor unfortunate John. No matter how hard he tried, he failed to get a word in edgeways and eventually with an apologetic glance in my direction, he bid a hasty retreat. After Elizabeth's withering glance I decided that discretion was the better part of valor and said nothing but picked up my pencil and got to work, while Johnny made good his escape and doubled back to Berlin.

Gloom hung heavy on our heads for the rest of the day where silence reigned until we packed up our work for the evening. It was quite a relief to trudge through thigh high snow into the warmth of the women's mess. Besides, it gave me a chance to think back and laugh with Jeanette, about my escapades in the capital. Then I remembered the cold and wondered how those in the Russian sector were faring, living out an existence literally under the rubble.

The Berlin episode lay dormant tucked away in the recesses of my mind for fifty years until one balmy California evening in 1999. As a volunteer helper with the Nortel Film Festival in Palm Springs, I mingled in the foyer before the show with visitors from all parts of the world. A man's gentle voice with a strangely familiar accent, attracted my attention, but I couldn't place its origin. I talk to him and heard he was from Germany.

"How interesting," I said "I know parts of Germany. Where are you from?"

"Berlin," he replied "1947—it was the coldest winter on record!"

"I know. I was there!

"You were there?" It didn't take long to be drawn into conversation as I lead him to his seat.

"I was a very small boy in Berlin in '47," he went on "We had no power at all in one of the coldest winters we had ever known—no light and nothing to cook with. If we wanted a hot meal we made a little fire in the open, with some bricks in the shelter of the rubble. We kept each other warm sleeping huddled together at night."

He went on to tell me of his beloved companion, a tiny white mouse he that adored. "The little creature would spend its time racing round a treadmill in his cage during the day and slept under my shirt for warmth at night." He paused for a moment, remembering his childhood, then continued. " One night I forgot and left him in his cage, and in the morning I found his little body dead on the floor of the cage—just stiff. He had frozen to death."

"Oh, no!"

"I was inconsolable," he went on with a smile, "I adored my little mouse."

"How strange life is" I said, "you on one side me on the other, in the same place all those years so long ago, and here today we meet as friends in Palm Springs, America of all places!"

"And that is as it should be," he replied softly as he and his companion settled into their seats at the end of a row.

"Yes," I echoed, "that is as it should be," and the lights went down for the start of the movie.

Although I searched for him at the end of the show, with the rush of people leaving the theatre it was impossible to find him. A pity—I would dearly like to have had a chance to continue that conversation—and find out which sector of Berlin he was in.

All was quiet as I walked home that night, the California sky filled with a spectacular array of stars. The moon shone down casting shadows as it had done over Berlin during the war, as it had so silently those tropical nights over men incarcerated in a prison camp in Singapore. There have been visitors to that moon since then, and if we should return—which assuredly we will—I for one, hope that we will be kinder to that far away moon than we have been to our own beautiful planet—Earth.

*****

That was not the last Liz heard from Captain Johnny Johnson! Exactly two weeks later he was back, having made the drive from Berlin alone. This time he bore a message from Perry to be deciphered and the materials with which to do it, in the form of liquid in a small glass bottle he carried in a trouser pocket. From the depths of another packet he pulled a scruffy blank piece of paper, handed it to the bewildered Liz and asked her to set about decoding it.

Nothing like this had come our way before and naturally it captivated our attention totally unnerving the older woman. As she and Johnny straightened out the rumpled paper the bottle tipped over, and in the excitement of the moment the lid came off, the clear fluid flooding the desk and everything on it, much to our merriment as we jumped to her assistance.

The confusion rose as words appeared in bold, black letters on the once blank, scruffy bit of paper. Liz—looking sheepish held up the dripping object by one corner, and apoplectically handed it to the Captain, as we in turn, mopped up the mess upon her desk! Obviously some agents in the war-torn capital knew nothing about figure coding as such, and certainly not our five figure groups!

But it did result in equal footing between our fearless leader and the Captain and once again good humor between the sexes was restored.

*****

Gradually the snow melted in the village of Bad Salzufflen leaving the marble statue of Aphrodite gazing out over the flow-off that formed a lake in the valley below our office. Her picturesque figure reflected in the water that would slowly recede, encouraging lush green grass to grow, as spring preceded the summer warmth.

For us in Germany, more seasonal activities took the place of nerve-wracking experiences on skis, speeding down mountains covered in snow. I struck up a friendship with a spirited, dark bay mare that few would ride. Monica often displayed the whites of her eyes: she was tough, she was strong and prone to bolting, invariably depositing her mounts on Germany's good, solid earth. But when she realized that I was used to this sort of behavior—having possessed steeds of my own—and was not about to become unglued, we had some wonderful times together racing through fields and forests, in the early morning breeze.

Even before the last of the snow disappeared, Monica and I became fast friends, our early morning excursions taking on exhilarating experiences. She never lost her desire to shy at shadows, both real and imaginary—including her own; to her this was just pure fun. Her strength was formidable, necessitating me to exercise both mind as well as body. In the early morning before breakfast sometimes we went out alone, but when in the company of others, she would strive to bolt and outdo everyone in sight. I was encouraged by the grooms to exercise her as much as possible and work out some of that excess energy.

At such times it was difficult to realize that trials of the atrocities resulting from the war were taking place at Nuremberg, in the American zone of Germany—where justice was at last meted out to the leaders of the so-called master race. But we were far from that in our small part of the British zone—a beautiful zone, now filled with British soldiers and civilian, hunting down those responsible for so much horror and destruction.

One of our secretaries did accompany her boss to Nuremberg. Although Jeanette was a friend of mine, our strict code of security prevented me from entertaining a thought of questions I might have and she offered no information in return.

More and more over the years, as accounts of this tragedy come to light, I realize that the reality of it all might fade as generation follows generation. That would be a pity—I hope World War II will never be forgotten.

We continued our work in the office during the day and spent the evenings dining at the officers club, or with an ever-increasing number of officer friends from surrounding units, punctuated by trips to interesting places. One of these I had a chance to visit when Perry was transferred to the Dusseldorf office on the outskirts of the area. I spent many happy hours alone, meandering through the woods in the near proximity, picking my way through patches of snow that had yet to disappear. The trees bereft of winter foliage, dripped moisture in my face. Everything was quiet and still with just a leaf falling, twisting as it and floated on its way. It was a time of year I loved.

When the snow finally disappeared and winter surrendered the land to spring, a magical change took place, filling the air with fragrance from the blossom that covered the trees; the song of the birds resonated through the sky. Every branch was filled with a cargo of life. With the French windows on my balcony flung open, inviting in all that was natural and beautiful, I spent more time with beautiful volume of *Shakespeare*, browsing through its pages.

Sometimes, insisted of riding, two or three of us drove to Lubecka to sail on the Duma See, where there was an opportunity to bring my Zeiss Icon camera into play. The yachts, the sails and the rippling water not only made for some pretty pictures, but also had the desired effect on working minds—it was impossible not to relax!

*****

Eventually, as summer approached, shirtsleeves became the order of the day. We noticed that our counterparts in the surrounding areas arrived from England wearing navy blue. At first glance we rather envied them, but soon realized the material was heavy and in no time at all looked hot and uncomfortable. We tended to gloat—a little 'one-upmanship' from those of us who were amongst the first to arrive in Germany!

During the heat of the summer Peter Morrison-Jones, a Captain in another unit in the British zone, invited me to take a trip to Hamburg. He had business there and thought I might enjoy the ride. Peter was not a handsome man, but charming and incredibly loyal. What's more he had the advantage of topping Liz's approval list and I must admit her opinion on this was sound.

It was one of those hot, midsummer days when all creatures—including mortals—prefer to be very still, when Peter and I set out on the autobahn; not in the luxury of the CO's car, but a British army pick up. It was enclosed and I have since learnt that the American open jeep, although seemingly devoid of springs, would have been more comfortable in such incredibly hot weather, wide open to catch any passing breeze. Discarding coats for shirtsleeves made things a little more bearable.

By the time we arrived at the outskirts of Hamburg in the late afternoon, we were hot, disheveled and my makeup badly in need of repair. Reaching into my bag on the floor at my feet I retrieved my cosmetic purse. The lipstick case felt hot, but not until I took off the cap I realized just how hot! The case was empty—the lipstick a puddle of red and Peter's untimely mirth was not appreciated. Bereft of lipstick, hot and sticky, all I wanted now was to relax in a bath, filled to the brim with perfumed water. However, for some reason best known to him, Peter stopped an M.P, and asked for directions to the army store; and thankfully, a well-stocked shop it turned out to be! Not only was my lipstick replaced but he presented me with a bottle of Worth perfume, which did wonders in restoring my morale.

Hot and disheveled we arrived at the Hamburg Hotel, went through the door and came face to face with an awesome sight. Although the town was heavily bombed by the allies during the war, there certainly was no evidence of this in the opulent foyer of the hotel!

The place was alive with officers, both men and women coming and going in all directions. Awe-struck by the sight of the impressive array of meddles and ribbons, I gazed in amazement at Peter, wondering what sort of "business" had brought him here! Our feet sank into the carpet as we followed a pageboy up the stairs and to a large, comfortable room.

Peter looked around with approval. "Yes, this is good" he said handing me the key and continued "My room is on the same floor, at the end of the passage. Relax have a good bath and rest. I'll give you a call later, and we'll meet in the bar for a drink."

"On the same floor *at the end of the passage*!" I am sure if Lizzie had had her way Peter would be on another floor altogether!

But I thanked him, closed the door, unpacked my case and flung open the windows to catch the breeze. I took off my uniform and replaced it with a flimsy robe, stretched out across the bed, relaxed and listened to the water filling the tub in the adjoining bathroom.

With water just the right temperature, the fragrance of Worth wafting through the door, the bath was ready to receive its grateful occupant. I sank down, closed my eyes and relaxed. What a relief!

After a while, but in no hurry, I stretched out an arm for the soap—it was just out of reach. Lazily, with a shade of reluctance I sat up, when something caught my eye. I glanced to the right and got the shock of my life. At the back of the wash basin and through an enormous hole in the wall I saw a pair of socked feet. Complete with suspenders pacing the carpet, backwards and forwards they marched in what appeared to be some agitation but not nearly as much as that now experienced by me—by no means had *all* the damage from the allied bombardment of this once beautiful city been repaired!

There were still holes, *enormous* holes in the strangest of places, and here, in my bathroom one large enough for a full-grown man to enter on his hands and knees. I was horrified! Covered in confusion, I sank down to my chin in the water to collect my scattered wits and plan an escape.

Had I not been of so naive I would probably have seen the funny side of this ridiculous situation. Who knows? I might even have thrown a towel around myself, popped my head through the wall and smiled a cheerful hello. But I *was* horribly shy. Sinking down again below the rim of the tub, the luxury of relaxation totally destroyed. I wondered if the owner of the socked feet realized there was a live body within sight should he happen to bend down and glance in the direction from where the sound of splashing water had rung out? Or was he some high-ranking Army executive, his mind on problems so far beyond those of my own—which however, seemed pretty gigantic at that moment—he was totally unaware of the very existence of a gaping hole in the wall of his sitting room. Surely he could hardly miss it?

I decided that a discrete and hasty retreat on my part was the better course of action. Following the next stroll of the legs, nipped out of the bath as silently as a nip from a large amount of water would allow, picked up a fair sized towel to throw around myself—Roman style—and bid a hasty retreat through the bathroom door which I firmly closed behind me. Inhaling an enormous sigh of relief I decided there and then not to breathe a word to anyone about this horribly embarrassing situation.

So much for my stay in Hamburg, and Peter never knew a thing! Thank heaven we spent only one night in the city; more would have played havoc with my nerves. We enjoyed a delightful evening of wining, dining and dancing. Afterwards I spent the night darting in and out of an unlit bathroom, too terrified to turn on the light—how do you scrub your teeth in silence? My saving grace was the old fashioned key in the keyhole, again my side of the door, turned to safety position before jumping into bed. Peter and I remained good friends for many years, and I hope still are, despite the fact we have lost touch since I moved to America in '62.

*****

Periodically I called my parents who were eager to hear of our activities. My experiences in Berlin must have left them wondering a bit, but they never wavered in their opinion that I was "a lucky little devil" to be having such an exciting time and visiting so many interesting places at no cost to myself.

They themselves were taking trips, staying at picturesque little pubs, enjoying the beauty of the English countryside as they walked across green fields and down country lanes. Soon they bought bicycles and went further afield, and all the time Jackie indulged in his new found delight—bird-watching, a passion formed in POW camp where sparrows shared his precious food, and became beloved unfettered companions.

My mother showed commendable patience on these occasions. A sparrow with a twig or blade of grass, would bring Jackie to a sudden halt. "Look Dory look!" he whispered, enraptured by the efforts of the little feathered creature, pushing and twisting the twig into place, as he and his mate built their precious nest. Gazing through binoculars he chortled with delight, whilst my poor mother battled with her glasses hanging round her neck. By the time they were pointing in the right direction and more or less in focus, the charming objects of all this attention had flown in search of more building material.

Invitations to formal luncheons and evening activities that arrived in the mail, were much more to my mother's liking. These resulted in trips to London, with stays at a charming hotel they discovered in Ebury Street. It was a chance to dress in her most glamorous attire, with Jackie sporting black tie and sometimes tails. If they stayed a second night in town they could indulge in a show in Drury Lane, or the ballet at Covent Garden, and meet with friends and former Prisoners Of War who, like Jackie, were reveling in their newfound freedom.

One document received with pride and gratitude by every returning prisoner of war was a welcome home letter from His Majesty King George VI. My parents' subsequent visit to Buckingham Palace was an honor well deserved.

The invitation to The Lord Mayors luncheon at the Mansion House, to meet the Admiral of the Fleet, The Rt. Hon. Viscount Cunningham K.T., G.C.B., D.S.O., Field-Marshal The Rt. Hon. Viscount Alanbrooke, G.C.B., D.S.O., Marshal of the Royal Air Force, and The Rt. Hon. Viscount Portal, G.C.B. O.M., D.S.O., M.C., gave them a tremendous boost to the morale, and a chance to meet former POWs who had also been invited, who had been until that day, out of touch.

Almost always when meeting friends, my parents were questioned about my own activities and, with delight, would give accounts of my whereabouts and lighthearted escapades. My mother never failed to remind her friends—nor me, if it comes to that—how fortunate I was that her contacts in high places used their seniority to draw me into the auspices of the Foreign Office, when girls of similar age on leaving school or college were drafted into factories, to perform *their* war work.

One thing she tended to overlook or preferred to forget, was the strain close figure work of coding had on my eyes. Not strong at the best of times—although my sight was good with glasses—there were times at the end of a day's work those eyes were grateful for a rest!

CHAPTER XIV
CHAMPAGNE, HIGH JINKS AND HORSES

Summer's colors are vibrant and beautiful in Germany. I spent more and more time before breakfast at the stables with Monica, my magnificent bay mare, riding in the early mornings, through the fields and forests, round vast areas of golden corn and oats. It made the days cooped up in the office pass more quickly until it was time, when all of us would interrupt our work for a stroll down the street to the officers' club for tea. Lizzie was as skinny as a rake and unaffected by the pastry puffs stuffed with cream that were placed before us, no matter how many she devoured. Phoebe was more circumspect and used discretion. As for me, I relied on Monica's assistance to regulate my waistline.

I grew to love that lady. Our times together were sheer delight those glorious summer days when we just roamed free, skirting evergreen forests a deep shade of green, trotting between fields of golden oats and corn swaying in the breeze, beneath blue skies peppered with puffs of silver clouds. There were no gates to maneuver no fences to bar our way—no barriers of any sort and life was *very* good. A pity it was all to come to an abrupt and disastrous end.

There was a party in our mess the night before. Both Ronny and Perry were waiting at the bottom of the stairs, champagne in hand when I floated down in a pretty evening dress.

"Here she is," smiled Perry, handing me a glass filled to the brim with bubbly liquid, "Happy birthday, Roo!"

I went ahead, leading the way to the room where the festivities were already underway. Each person had drawn on their reserves of liquor from their generous ration allocation, the food had previously been prepared by the German staff. Dance music of the time blared out of the gramophone—records chosen and changed by anyone passing at the moment. It was a happy occasion with dancing into the early hours of the morning. Looking back it amazes me what reserves of energy we possessed on which to draw when we are young. Dancing the night away on a few glasses of champagne, then up at the break of day, to witness the sunrise in the magical company of horses, followed by a good day's work—and probably ready to dine and dance the following evening. No doubt we pulled on emotional reserves created by the events of the times, added stimulus following the war, and excitement of just being where we were, alive and young.

Sometime during the evening a voice rang out across the floor: "Annette, how about a ride?" Ryan with his arms around Rosemary swirling in the opposite direction, laughed across at me as I danced with Perry. I didn't know whether or not he was serious, but of course I jumped at the bait.

"It's a crazy idea, but if you must, go upstairs and get some rest." Ronny was worried and as I bid them goodnight, both he and Perry wore anxious faces, muttering together about the sanity of that man Ryan from a unit in Minden. Besides, he was too suave, too good looking for any man's peace of mind. He was considered an outsider, almost an intruder by the members of our group, accepted only out of respect for his close friendship with Rosemary. Taking their advice I went to my room to snatch some sleep. Then donned my riding habit—jodhpurs and riding boots, with a shirt and tie—and picked up the riding crop as I left the room.

Ryan and I drove to the stables as the sun rose on another beautiful day, filling the sky with a magnificent array of reds and gold. Monica had just been groomed and her dark coat gleamed in the early morning sun. She looked magnificent, champing at the bit and prancing with excitement at this unexpected treat, showing the whites of her eyes as a challenge and a warning to me. Once I was up, Ryan mounted his own large, well mannered, light bay beauty—and we were on our way. Both Monica and I were in high fettle, the thrill of high jinks from last night's champagne transferred to her from me—she promised to be a handful and I was prepared for an invigorating ride before returning to our digs, to bath and change for breakfast followed by a good days work.

Our path ran between vast expanses of golden wheat and corn, before reaching the trees where we turned left for the run down their side on our right. It was a perfect spot for a canter, or in Monica's case, a splendid gallop. I let her have her head and away we went, the wind rushing through her mane and tail, through my hair and in my face. It was refreshing after last night's party! I could hear the thunder of hooves from Ryan's horse close behind—and so could Monica. Her ears went back flat against her head, her neck stretched out, her speed increased as she took the bit between her teeth and bolted—no amount of strength on my part could stop her now. We battled together as we reached the end of the trees, turned right with the path without a pause, and by now I too got a thrill with the speed.

We raced down the far side of the wood until the trees stopped, where before us lay an endless sea of golden corn waving in the early morning breeze. Monica was surprised at the sudden change of scenery. With no path to follow her neck arched, and her ears went forward in curiosity, coming to a sudden halt taking me completely by surprise. I sailed over her head in a somersault, landing flat on my back on the ground. I made no impact on the corn, which parted and swallowed me up, then went on waving undisturbed in the breeze.

I lay there breathless for a moment and listened to Ryan floundering around, up to his waist in corn, calling my name: "Annette, where are you?" his anxiety increasing, "Annette, are you alright? Where are you?"

I tried to call out but the wind had been knocked out of my body, the only audible sound—a faint squeak. Hearing this my imagination ran riot—what if a wide-eyed rabbit appeared through the stems of corn to see who had made such a curious noise? The thought of it made me laugh, and that was not good because it hurt. From the tone of his voice, Ryan was getting more anxious by the minute; I tried calling again, this time with more success. Within moments the corn parted above and he looked down.

"Hello Ryan! I'm all right. Let me lie for a minute. The wind was knocked out of me. Where's Monica?" My thoughts were immediately on my horse, afraid she might run off. What an idea! Ryan looked across the corn and smiled "She's alright. She's over there—eating."

"Eating? You mean gobbling it up as fast as she can."

Ryan gave a little laugh, "Yes."

"Trust her!" I said, "As if she hadn't had enough already." Then after a moment, "Where's yours?"

"He's near," he said.

"Eating too?" I felt a little better.

Ryan looked across at the large bay. "Yes," he said "but not as fast." Then looking down at me "Annette, can you bend your legs?" I tried. They seemed to want to bend. "Alright." He took command of the situation. "Put your arms round my neck. I am going to pick you up." He bent down and with ease I put my arms around his neck and held on tight as he slowly and very carefully picked me up, talking all the time, "Now, I am going to put your feet on the ground, very slowly. See if you can stand." Gently Ryan eased me onto my feet, allowing me to test my weight.

"Oh, no! Ryan," I gasped. "No."

"It's alright," he said taking my weight in his arms. "Hold on." There was no strength in my legs at all—just excruciating pain.

"Phew!" I said, breathing hard, "that wasn't a good idea at all! My! I'm going to be stiff tomorrow." I laughed playing for time as Ryan carefully laid me back on the ground. "Ryan, I'll be all right in a moment," then after a pause, "you know I should get back onto Monica right away after a tumble? It's only a bruise. I'll be all right, really I will. Just give me time to work off the stiffness." He straightened up slowly, realizing that I had not grasped the seriousness of the situation, or possible implications of this fall.

He gazed around. Not a sign of civilization was to be seen—just mile upon mile of cornfields uninterrupted by hedges, and close by two horses in their element, determined to take advantage of the situation and eat as much as possible while the going was good. Here he was with a badly injured girl lying at his feet—a girl not even from his own unit. How was he to explain *this* to Julian? It was something to which he was not looking forward. The most important thing at the moment was not to allow any sense of panic to enter her mind and secondly—to get help. He searched for signs of human life. As luck would have it, in the distance he spotted the roof of a small, isolated farmhouse.

"Annette, listen to me. There is a farm over there. I am going to take the horses and get help. Lie still and don't try to get up." His quiet tone of command in handling this absurd situation had the effect he was seeking. I heard him cross to the horses talking quietly to Monica as he caught her, and with her bridle in one hand he mounted his bay, leading her out to the path and away. I was completely at ease, trusting him implicitly to put everything right.

I relaxed and watched the clouds overhead and wondered about Liz's reaction on our return, hoping that she would not worry unduly or imagine that I had hurt myself too badly. It was important now to move with care, probably some knee bends and a few stretches would work out the stiffness and the bruises were out of sight anyway. A fly buzzed in and out of the corn stalks, then flew away. I closed my eyes and relaxed as much as possible, twisting slightly to relieve the pressure on my back, but that was not wise! Eventually another sound broke through the silence of the morning—a motor coming closer, then the voices. One was recognizable as Ryan speaking in German and the other belonged to the farmer—the owner of the distant house whose assistance Ryan had enlisted.

For my benefit a number of empty sacks covered the floor of this strange open farm vehicle. They helped to absorb the shock of the bumps and jolts as I lay on the floor behind the two men. They made an unlikely pair Ryan, in his smart officer's uniform, perched up alongside the farmer in work-a-day clothes, silhouetted against the sky as we lumbered back to the small farm in the middle of nowhere. The horses tethered to a nearby post had not long to wait. Once I was settled on a couch, Ryan was off again with them both, heading towards civilization, and our unit.

Under the watchful eye of the anxious farmer and his wife, I closed my eyes and tried to relax, but worried about the trouble I was causing. These two were poor and had little to offer but kindness and a hunk of black bread. The first I accepted with gratitude, the other I declined with thanks and by the time Ryan returned with a car was more than a little despondent. However a happier mood picked up again on arriving back at the mess where familiar, friendly, if somewhat somber faces were around. I tried to cheer them up by joking about the stupidity of the situation as Ryan laid me flat on the hall table and turned to talk to Liz. "I'll carry her up to her room," he said, turning back to me, and bending down.

"*I'll* carry Annette up to her room!" Softly but clearly the words cut through the air like a knife. Framed in the doorway, Perry's tall figure stood motionless with his icy gaze directed at Ryan. For a moment no one spoke, but the atmosphere was brittle. Perry was furious!

"Perry! I am so sorry," I said, "I fell off. So stupid of me." It seemed an eternity before his eyes dropped to me and his voice softened "It's not your fault, Roo." He smiled, crossed over, reached down and picked me up in his arms. "Gently does it. Here we go!" Had I been a little older and less naïve, I would have been more able to compete for the love of this man.

As we went towards the stairs I heard Mary talking quietly to Ryan, trying to reassure and comfort him. "You had better leave before he comes down. Besides the others will wonder where you are if you are not in your office" Out of the corner of my eye I saw her give the poor man a hug as he left. "Call me when you have a chance."

We started up and I looked at the firm, set jaw above me. "Perry," I said. "It's a bump, just a bump! I have to be up and about by Friday anyway!"

He knew only too well *why* I had to up and about by Friday! A number of us were planning a weekend trip to the mountains with the horses—an expedition we were all anticipating with great excitement. I lived for horses, as the saying goes; even the thought of the weekend thrilled me. Skiing? No! But when on horseback I was in my element.

We turned the corner at the top of the stairs and down the passage followed by Liz and four or five of the girls, each lost in thoughts of their own, not one of them saying a word.

"The first thing to do is to get you up and about and back on your feet" Perry carried me carefully through the bedroom door. He crossed to the couch, bent down and gently settled me onto it, then straightened up. Turning to the older woman standing silently in the doorway backed by the others, he said "Take care of her, Liz." Then in an undertone,

"Help is on the way." He glanced at his watch. "They should be here in about fifteen minutes."

Liz was speechless! She took her self-imposed responsibility, keeping an eye on my welfare, very seriously. I would not have succeeded in getting my parents authorization to go to Germany in the first place had she not accompanied me. She looked at Perry helplessly. "Don't worry," he said "I'll go and see Julian!"

"Her mother!" Poor Liz, she was not looking forward to making that call to England, and to tell the truth, Lizzie was not relishing the thought of the inevitable interview with her commanding officer.

"Julian will handle it all." Although he spoke with authority, it did little to comfort the poor woman.

"Perry," I said urgently. He turned, looked down and gave me one of those smiles that I loved so much, and left the room.

That was the last time I saw Perry until Julian's party given for me in London, five long years later. By then I had experienced a marriage that was to end in disaster.

CHAPTER XV
A CHANGE OF SCENEARY

Crushed in the doorway with the other girls stood Jean, Ian's ever efficient secretary and it was she who now took command of the situation. An ambulance was on its way, and army medics were expected to arrive in approximately fifteen minutes according to Perry. The girls knew it was essential to get me out of my tight-fitting riding habit—medics were no respecters of delicate females in a little pain, and a considerable rough handling might unintentionally, but inevitably ensue. But as Jean approached with a large pair of scissors I remonstrated, "No, Jean, no! Not my jodhpurs"

"Annette, we've got to get you out of them, and quickly." she said.

"Alright, but *don't* cut my beautiful jodhpurs." I was emphatic.

"Very well," she replied "but hold on tight."

By the time the boots and tight-fitting jodhpurs had been removed, I was breathing hard, feeling somewhat hot under the collar, and muttering half-hearted protests as the undergarments were cut to pieces. This was just the beginning as far as discomfort was concerned. It was no an army medic that called for me, but a truck driver who had the amazing ability of handling me as if I were a sack of potatoes. I gritted my teeth as we jogged down the stairs, and kept them clenched as he strapped me to what appeared to be a stretcher of sorts running down one side of the army truck. Some poor soul presumably in similar circumstances occupied the opposite side. Neither of us spoke for the entire, unbearable trip. We did not take a direct route to a hospital, but sidetracked down a rough country lane, where every jolt and bump reverberated through my body, emphasizing the fact that this terrible vehicle was totally devoid of shock absorbers.

It remains a mystery to this day why we had to cross trackless fields and explore rough country lanes to reach a small cottage, or why my unfortunate companion and I were subject to an agonizing wait; strapped down, unable to move and longing to turn from the pain to a more comfortable position. Suffice to say our driver departed for a good forty-five minutes or more—for me each minute felt like an hour—eventually returning looking smug and pleased with himself as he leapt into the driver's seat and backed down the lane. Was that a young German girl I glimpsed in a pretty cotton dress waving to him from the front door as he turned onto the road and drove like the devil to make up for lost time?

I don't remember what happened next, not until I lay between the sheets of a hard, uncomfortable hospital bed.

"Hello, Annette. What have you been up to?" a familiar voice reached me from the only other occupant of the room.

"Phyllis! What on earth are you doing here?" Phyllis, one of our secretaries, sat upright in the bed next to mine putting lacquer on her nails, and I learned that she was recovering from a chest infection. I can't say that I was pleased to see her in that situation, but I was surprised and delighted for her company. After a drive like that I was only too thankful to relax and remain immobile.

The following day things were different. Friday was drawing close and nothing seemed to be happening—no visit from a doctor and little time with any nurse—they obviously had more important cases on their minds, so I decided that a some help from me would not go amiss. Reaching up to the head-rail at the top of my bed, I held on, gently pulling myself up for a split second, then eased down again, perspiring profusely from the reaction in my back.

"Annette, what do you think you're doing?" Phyllis was aghast.

"Just—working—out—the—stiffness." I explained.

"You are crazy," Phyllis said, "you might make it worse."

"I have to be out of this place by Friday," I said with a laugh. "Up and back onto my horse."

"Yes" she agreed "I'm supposed to be on that trip as well, but I don't think either of us will be there."

"Don't be too sure about that," I replied. Phyllis knew that her words would fall on deaf ears and said no more on the subject.

Next morning, after breakfast when the nurse had left, anxious to see what progress had been made, I eased my legs over the side of the bed, reached down as carefully as possible, putting the weight onto my feet. "Why," I wondered, "are hospital beds so high?" I was surprised to find myself sitting on the floor.

"Annette, for goodness sake get back into bed. If the nurse finds you on the floor, you'll be in trouble!" Wise words from a friend, but easier said than done. Getting up was not as easy as falling down, especially when it seemed necessary to complete it in record time to avoid the displeasure of the nurse! However, the battles with Monica over the months had strengthened my arms, and once again I was able to reach up and get hold of the bed-frame, and by trial and error—and an abundance of laughs—was back where I started when the nurse walked in.

Although we were not out by Friday, both Phyllis and I left hospital together—she because she was well again and me because I refused to stay. Neither of us made it to the mountains, nor for that matter did anyone else. My fall dampened the spirits of my friends to such an extent they had no heart for the ride, which was a pity. If they knew that my spine had been fractured, they kept it a secret from me. Almost forty years went by before an ex-ray was taken of my spine, and then I realized that I had a permanent memento of Monica!

There were further repercussions from that escapade. Although I did not appreciate to what extent the accident had on me physically, as far as my employers were concerned their young charge needed time to recoup. And so, after sixteen months, my two year posting in Germany right after the war came to an abrupt and untimely end. Disappointed at having to leave my friends, I was sent back home to rest under my parents' care before resuming my job at head office in London.

*****

Hardly overjoyed to see me under such circumstances, my mother made the most of it. Drawing on her experiences as a VAD in the First World War, she soon had me up and about again, which was crucial, owing to the fact that at last the time had come when she and Jackie were preparing to return to Singapore.

Although there would be the inevitable moments of depression, Jackie's physical and mental health had improved in mind and body. Under my mother's eagle eye, coupled with rest and plenty of good home cooking he had put on weight. Laughter—never far from the surface—now bubbled over with a new zest not only for life, but life abroad. He made the necessary telephone calls, was passed as fit by the doctors, and those in charge at Guthries were pleased to grant his wish to return to their office in South East Asia. Not only was Jackie popular with his fellow workers, but also with those of the local population. He had a way of endearing himself to all that he met. His keen sense of humor, ready wit and contagious laughter was enough to make him instant friends wherever he went; ideal for their offices in Singapore.

The excitement of preparation for such an extensive trip was enormous. Winter clothes were now stored, sold or given away, to be replaced by tropical kit. Furniture had to be disposed of and arrangements made for the sale of the house. Although they never showed it, it was obvious to me that I was in the way.

Sadly, I bade them farewell and rented a small room in a private flat in London in the Bayswater area, owned by an elderly lady who followed on my heels my every move. There was no key to my bedroom door, and personal things were moved in my absence. Working in the austere London quarters and the bus rides to and from the office, not withstanding the dreary London smog, all combined to drag the spirits down. More than ever I missed my friends in Germany, my horse and the delicious fragrance of the countryside. Now I missed my parents too and the home that I had enjoyed for so short a time. I asked for another posting abroad and to my great surprise my wish was granted.

Although her name escapes me, I well remember the kindly face of the admin officer as I tentatively opened the office door. A middle aged woman, well suited to cope with the whims of men and women of all ages, she invited me in. I approached her desk with my request, she smiled and said, "Annette, you worked well in Germany!" Then she asked, "Where would you like to go next?" After a few moments, on seeing my bewildered face, she added, " We do have an opening for you in Moscow or would you prefer Istanbul, or Rome? Which would you like?" Expecting a firm rebuttal as a result of my riding escapade, I was stunned into silence.

She laughed at my surprise. "You did your work very well you know! Coding for the SIS is a very important job. You never talked—you never said a word about it and what's more, you were so persistent in working out muddled five figure groups! Go and think about it and come back in three days and give me your decision."

I left the room in a daze—Moscow, Istanbul or Rome instead of the depressing little room in Bayswater! The whole idea seemed incongruous—unbelievable. Where most people would be delighted to have a choice of job offers in other towns within the country—London, Edinburgh or Oxford—I was to choose not only between three cities, but three very different countries. It took time for my brain to accept the situation, but when it did, I walked on air.

I suppose it was a foregone conclusion but I pretended otherwise, even to myself. Moscow? Plenty of snow but much too cold and besides—as a Secret Intelligence Service codeist for all my short working life, I did *not* fancy the idea of an intensive stay in Russia! But the ballet—the glorious Russian Ballet! It was a tempting thought.

Istanbul—hot, very hot and besides I sensed that some day I would join my parents in Singapore. The Middle East was set aside, but it would have been interesting and certainly very colorful. But Rome—now that was a different story.

I wandered into the office of one of my former colleagues from Germany, the man we knew as the Wing-Co, the only one to the best of my knowledge to be sent to the Neurenberg Trials after the war. He too had returned to England and was now working in the London office.

"Oh Annette," he laughed on hearing my dilemma. "There's no comparison! Go to Rome. You'll have the time of your life, and what is more, I'll give you an introduction to Col. McNabb, the Military Attaché. He'll get you a horse."

A horse! If there were any doubts before, they were banished from that moment on. Still under the age of twenty-one my mother's permission was sought and granted. In her absence the assistance of her friend and former department boss, Phoebe's mother bore me off to Harrods for a spending spree. It was not for uniform this time but pretty little summer dresses—I was due to fly to Rome in spring—the most beautiful time of year in Southern Italy.

*****

The first experience at flying on my own was one of comfort and pleasure. I had a window seat and was able to gaze out at the great billowing clouds as they passed beneath us, the sun painting them with silver and wisps of pink. The Italian gentleman on my right took me under his wing, the first of many wings during my sojourn in Italy. The main point of interest he pointed out as the pilot flew low over the coast, was the little Isle of Elba, clear and distinct. Just a rock, surrounded by giant silver spray from mighty waves that crashed against it—dramatically beautiful, the spray shimmering in the sun. "But how," I wondered, "how did Napoleon *ever* manage to escape from that inhospitable place?'

CHAPTER XVI
ITALY

A car with GB (Great Britain) Office diplomatic plates met me at Campagnelli Airport. When my luggage was stowed in the trunk, the driver introduced me to bedlam—the traffic of Rome—chaos to which I became well used in a very short space of time.

The charming little hotel—the Continentalle—that was to be home for the next few weeks stood back from the street behind shady trees in one of the more peaceful quarters of Rome. It was there, over breakfast, I met Barbara—a secretary—another new arrival to the British Embassy. By using the same transport, an Embassy car, exchanging early morning greetings over cheerful red and white checked cloths of the little breakfast tables, it was inevitable that we should strike up a friendship, and before long were visiting estate agents with the intention of sharing an apartment.

An imposing, tall slender woman with strong, unsmiling features owned one of these agencies, and surprisingly proved to be the pivot on which our future social life in Italy would revolve. The Principessa Soldatankoff, a former white Russian with an impressive title boasting one large and two smaller villas on her property in Sorrento, brought us success in more ways than one. Thanks to her, Barbara and I enjoyed the freedom of a spacious two-bedroom ground floor apartment, on the elegant Via de Villa Emeliani for the duration of our adventurous sojourn in the country.

Like so many of the more elegant streets of Rome, the Via de Villa Emeliani was bordered by trees, running the incline to the summit of a hill, where a spectacular view overlooking the River Tiber and the valley below could hardly fail to hold one's attention.

The landlord of our charming establishment was an overseer of the open-air market of Rome, so it was not unusual for flats of figs, persimmon and other delicacies to find their way to our door, and from there to our dining table, by way of an excellent maid. Palmara not only took charge of all the kitchen activities—she was an excellent cook—but she also looked after the apartment and our personal clothes.

In time, I was invited to the apartments of other secretaries and all were outstanding, spacious and filled with magnificent antiques of the country—each in its own way, quite perfect.

From the start, we were steered in the right direction and introduced to the atmosphere and wonders of Rome. One late afternoon after work, leaning against the soft upholstery of a *carretta*—a charming little horse-drawn carriage with a comfortable fit for two—we swayed in time with the horse's hooves as it jogged down the cobbled streets in one of the older parts of the city. Seeped in history, the very walls exhumed the romance of bygone eons; lights glowed from tables of the sidewalk cafés as evening drew in, enfolding its shadowy mantle around us. I said not a word but relaxed and drank it all in. Barbara too was silent for this was also her first *carretta* ride. Eventually the driver pulled up and let us off. We paid and probably over tipped, partly out of ignorance of the value of Lira at this early stage of our life in Rome, but also from gratitude for an enchanting introduction to his city.

Work was foremost in my mind those early days in Rome. It took time to get used to the routine of the new office, but the weekends were my own to explore the surroundings. My colleagues at the embassy, although much older than I, were patient to the extreme and looked on me with a patronizing air, still naive and under age. They were of a more serious disposition, but seemed to take a delight in expanding my education and intellect. The historic buildings, the coliseum and Roman baths; the magnificent statues—works of art by the masters of old, Michelangelo and his contemporaries, were all were included on the agenda. I lost my heart to Rome!

Further afield Astia Antica, although not as well known as the ancient ruined city of Pompeii, was every bit as interesting—food for thought and the imagination. I stood on the outskirts of this fascinating area, and gazed over what was once the thoroughfare of a busy community, now deserted and home to lizards and insects living beneath the stones. Ovens were clearly visible where women once baked their bread, and doorsteps where people stood and passed the time of day as children played. All was silent now except for the occasional bird, and other small living creatures.

We were four girls meandering in different directions, each lost in thoughts of our own. I sank down on a rise of bricks, and wondered what it was on which I sat! The grass waved gently around my legs; a grasshopper landed on my knee, as one of its kind must have on another knee hundreds of years ago. Sheila was busy taking photos of the ruins, none of which was more than three feet high. I pondered on the cause of this disaster, devastating for both man and beast alike. The grasshopper, having had enough of human contact, jumped off my knee to land on a blade of grass that dipped momentarily under the weight of its tiny body. It was a peaceful afternoon beneath the blue Italian sky; the sounds of war and natural disaster, for the present, things of the past.

Eventually we made our way to the outskirts of the area, reluctant to leave. It was time to head towards Rome, yet no one was in the mood to return home. Instead, we digressed to tour the fountains of the city, where Sheila's camera came into play once more. The magnificent fountains were a joy to behold—the spray fascinating to watch, shimmering in the sun, the sound of falling water music to the ears. We threw coins into the waters of the Trevi Fountain and made a wish, ensuring our return to this beautiful place according to Italian superstition! There were so many magnificent statues on which to feed the eye—so much artistic energy put into so much beauty—it seemed to immerse itself into one's very being.

At last, tired but happy, we chose one of the sidewalk cafes to relax over *cappuccino*, or—as in my case—*cassata,* a deliciously rich, creamy filling incased in a crispy layer of ice. Although I have searched, nowhere in the world other than Italy have I found this delicious dessert. We watched the ever-present horse-drawn *carrettas* and pondered the events of the day. Oh yes! It was easy to fall in love with Rome, the Italian way of life, and its people. Strange to think that not so long ago Germans soldiers walked these self-same streets, gazing at the statues, their army boots rasping on the floors of the buildings, echoing from the walls and in the Embassy in which we worked! The irony of it—the British Embassy so short a time ago housed the enemy; the Villa Volksonsy was forermly the Germany Embassy.

*****

To me Rome was akin to a dream city and none the least was its music. The people burst into song seemingly at every conceivable opportunity—on the streets, on the beaches, and best of all—the opera.

Introduced to Italian opera at a spectacular performance of "Manon" performed at Rome's opera house, I listened and watched as music and song flooded the theater. From a box, I gazed spellbound at the spectacle on stage, enthralled by the color and action. From the audience to my left came another sound, faint but clear to one unused to the Italians so appreciative of their music, a distinct hiss—not on the outward breath as one of disapproval, but on the intake through lips and teeth, audible to the uninitiated such as myself.

"Why are they hissing?" I whispered to my escort.

He listened, then replied somewhat surprised. "You know, Annette, I never noticed it before! It's obviously a mark of appreciation. The Italians love their music." Not only music *per se* but also the spectacle! I could hardly believe my eyes when a pair of horses crossed the stage. Frank went on, "You know, Annette, this is not grand opera. You will have to see "Aida" or "Il Trovatore" for the really spectacular in Italy." But at that moment I felt that anything more grand would be too much for my senses. However, in time I came to expect more and even more, until it culminated one most wonderful evening.

On a cool and beautiful night, with the stage filled with light, offset by battlements on which three soldiers representing a bygone age and patrolled back and forth, high overhead, outlined against a starlit sky—all went to make up an atmosphere filled with anticipation at the Terme di Caracalla. Barbara was as excited as me. The two of us had excellent seats by the center aisle, in the third row, to see "Il Trovatore." As people filed in searching for their places, there was surprising activity on stage. Two burly individuals dressed in dark brown leather, muscles bulging, hauled a brazier filled with red-hot coal to the far right of the stage. There they fanned the smoldering embers, persuading flames to rise until the whole thing looked thoroughly dangerous!

Despite its size, the open-air theater quickly filled to overflowing, except for the front row held open by the officials for VIPs. The general hub of conversation gradually subsided as we waited for the orchestra to take its place. Barbara was reading the program, translating it to me, when movement took our attention in the front row as men in black dinner jackets filed in to take their place. One young man, dark and very good looking, turned towards the audience as he followed his companions to his place; his gaze ran over the crowd and finally fell on me. A smile spread across his face, he said something to his friend, who turned and smiled as the young man retraced his steps and made his way to my side. Taking my hand and with a little bow, he said a few words in Italian which I failed to understand, but was painfully conscious of Barbara's suppressed mirth. It was the same young man who had paid me marked attention when we first arrived—a guest in the same hotel.

As he returned to his seat, a lady in the row in front looked back, much impressed, and said in broken English, "You know who that is, don't you?" I shook my head. "That's the son of the Argentine ambassador."

"Oh! Thank you." I replied, wishing that Barbara would control her laughter, and thankful that the lights were being lowered.

Meanwhile action took place on stage; the two giants stood back and surveyed their blazing handiwork as the orchestra burst into glorious sound, and then we were able to see their primary role! In time to the beat of the music, enormous tools swung high overhead and there followed a crash on red-hot steel from the brazier. Sparks flew in all directions! Music and song flooded the Caracalla filling the night skies with its magic. It was indeed an inexplicable evening and the start of my life-long passion with opera.

…

Although there seemed little time in which to draw breath in this wonderful new life of mine, there was still that unmistakable hankering in the depth of my soul for the companionship of a beautiful four-legged steed—to feel the powerful motion of her stride and revel in the sound of hooves on the ground. I missed the fragrance of a shimmering coat and soft velvety touch in the palm of my hand as she nuzzled in search of a carrot. The well-polished jodhpur boots stood forlorn beneath the riding habit hanging in my wardrobe, whilst the rays of the sun reflected in the silver rings on the handles of both riding crops, suspended on the bookcase by my bedroom window, in good view, as if there to remind me of my love of life.

"Annette—get in touch with Col. MacNab! He will get you a horse." The words of my friend at head office still echoed in my ears, and needless to say, I took him at his word.

In answer to a tap on his office door, Col. MacNab looked up, somewhat startled at the sight of the newly-arrived little codest who approached his desk with an unusual request—a horse, please! The large green eyes gazed at him in absolute confidence that one would be forthcoming at a moment's notice at his command.

He got up from behind his desk, strode to the window and looked out at the peacocks strutting the lawns—why had his old friend and colleague in London done this to him? What was he doing in London anyway? The last he had heard of him he was in Germany!

He frowned at the peacocks, turned; I was still there, patiently waiting for the improbable, when an idea suddenly entered his head. He crossed to the desk, jotted a name and address on a slip of Embassy paper. "Go to this address" he said, still writing with a glimmer of a smile on his face, "and I'm sure you will get your horse!"

I took the paper from the outstretched hand, thanked him without glancing at it, and left the office.

Quietly, without confiding with even my closest friends at work, I slipped out one sunny day at lunchtime, hailed a taxi and gave the driver the precious slip of paper. No doubt impressed by the address to which he was directed, he turned the taxicab and cut a precarious course across town, coming to rest with a jolt outside an impressive looking building, of whose importance I was in total ignorance. However, undaunted by the uniformed policeman on guard at the door, who seemed duly impressed by the name on the colonel's note, I followed him down passages and was ushered through a door into the holy of holy's—the inner sanctuary of the chief of *polizia*. Unfortunately, the effect of this first introduction was somewhat diminished, for like me, the owner of this imposing office was also on his lunch break but, unlike me, he was taking it in true Italian style. With his feet in highly polished boots propped up on a spacious desk, spotless white shirt open at the neck, chin resting on his chest and hands folded across his stomach, he lay back in his chair deep in slumber. Touched on the shoulder by his grinning subordinate, the astonished man awoke with a jolt to the sight of a young *signorina* wearing an enchanting summer dress, bearing a note from his highly esteemed friend at the British Embassy, the Military Attaché.

He whipped his feet off the desk, buttoned his shirt and beaming all over his congenial face, took my hand in his and bowed me into a chair, all the while talking in rapid Italian, little of which I understood. After the initial confusion, during which he was all smiles, he assured me that a steed would be forthcoming.

"Really," I thought to myself, longing to know exactly what it was he had said, "I *must* learn this wonderful language!" And he, bowing his delighted concern, instructed his astonished minions, to escort me to my taxi.

Returning to the Embassy for the afternoon's work, I could hardly forget this extraordinary interlude, but it did get banished to the far recesses of my mind for the time being as life was to become increasingly lighthearted and packed full of adventure.

*****

The Principessa Soldatankoff's interest in the two British girls working at the Embassy in Rome stemmed from a possible more prestigious position in her own circle. Should her eldest daughter become acquainted with us, her social standing would rise, and to her great satisfaction Tatiana and I soon became good friends—we were of an age. She swept both Barbara and I into the whirl of life amongst the young Italian set, whose parents based in Rome and boasted villas on Capri or, what became my favorite haunt—Sorrento, nestled at the foot of Mount Vesuvius.

Tatiana introduced us to her friends of the intellectual set, led by a quiet young man with smiling features who made us welcome and was quick to take me home to meet his charming parents. Bebo spoke good English, which was fortunate—it got me out of many a difficult situation.

One memorable day, when my knowledge of Italian was still virtually non existent, Tatiana and I were riding on a crowded bus in Rome with Bebo and two other members of this intrepid group, Mario and Marco, the latter having an irrepressible sense of humor. He spoke no English but took a delight in teaching me on-the-spur-of—the-moment Italian. It was obvious from the looks on the faces of his companions that some of what he taught me was 'dicey', to say the least. Although they remonstrated with him, Marco gleefully laughed it off and I was none the wiser. On the bus that particular morning I repeated to all and sundry in audible tones a remark that he had taught me, and to my amazement found that I was alone without a friend to my name. All turned their backs on me and pushed their way through the crowded bus in different directions, struggling to control their mirth, whilst other passengers cast disparaging looks in my direction. It was then that I realized classes in the Italian language by a valid instructor were imperative.

It was the tall, blond, blue-eyed Mario who spoke no English at all, who steered me in the direction of a professional Italian instructor. If *I* learnt *his* language, at least we would be able to communicate one way or the other. The lady in question was a charming, soft—spoken, amply built Hungarian, whose name slips my memory, if I ever knew it. Three evenings a week, after work, she kept me occupied until such times she deemed me adequate to understand the fundamentals of the language necessary to ease life in my new surroundings, and be able to stand my ground amongst my group. This her classes did with a certain amount of success, though looking back in retrospect I sometimes wonder what my Italian must have sounded like coming from the lips of an English girl, taught to speak Italian by a woman with a strong Hungarian accent! However, it worked wonderfully until I left the country, when I wrote lengthy letters to my friends in moments of great nostalgia. One received from Bebo in return—suggested that I write in English instead of Italian—it would make it easier for them all to understand. So much for that!

These young men and women's zest for life knew no bounds. They welcomed us into their daily activities seemingly without a thought or care in the world; energetic and light-hearted they brought laughter into what might have been a more somber existence. The moment our transport left the peacocks to their domain, drove past the guards and through the gates into the chaos of the Roman traffic every other Friday, the cares of work were dropped.

Early every other Friday morning, with the apartment left in Palmara's capable hands, it became a habit for Barbara and I to leave Rome by bus for the drive south towards Naples and the coast. It was a pretty drive, we bypassed the Monte Cassino and the ruins of the monastery high on top of the hill, blasted by the allies to overcome Hitler's forces in the area. Many years later, I was to meet one of the British officers from that battle C.Ormond L.Salvesen, the man I eventually married—but in Italy in 1948 marriage was the last thing on my mind. Surrounded by happy, friendly faces in this beautiful land, the one thing that did bring back thoughts of the last ten years was—when sitting at sidewalk cafes in Rome, strolling down the promenade in Naples, or swimming in the brilliant blue Mediterranean waters. All these lads and lassies were doing exactly the same with German soldiers not so very long ago!

Arriving in Naples, the two British girls from the Embassy were welcomed with open arms at the Hotel Continentale, where our suite overlooked the picturesque Santa Lucia castle in the bay.

After unpacking our cases and settling in, our custom was to stroll down the waterfront and lunch in the open at the See Teresa Restaurant. There the resident 'song—bird'—a man with a surprisingly pleasant voice, habitually serenaded us with his rendering of "*O Santa Lucia*". Although no Pavarotti, it went down well over a glass of wine and a *mozzzrilla frittata* to the accompaniment of the lapping of little waves on the shore. What better way to totally relax in the peace of the moment? Then there were enchanting shops to explore in the arcade, where strands of local coral were sold in abundance, some of which I have to this day.

After a late afternoon nap, we changed and stood on the balcony as the sun dipped and dusk took over from the light of day. One by one, lights began to twinkle in the tiny castle in the bay, their reflection danced on the water. Soft music from other restaurants acted as a background for our troubadour as if to draw us under its spell. These moments on our own away from the crowd were a pleasant respite, relaxing to the nerves, refreshing the senses as we gazed out over the water—the horizon closing in as darkness fell. These were precious, peaceful moments, the memory stored to draw upon later in life from other shores and distant lands, under other circumstances, not just forgotten and discarded. A quiet dinner, followed by a stroll along the waterfront, the strains of "*Torna a Sorriento*" fading in the distance, and an early bed to sleep and rest in readiness for a very early rise the following day.

A tap on the door of the adjourning room next morning announced the arrival of a smiling buxom maid bearing an enormous silver tray, which she placed with great satisfaction on the table in the middle of the room. Might well she be pleased as it was an impressive sight—a mountain of fresh fruit, croissant, butter and marmalade, jugs of steaming hot coffee and milk—what better way to embrace the activities of another exciting day?

A taxi drove us to the docks and so to the little boat berthed alongside awaiting her passengers. When everyone was aboard and all was shipshape and ready to go, she pulled out and made her way slowly across the Bay of Naples. The dancing waters rippled as far as the eye could see, each ripple reflecting the early morning sun—a sea of sparkling diamonds. What few people that were on board besides ourselves stood at the rails talking in undertones, as if reluctant to break the spell although they must have witnessed this a hundred times before. To our port side villages lay sprawled in silence, basking in the sun at the foot of Mount Vesuvius, a huge magnificent backdrop reaching to the blue Italian sky with a tiny white puff—a cloud—suspended over the head of the volcano.

Approaching Sorrento sometime later, the villas, like the cliffs on which they were suspended, shone pink in the early morning sun. We docked, hailed a *corrotta* that took us up the hill to our hotel beyond the village—the Hotel Royal—that became our home away from home.

CHAPTER XVII
SORRENTO AND CAPRI

Reflecting pink in the sun, the Hotel Royal stood perched on top off a rocky cliff overlooking the vast expanse of the calm, crystal-clear waters of the Mediterranean Sea. Purple bougainvillea grew in profusion from every nook and cranny in the rock—a glorious sight that blended with the color of the buildings of Sorrento, adding to the lazy atmosphere so characteristic of the place. Railings around the terrace of the hotel served as a deterrent for a dangerous plunge to the beach far below. Fortunately, this could be reached by steps winding down the cliff face, or—what was probably a little less intimidating—by elevator, the shaft chiseled through solid rock. It was impossible *not* to relax and to realize how fortunate we were to be working for the British government in Italy.

Our cases unpacked and wearing light summer dresses we strolled to the village along a road normally deserted, until we reached the main piazza. Tatiana had previously introduced us to Biga Yanuzzi, a dark eyed, good-natured Italian girl, who took life at a leisurely pace. In a very short time, we found ourselves welcomed into her set and the easygoing way of life enjoyed by the natives of Sorrento, a sharp contrast to the activities of our friends in Rome.

The eldest of nine children, Biga met us outside the family store whilst her parents sat at ease in wicker chairs and watched the world go by as the younger members of their brood romped together in the plaza. Their mother kept an eye open for any potential customer, always ready to assist a tourist who, like ourselves, wandered into the shop. This was filled to overflowing with the most beautiful merchandise. I was fascinated by the figures dancing the Tarantella inlaid on rosewood tables, the soft colors of their local costume similar to those of lovely flowers on the surface of smaller tables. One felt impelled to reach out and run a finger over these beautiful works of art. There were also delicate handkerchiefs and table linens all exquisitely embroidered by the local girls in sewing factories. The lingerie was the ultimate in beauty and glamour—an occasional peignoir set departed from Sorrento and accompanied me to Rome.

Sandy beaches invited us to laze and sun ourselves and turn a golden brown, or just meander along the shore splashing our feet in the water's edge. There were lemon and orange groves to visit stretching for miles far into the distance, lending shade, peace and privacy—a retreat where we could spread our towels, relax and read undisturbed, until one day Barbara's voice broke the silence.

"Annette," she whispered in hushed undertones, endeavoring to suppress her laughter "Annette! Do look."

Pausing only to finish the line that I was reading, I glanced up and received a shock. Advancing cautiously on hands and knees, stripped to the waist and hampered by ill-fitting sandals that threatened to desert the two men who, a pair of would-be Romeos, Atelio and Mario attempted to make their way surreptitiously towards us. They muttered under breath as they battled with the vines, their giant sombreros causing even greater difficulty than their impossible footwear. Realizing peace would no longer prevail in this secluded arbor, we laughed as we packed our paraphernalia and bid a hasty retreat to the hotel. Our picnic now so rudely interrupted, we found chaise longues in a deserted spot on the terrace where we could sit and read, and at the same time appease our appetites and our sense of humor at the expense of a poor unfortunate waiter, by ordering a *mozzarella fritatta*. We waited in delightful anticipation of his reappearance bearing an enormous oval platter on which this fat, delicious repast lay. Balanced on one hand, he attempted to serve it with the other. We watched him wield the spoon and slice the omelet equally in two; then scooping the fluffy golden mixture between spoon and fork, he raised one half to ease it onto my plate—easier said than done. When hot, mozzarella cheese stretches in long, spaghetti-like strands that refuse to snap. The farther he reached the thinner the strands, and by the time he stretched a full arm's length at shoulder level, over the head, around the side, or just out in front, the expression on the poor man's face was well worth the watching. Caught up in the mood of our hilarity, he too began to laugh.

After lunch, still laughing, we wound a precarious treck to the shore, down the uneven steps of the cliff that threatened to send us sprawling headfirst to the beach below. Once there we spread our towels, lay down and gazed out over the vast expanse of water. How incredibly blue it was. There is nothing like the brilliant blue of the Mediterranean on a calm summer day. Far out in the distance, their white sails caught by a gentle breeze, the little boats went skimming across water, and as they danced and dipped, their magnetic spell beckoned us to join them! Soon the very sight of them made me feel drowsy, my lids felt heavy, and seemingly powerless to resist, reluctantly I let them close.

It must only have been a few moments before I awoke, fully refreshed and ready to take on the world. The sky was still as blue as the sea that invited me down to the water's edge and into its fluid embrace. It was crystal clear and surprisingly warm as I gazed down at my feet, the little pink toes sinking into the sand. I stooped and allowed the clear, salt water caress my neck and shoulders, then waded still farther out from the shore. Glancing back Barbara had not stirred; face down prone on her towel, she passed into happy oblivion, the sun enfolding her in its comfortable, warm embrace, gradually transforming her body from white to a golden brown.

I turned from the shore and with long, even strokes swam on towards the small boats ahead; it was impossible to resist their magnetic draw. Upheld by the buoyancy of the water, my mind wandered to events and places far beyond the present environment—once again to my parents now well-settled in Singapore. I thought of Jackie's reaction—returning to the land he loved where so much misery had taken place, and this alone would bring back untold memories. Although he never discussed it with me, I knew that my mother was the release for his mind. They sounded happy from their letters. Recently she had sent me a dozen enchanting little summer dresses, made to measure by her local Chinese tailor. How fortunate we were—almost identical in size! I swam on, lazily dreaming and wished that both she and Jackie were here to experience the beauty and peace of this wonderful place.

The boats were larger now, faces clearly discernible. They were sailing around me! I laughed happily as someone waved a greeting, and turned to watch their course, but in so doing I glanced towards the shore, and to my horror realized the distance was farther than I dreamed. Sorrento's beach was indistinguishable from any other on the coast. All blended into one, little pinpricks in the distance. Poor eyesight? Who knows? I up-kicked and started the long stretch back, the water itself held me afloat.

Barbara's wrath was justified—she had a fright on waking when I was nowhere to be found—not on the beach nor the hotel terrace; she searched the village, inquired at the Yanuzzis's without success. I was in disgrace for the next couple of hours, but it passed and back in Rome we laughed over our exploits and settled down to work for the next few weeks before our next trip south. But even here life had its unexpected adventures.

*****

The aroma of coffee wafted through the apartment as Palmara prepared breakfast. Bright green chopped parsley topping a mound of fluffy yellow scrambled eggs on toast was on the menu for Barbara, fresh fruit—persimmons, figs and pears—and a glass of milk and coffee for me. The early morning sun heralded another perfect day in this beautiful city. All was quiet on the Via di Ville Emeliani, bordered by blossom trees, separating the sidewalk from picturesque buildings, and devoid of human contact at this early hour.

Unhurried and at ease in our respective rooms we girls prepared for another day's work, at first oblivious of something unusual in this quiet neighborhood. Gradually, against the background music of sparrows twittering in the blossom on the trees separating the pathement from the modern, but picturesque buildings standing back from the street, a much loved sound captured my attention—the unmistakable clatter of horses hooves—music to my ears. As they approached, ascending the incline, heads appeared at the windows to catch a glimpse of the pretty sight. Three pairs of horses, their heads held high, well-groomed coats glimmering in the sun, made their way up the center of the street. Their riders, all members of the Italian carabinieri, immaculate and proud in their unique black uniform with their highly polished boots gleaming in the sun, were led by a familiar figure. No longer at ease on a luncheon break but mounted on a magnificent stallion, the Chief of Police himself now led his men, riding at the head of this little brigade. With one strong hand on the bridle, the other resting on his thigh he was every inch the picture of the man in charge of the situation.

As we gazed from Barbara's window, we began to realize what this was all about. In the center of the group, on a leading rein held lightly by one of those handsome men, trotted a mare saddled in readiness for her mount. I blinked, speechless, as the procession came to a halt beneath the window.

Obviously enjoying himself enormously the chief looked up at me a smile spreading across his face. He nodded his head in acknowledgement saying "Bon giorno, signorina." Of course, my impossible friend began to laugh. Where but in Italy would a maiden be so romanced in such a wonderful way? This was the escort for my early morning rides!

Collecting my composure, "Bon giorno!" I replied, and with Barbara endeavoring to control her mirth and chatting away in excellent Italian, I disappeared momentarily to the recesses of my room to make a rapid change into my riding habit. If Barbara's life was filled with laughter, mine was full of surprises. And I was *not* about to lose this opportunity!

*****

Rome—oh Rome! I look back with great nostalgia to my life in Italy, the romance of such enchantment! Surrounded by so much artistic beauty, its depth of history, and the warmth of the people themselves who opened their hearts and homes to Barbara and myself with such deep sincerity and love. I performed my work at the Embassy, trying not to allow my private life to interfere—but after office hours, that was a different story. We totally abandoned ourselves to our other life. When not with our Italian friends, or more reserved colleagues from the Embassy, Barbara and I continued to explore. We roamed the streets, the piazzas the alleyways, peering into shop windows, so elegantly displayed with merchandise the like of which I had not seen for years, dubious thanks to the 'duration'—so much time was lost to the war! There were clothes of exquisite colors and textures, leather goods, shoes, handbags and belts fashioned painstakingly by hand—all to be gazed upon but unfortunately out of reach of our pockets.

The contents of one window captured my attention and refused to let it go. The name slips my memory but this shop stood in the Piazza de Spagna, just to the right of the Spanish steps. At times, these steps gave the appearance of reaching up to the little white clouds that hovered beneath a blue Italian sky. Couples took advantage of this romantic place to sit, talk and laugh as lovers do, and pass the time of day or feed the pigeons that milled around their legs, with crumbs from their luncheon bags.

Alabaster! Behind the glass of this particular window were displayed magnificent statuettes carved out of pure white alabaster, some were large and some small but each exquisite painstakingly chiseled, lovingly polished by its creator until it glowed. Taking center stage side by side, their necks well arched and fashioned in a prancing gait, two pure white alabaster horses proudly accentuated the majesty of their kind. Each mounted on an individual black marble base they stood about one foot in height. My eyes feasted hungrily on these two magnificent works of art.

"Look Annette, Shelly's home!" Barbara pointed to the sign over an unobtrusive, brown narrow door the other side of the piazza. Reluctantly I dragged my eyes away from the statuettes to glance across to the opposite side of the street. "Oh, yes." I exclaimed, and realizing that this was indeed a wonderful place in which to be living.

We returned more than once and never failed to pause and gaze at the horses in the window. One day a pair of alabaster dogs—Alsatians—joined them, each mounted like the horses, on black marble blocks. Barbara asked which I preferred, the horses or the dogs, and I replied with a laugh, "The horses of course." But then they were gone. The dogs stood alone—beautiful and fascinating, but alone. Well, it was inevitable but my disappointment reached rock bottom.

*****

With Tatiana and "the gang" we continued to explore, riding on the crossbar of the boys' bicycles, hardly a mode of travel that might have the approval of the powers that be in the Embassy—especially in the bedlam of Roman traffic—highly dangerous; but we were young, carefree and ready for fun. We visited the Coliseum, and by contrast the magnificent artifice of San Pietro. It was a never-ending exploration for our insatiable appetites.

One weekend Barbara and I decided that an alternate route from Naples to Sorrento might ring the changes. Instead of an early morning crossing of the bay, we decided to take the local bus that wound its way through villages nestled at the foot of Mount Vesuvius—the same little places we saw, and wondered about, from the ferry as we crossed the waters of the bay. They had always fascinated us from a distance, and with a close up view with which to feed our inquisitive natures, who knows what other escapades this might lead to? We were not disappointed!

Arriving early at the station, we took our places at the back of a somewhat dilapidated bus that gave us a bird's eye view of all that might take place. It was not uncomfortable, and we settled down to enjoy what we thought would be an uneventful drive. What a hope! As our fellow passengers began to climb aboard it was plain that they were on their way to various local markets; old acquaints, they greeted each other enthusiastically in rapid Italian, each outdoing the other in volume as they vied to make themselves heard above the ever increasing din. Some were hugging baskets or bundles, puffing as they maneuvered their ample forms through the narrow door and up the steps. Others were followed by miniature replicas of themselves, the latter sucking lollipops and other sticky goodies. Almost all were bearing baskets filled to overflowing with fruit and bread and other sweet smelling morsels. Some handled their merchandise with a certain lack of dexterity—clucking, squawking, quacking and fluttering in indignant protest, the merchandise obviously preferring to remain in its own backyard than undergoing the tiresome trip to some unknown location. Barbara and I realized that we were in for an interesting ride.

Once the bus was full with chattering humanity, the driver took his place, and looking back to view his assortment of passengers running his eye over each and every one, revved up and with a jolt, a cough and a splutter we were on our improbable way.

The coast road winds like a snake around the foot of the slumbering volcano, oblivious to the ant-like movement along its path. The driver, well used to his charge, clung to the wheel with a heave and a pull as he rounded the curves, his foot pressed near to the floor we lumbered along, rocking from side to side. I grabbed the edge of my seat as Barbara collided into me and we realized that we were in for the ride of our lives. The weather was glorious, the scenery beautiful; the sky clear with the familiar little white puffs-clouds hovering over Vesuvius to our left and the Mediterranean stretching to the horizon on our right. As we came to villages, dogs scampered out of the way, then turned to give chase voicing their joy or indignation when our rackety coach came to a halt allowing one person off, another on, with cries of farewell to those still aboard, and greetings for those now climbing the steps. Off we went towards the next port of call and it started all over again. Then the inevitable, but seemingly unpredictable took place. Bounding along at a hair-raising pace in the middle of nowhere, there was heard an ominous hiss, and with steam rising up through the floor our gallant vehicle came to a resounding halt. Amidst the crescendo of feminine voices, the clucking of ruffled hens, the quacking from indignant ducks accompanied by occasional grunt of protest from the goat, we were summoned out by the frustrated driver, ordered off to stretch our legs or just mill around while he maneuvered his lithe body under his troublesome charge to put things right beneath the boards. This was brought about in a surprisingly short space of time, and we all clambered back, complete with menagerie, and on our way once more, eventually reaching our various destinations without further mishap.

For Barbara, that was enough excitement for one day! My more serious, bespeckled companion now chose to relax with a book on the terrace while I was ready to roam. Leaving her lost in the depths of some imaginary adventure I made my way towards the village in search of Biga, and once found, followed in her wake between the crowded tables of a restaurant frequented by the local population. Tatiana, Mario, Ateilo, and Giovanni hailed us from a table at the far back of the open-air plaza. Biga began to maneuver her way through the crowd when, one by one, the male patrons rose to their feet, their faces wreathed in smiles and murmuring something in Italian, each gave a small bow as we passed. With a quick glance back at me she too smiled, acknowledging first one and then the other with a "Grazie, grazie signor!" until we reached our grinning companions.

"Oh Annette, Annette" she laughed and sat down at the table.

"What was that all about?" I asked as Mario pulled back my chair.

"They were *saluting* you!" he said, "We Italians appreciate beauty!" *There is no other place like Italy*!

A visit to Capri was in the offing. Over coffee and casatas we finalized the plans, taking our time, enjoying each other's company with the congenial atmosphere of easygoing friendship. Still chatting and laughing we pushed back our chairs and made our way down hill to the jetty where the little boat bobbed at her mooring in the harbor. The water lapped against her bows as we clambered aboard and pushed off with two of the boys at the oars to row across to Capri.

It was a glorious, sunny day. Like other visitors to Capri, I had previously experienced the mystic beauty of the Blue Grotto, or Grotto Azzura, as it was known in Italy, however Biga was anxious to introduce me to its smaller, but every bit as beautiful companion. This little cave, its privacy protected by the sea, discouraged visitors. No boat could penetrate its secret underwater entrance. Those who wanted to explore its watery depths must dive, swim through the opening, to surface inside the mysterious, ethereal rocky cavern. We passed close to the Grotto Azuria where two or three small boats waited patiently before disappearing one by one through the entrance of the grotto. We watched and passed them to our right, the boys resting momentarily on their oars, then went on until we reached a spot that looked like any other on the cliff, its rocky face uninterrupted by any unusual physical feature, stark and forbidding for anyone foolish enough to try to climb ashore. One by one my friends stripped of their shirts and shorts to reveal their swim suits underneath. I followed suit and dove over the side to join them. They turned and swam towards the rock leaving Tatiana in the bows to look after the little boat.

"Dive, Annette, dive and follow me!" Giovanni led the way then disappeared beneath the surface. I took a deep breath, dove with eyes wide open and followed his shadowy form through the underwater opening, then onwards with slow, steady kicks rose to the surface. The need for air was great, but my gasp was for the sheer beauty of the exquisite little cavern. A brilliant iridescent light seemed to reflect from beneath the water and onto the walls, flooding the place with a mystic power that even our bodies glowed beneath the surface.

The others joined us from the outside world one by one, and laughed as they saw my face and witnessed my incredulity at this extraordinary little place—were our legs turning into fins? We swam and splashed each other, and as we did the drops of falling water glimmered like a thousand falling stars. I laughed in sheer delight and wished that Barbara was here, but swimming was not her forte; she shunned water of any great depth—and this was deep! There was no ledge on which to rest, but the buoyancy of the crystal clear water kept us afloat without exerting ourselves unduly; a steady dog paddle was all that was necessary. In time, reluctantly, we left "the little grotto" the same way as we came—diving to reach the entrance and surfacing outside where Tatiana sat patiently in the boat. With imminent danger of capsizing, her indignant shouts of protest rang out as she did her best to hold it steady as we scrambled aboard. If this was the beginning of the festivities for my birthday celebration it proved to be a good one!

*****

Only once in a lifetime does one come of age and the twenty-ninth of September fell during the week. Aware that a package from Singapore sat on the breakfast table, I dressed for work as quickly as possible and went skidding on the parquet floor as I raced to join Barbara in the dining room. Beaming all over her face, delighted that at last her well kept secret was about to be revealed, she greeted me, while Palmara poured coffee into the cups.

"Happy birthday, Annette." She grinned when she saw my face, for there, beside my mother's unwrapped gift of a beautiful strand of pearls, the two alabaster horses from the shop in the Piazza di Spagna took pride of place in the center of the table! I stretched out my hand, not daring to believe my eyes, and for the first time felt the smooth, cold backs as I ran my fingers over their beautiful forms. An envelope lay on the table beside this magnificent gift. "Open it Annette," Barbara's voice brought me back to my senses. I slit open the envelope and drew out a page of Embassy paper bearing the signatures of everyone who worked in the department. I was elated, and to this day treasure this gift that brings back so many happy memories.

*****

The evenings were drawing in as winter wrapped us in a frosty mantle of bitter cold, and with the icy blasts came a general exodus from Rome. Some went south to the Riviera and warmer climes, others north armed with skis and skates to frolic in the snows of wondrous places such as the Blue Dolomites and show off their expertise on ice.

In Rome, we girls worked, shivered and wondered just how long the bitter cold would last. The change came more rapidly for me in a very unexpected way. My eyes began to give me trouble; the vision blurred as I bent over my work my head ached a little at first, but as the days went by it worsened. A swelling appeared beneath the brow as an abscess formed, ever increasing in size, discomfort and pain. No amount of poultices—Epsom salts in hot water—would bring it to a head and subsequent relief; on the contrary, it showed a disquieting tendency to form an outer crust as the poison penetrated further in towards the brain. Work became impossible when a fever took over. Dizzy and unable to stand, I lay in bed, really not caring if I lived or died.

Sheila discovered me in that state. A competent and caring person, on finding me absent from my desk, she went in search, first around the Embassy and finally at home. One look and she took matters into her own hands. With Palmara's help, she bundled me first into clothes and then a waiting car.

The ride across town is wrapped in oblivion, but not Rome's emergency section. Oh, they were good—so very efficient! There was no wait—a doctor took one look at me, snapped out orders in rapid succession in Italian which I didn't even try to understand (although the comings and goings of the general public might have surprised me had I been interested.) Whipped out of my chair, I lay on a table surrounded by white—clad men and women, still vaguely aware of Sheila's face amongst the throng; I gave her a smile and relaxed. It never occurred to me to wonder how she managed to be in an operating room in the first place, but the talk was in Italian and I made no effort to understand. Standing at my head the doctor was in full command. At a word from him, the white-clad figures sprang into action, each taking a pre-arranged part of my body—my shoulders, arms, hips, legs and feet—in fact, any part of me that moved, they forcibly held me down, motionless in a vice-like grip, and my head—especially my head! I was surprised, but past caring. Something rasped across the mound on my face. The doctor swore softly in his native language, turned to his assistant and demanded a sharper knife. He sawed again with more success and as the poison streamed out I felt an unmistakable tear overflowing and trickle down my cheek. How embarrassing! In front of all those people too. Looking up into the doctor's face "Excuse me, signor," I said in the only Italian that would come to mind. "This is very stupid of me."

"Molto stupido?" he said with a laugh, then turning to his staff, said in amazement "Molto stupido!" The tension relaxed and all laughed in deepest sympathy.

I noticed that Sheila had disappeared. She told me later that she had found a far more interesting operation in progress, in one of the adjoining rooms! She was joined by other onlookers, people passing in the street who had the time to watch and while away an hour or so—a common practice in those days.

As the abscess burst the pain diminished, the relief was overwhelming, and recovery swift. The doctor had opened a good inch with his knife above the eye under the brow, but determined that no scar would remain to mark the skin, he used no needle or thread. Instead, he insisted I return each day for treatment, which proved incredibly painful, but effective. First, fifteen minutes with a steam poultice, then a young assistant doctor rolled back the flesh on what looked remarkably like a Q tip and swabbed beneath the flesh. To this day not a trace of a scar marks my face. They do beautiful work, those men and women in the Italian hospitals.

My recouping stage seemed unbearably lengthy. Unable to use my eyes for the necessary close work, we were short handed and needed a replacement. I went to London to recoup and was eventually offered an opening in Trieste, but my eyes were tired in need of a change. I realized a less demanding occupation for their benefit was imperative.

Loath to leave Italy—a place I loved—and my wonderful friends, I decided to join my parents in Singapore. To my surprise, I found a compassionate friend in the head of the admin department.

"Annette," she said "at Bletchley we all thought your mother should have made a home for you both, instead of her living in that enormous country house, putting you in the hostel."

"She thought it would be more fun for me there. To be with people more or less my own age and to enjoy the dances," I replied.

"Well, we were a little upset with her not taking you with her—it's time for you both to be together."

I was overjoyed to be blameless for leaving, but my mother was not amused! In fact she was downright furious! The very idea that I—her daughter—would leave so prestigious a situation in the Civil Service was unthinkable.

"Why, in years to come Annette could retire with a generous pension at a ripe old age, not forgetting all the travel to foreign lands she would experience. She might, with luck even get married. A senior diplomat would be a very pleasing son-in-law."

Of course the thought I might prefer some other profession was too awful to even contemplate; as for the strain on my eyes—what a fuss to make of such a little thing. Messages zipped back and forth across the wires; words were brittle and the outlook bleak.

CHAPTER XVIII
EN ROUTE TO SINGAPORE—1948

I watched the flame sputter and turn blue as my shillings ran out as did the gas fire that warmed my little bed-sitter called 'home'. Without more 'bobs'*****with which to replenish the warmth, I threw on my raincoat and emerged into the fading light of a wet winter's evening to wander the pavements of London, oblivious to the honk of horns, the slamming of doors and occasional grating of brakes as traffic splashed through puddles in the road. I felt thoroughly miserable, unwanted and alone. Finally, I made my way back towards my dreary little room wondering how God would get me out of this mess.

Climbing the steps of the building I pushed open the heavy oak door, and momentarily dazedly by the brilliant light in the hall, I found myself the center of a bewildering bustle of people.

"Annette, where have you been?" My landlady was in a whirl—she and her husband ran up and down stairs to my room and back, a stranger following in their wake.

"Oh, Annette!" he gasped, relief in his voice "I have been searching for you all over town." I blinked in astonishment—who on earth was he?

As if in answer to my unasked question he went on, "I'm Guthrie's agent. Your parents have booked your passage on a P & O ship—it's *waiting* for you at Southampton docks. It must sail this evening! Are you packed?"

*****The one-shilling coin commonly referred to as a 'bob'

"No," I answered, completely taken by surprise, "I didn't know that I was going!"

"Well, finish your packing, and I'll be back in an hour." With that he vanished through the door into the soggy London night as I turned and raced up the stairs followed by my landlady and her daughter, both entering into the excitement of the moment, anxious to help at this sudden change of events.

The old-fashioned cabin trunk stood open, ready to be filled with all my worldly belongings by those two dear people as I changed into suitable clothing. Right on time, the agent returned in a taxi to escort me to the station and board the boat-train for Southampton. We were on our way, and for a short while I was able to pause and collect my scattered wits. The situation now looked far more rosy! As the train raced through the dripping night, the young man handed me my ticket, passport and other relevant documents and with verbal instructions as to my cabin number and length of voyage. He was also able to answer questions thrown at him in my excitement.

Arriving at the docks we got off the train with few late passengers. Their luggage together with mine, was swept up by a bevy of waiting porters and taken aboard in preparation for departure. My smiling escort took his leave and wished me bon voyage as I finally climbed the gangplank to what was at that time, the epitome of my dreams—the huge expanse of floating 'home.' I was aboard a P & O liner and on to the next phase of my life.

The moment we stepped on deck the gangplank was raised. Shouts from the shore rang out as the moorings were cast away with a mighty splash. The engines began to vibrate through her structure as the great ship slowly turned to nose her massive form away from the wharf. The docks were almost deserted that dark, uncomfortable night. A steady drizzle, which threatened to develop into a downpour, played against the dim electric lights of the buildings. Soon my attention was drawn away by a touch on the elbow, and the voice of a smiling, darkclad steward asked me to follow him down narrow corridors to my cabin, where he stowed my luggage and introduced me to the small surroundings that were to be mine for the next three or four weeks. The vibrations increased, the engines began to pound in earnest as we headed out to sea, leaving the shores of England behind.

I tucked myself between cool white sheets of a narrow bunk rocked by the waves and rolling ship. What had changed my mother's mind remained a mystery, but I suspected that Jackie had a lot to do with her grudgingly submitting to persuasion as she prepared to accept me into her home.

Eventually, on-board life soon took on a rosier hue. Bundled up in winter clothes I stood at the rail and watched the waves break against the bows as we plowed through the waters of the Atlantic Ocean. The wind crashed against every object in its path, including myself, rain and salt spray drenched my face and scarf over my head. The seas were rough, the wind howled whilst rain lashed down, soaking everything in sight. For those who ventured out on deck when exercise and fresh air called, the intrepid few wrapped themselves in raincoats to battle an unsteady course on deck, or cling to the rail to witness the drama played out by nature. A lone gray and white gull, deserted by its fellows for safer climes on shore, clung to the halyards as it too braved the elements. Below deck, chairs, tables and even the grand piano were securely lashed to prevent them hurtling into people in passing,

Two days of this and then it was over. The winds died down and the seas—more or less calm. Gulls followed the ship and some passengers, somewhat shaky on their legs a little for the worse for wear and looking slightly groggy, reappeared one by one on deck, giving those of us who had positively enjoyed the experience, anguished glances. We, who had braved the storm on deck, discarded our wet weather attire for warm but more comfortable clothing. Stewards appeared on deck mid-morning bearing trays loaded with welcome cups of hot beef tea as passengers greeted each other, became acquainted and formed groups—friends which lasted the duration of the voyage and often longer. And so the initial stage was set for the next few weeks.

Lost in thought, at first I was unaware of a tall young man leaning against the rail at my side, until he introduced himself as John Watkins, one of a group of eight civil servants traveling to their various destinations in the Far East—their first postings for the British Foreign Service. Through him, I was drawn into the company of civil servants. Two were married, their wives accompanying them on their postings; no longer did I feel alone but one of a happy little band of travelers. They were interesting and interested in everything they saw, prepared to grasp life to the full, hold on and enjoy it. Their sense of humor was contagious and the days flew by in rapid succession.

In rough weather, we had bundled up in rugs provided by the ever-attentive stewards, but soon, weather permitting, we played deck tennis, quoits and shuttle-board then lazed in deck chairs, forever gazing out to sea and the endless horizon. In the evenings we drank at the bar and took our meals in the dining room, where whiteclad waiters catered to our every need, carrying enormous trays of plates containing a mouth-watering repast each topped with a silver cover on which balanced more platters. I was filled with admiration for the waiter's sense of gravity, which must have been acquired through months of training. Altogether, life was lighthearted and thoroughly delightful.

We approached Gibraltar and entered the Mediterranean, and still the weather improved the farther we sailed east. We spent the daylight hours basking in the sun and as we did, became better acquainted. One young man, whose features kindled something in my memory from my childhood days, was indeed someone from the past, and not a figment of the imagination. Michael's family hailed from Shropshire on the Welsh Boarder, a beautiful part of England, where I too spent years as a child with a family who kindly took me in as one of their own, and cared for me when my mother returned to Singapore following my father's death. Each member of this family owned a horse, including me—a little gray pony called Katty—and we followed the hounds—fox hunting. It was there that I first met Michael. Now here we were traveling on the same ship to South East Asia! But Michael looked at me somewhat aghast.

"Annette," he said. "That was years ago. We were children then."

"I know," I replied "but it *was* you!" Four of us were lounging in the shade on deck chairs.

"What sort of a memory do you have?" it was more of a statement than a query.

I glanced at Patrick another of our number, who sat between us, chuckling "Oh, don't look at me!" he said, "don't you bring up my past!"

"No, Pat," I laughed. "We've never met before." And so life continued in a light-hearted vein, but Michael continued to cast bewildered glances in my direction for sometime afterwards! I hasten to add I now abhor the very thought of fox hunting!

We reached Suez and made our way slowly along the canal, fascinated by the close proximity of the sand dunes on either side—

Egypt and Asia to our left and Africa on our right. We stood at the rail in awe, saying little as we passed such unfamiliar scenery, each lost in thoughts of their own. Mine whirled in a romantic vein wondering what T.E. Lawrence must have experienced crossing the vast expanse of the inhospitable Arabian Desert and sighting the Suez Cannel for the very first time. I made a mental note to acquire a volume of his "SEVEN PILLARS OF WISDOM" at the earliest possible moment. There were future trips down the Suez Canal for me later in life, but I never ceased to be amazed by this extraordinary feat of man's ingenuity.

The weather heated up as we sailed through the Red Sea, and summer clothes were then the normal wear. Some of our party went ashore at Aden, but time was short and I remained on board standing with others at the rail, fascinated by small boats farther out in the bay where fishermen cast their lines. No gentle puff of breeze disturbed their single sail as the hot sun shimmered on the water around them; it was a quiet and peaceful scene. I looked down at the medley of little boats that swarmed around us, filled with tropical fruit—huge branches of golden, ripe bananas—or trinkets made by the local people, all vying for our Western currency.

We stayed only to refuel, before crossing the Arabian Sea to pull in at Bombay where the rich colors of the East were very much in evidence. There we went ashore and, used to the rolling motion of the ship, were surprised that finding ourselves on solid ground, we felt uncertain of our legs—it was difficult to walk, to regain our balance! The feeling soon wore off but steering an unsteady course down unfamiliar streets gave rise to great surprise and laughter. We wandered through the bazaars and shops flooded with exotic fabrics and Indian *saris* of exquisite colors also worn by the local people. If *only* there had been more time! I would dearly like to have spent several days exploring further afield, searching for a glimpse of India's magnificent wildlife. But that was not to be, although we did roam the gardens round the Taj Mahal to gaze in awe at that amazing monument to love.

We settled down to life on board once more, regaining the balance required for the slow rolling of the ship under way. We spent time in our cabins inspecting our first samples of objects bought in foreign lands, laughing at photos taken ashore—keepsakes of our visit to the tropics—treasures to be mused and mooned over in the years to come. I was sorry to see the shores of India disappear over the horizon and disappointed that Ceylon was not on the itinerary with its vast, golden beaches, but nevertheless this would be something to look forward to in the future. Then it was the flying fish held our delighted attention; deep clouds of sparkling silver that could fly—little silver creatures that rose from the dark green waters of the Indian Ocean, skimming across the waves then diving down to the security of their watery home. They made a truly fascinating picture for those who love to watch the beauty of nature's creation.

Then, of course there were the nights! Nothing could have given me more pleasure than to stand alone on deck wrapped in the mysterious beauty of the sea at night—the salty fragrance of the water that mingled with the unique smell of a ship. High overhead the dark sky filled with a myriad of stars, their names unfamiliar to me, but to my father silent and friendly companions to guide him on his course as he steered his ship through the night so many years ago. He seemed close as we headed towards the land that held so many memories of him in my childhood days.

We were on the last leg of our journey when we reached Penang on the Malay peninsular. There I realized that this was our last stop before disembarking! On shore people waved to passengers on deck. John Watkins said his farewells, and headed for his post in Alor Star in North Malaya. The first of our group to leave, he little realized that trouble lay ahead in the not too distant future—that he would lead his local men in jeeps, well armed against the Communists terrorists in the jungle, on the border of Siam.

I went to the far side of the ship, despondent that the voyage was finally coming to an end. Lost in thought, I was surprised to hear myself paged and returning to the throng boarding from the shore, came face to face with a gentlemen from Guthrie's—Jackie's firm—who was to introduce me to my first taste of night-life of the East. Arrangements duly made, he returned early in the evening, dressed in the white dinner jacket commonly worn in the East, to escort me as I made my way down on shore for my first enchanting evening wining, dining and dancing to the strains of romantic music in the tropics of South East Asia.

Next day it was all over as we arrived at Singapore. I bade farewell to my friends as my mother came aboard. After collecting the luggage we were on our way to Jackie and their lovely home at Ardmore Park.

CHAPTER XIX
SINGAPORE—1948

Working again with Guthrie & Co. after the war, enabled my parents to take over one of the company houses at Ardmore Park which my mother soon turned into something exceptional, thanks to her outstanding sense of the artistic. Between her and the *kubun,* the Indian gardener, (both seemingly blessed with "green thumbs"), the place became a haven of color and peace. A large purple bougainvillea tree gave shade to a grassy round-about encircled by the front drive, while Hibiscus and Gardenia bushes bordered the lawns, and brilliant yellow, red and salmon-colored canna lilies filled the beds outside the perimeter of the drive. Herbaceous borders of blue, pink, mauve, white and yellow flowers covering every inch of earth bloomed gloriously in that tropical climate, but no reds—in my mothers opinion red would have clashed in those particular beds!

When I arrived, a badminton court was laid on the spacious lawn where Jackie coached me thoroughly into the art of the game he loved so well. Although no longer possessing the stamina with which he was formerly blessed, courtesy of the Japanese, and forever watched over with an eagle eye by his adoring wife lest he should overtax himself, he still played an excellent game, his face lighting up with enjoyment and some pride at my own prowess. He welcomed the young people who flocked to our home for an evening game of badminton. I can see him now in my mind's eye, driving up after a hard day's work, his face alight on seeing us on the court, laughing and calling to each other as we chased that elusive shuttle. He would greet my mother with a kiss and laughing, call to the "boy"—the Chinese servant—in excellent Malay (the universal language of the area) to bring out chairs and cocktail glasses, while he himself vigorously attacked the cocktail shaker filled with ice, grapefruit juice and gin, preparing a refreshing drink as the sun rapidly disappeared as was the way so close to the equator.

Not long after my arrival I went in search of a job, and with the benefit of an introduction from a friend, approached with some trepidation,

the imposing building of the CID. There I met a Mr. Carringdon who wrote down the name of my former place of work—that of four years standing as a Civil Servant—my own name and that of my parents; he then disappeared through a door leaving me to sit patiently until his return. This took place after a remarkably short space of time, and holding out a friendly hand, he asked me to report to his own department the following Monday. To my surprise, I was in as a secretary, with no shorthand or typing tests, no papers to fill out—no further ado at all.

And so I took my leave, walking down the uncarpeted stone passage to the main entrance watched, unbeknown to me, by a pair of brooding eyes through a half open door of another office belonging to the "big man" himself, Col. John Daly. I caught a taxi that took me home to break the news to my mother and Jackie. To my astonishment it had a very strange effect on the latter who was both surprised and delighted.

"Without our help too, Dorothy! She did it on her own. She got in there on her own, the CID of all places. Well done Annette!" I couldn't understand what all the excitement was about. It seemed perfectly natural for me to go in search of a job but his next remark explained it all. "I'll give John a call and ask him to keep an eye on her."

The moment John Daly saw Jackie's name on Mr. Carringdon's card, I was in. Many years were to pass, and later in life I was to learn that this was not the normal procedure of getting a job, and that employment was not so easy to come by. My rapid success in job-hunting had been influenced, to the surprise of my parents, by they themselves.

As the Japanese advanced down the Malay peninsular during the first days of the invasion, Col. John Daly walked over the causeway from Singapore onto the mainland to Johor and slipped quietly into the jungle. There he gathered around him the local Chinese and Malay inhabitants, who too had disappeared like shadows into the dense foliage. He quickly established a force to become known as Dalforce, with the aim to combat and harass the advancing enemy anyway possible. Unfortunately it was too little too late. The men needed more training, and eventually their leader was captured, to find himself reunited with his British friends in Singapore POW camp!

Work in Mr. Carringdon's office was far from taxing—just infernally dull. Pounding away on a heavy old typewriter, entering seemingly endless names onto separate cards was monotonous, especially as I had no idea to whom the names belonged. Not my idea of 'interesting work' at all. After about three days Mr. Carringdon explained the situation more fully—the names were those of individuals who harbored aspirations of harassing the British and to cause as much trouble whenever possible—people who we needed to keep an eye on. This was the prelude to the Communist uprising later in the decade—the riots of 1949, when cars were overturned and property set alight, and violence raged against the Europeans. The police engaged the assistance of the volunteer police, of whom my future husband was deputy commandant. This "State of Emergency," as it was to become known, continued until 1960.

In those early days boredom from the monotony of card indexing was relieved by the attention of the Malay detectives whom I seldom met—handsome young men with black hair, eyes flashing in dark-skinned faces and broad smiles revealing pearly-white teeth. They came surreptitiously to my office early, before I arrived and graced my desk with vases of white gardenias that filled the place with their heady perfume. I never knew who had left these beautiful offerings, so welcome and gratefully received, but I did hear laughter as they recited to their colleagues exploits of falling head-first over bushes, warding off the unwelcome bark of dogs as they tried to pick the lovely blooms over the hedge from other peoples gardens. I thought it best to turn a blind eye and deaf ear to these delicious bits of information gleaned in moments of delight!

At home one day after work, I casually remarked that Col. Daly had invited me to accompany him on a drive over the causeway and up the jungle road on the mainland. This would be a new experience and I was eager to find out what a jungle was like. I had already fallen captive to the *sounds* of the tropics, the medley of unseen insects and birds, so I anticipated an interesting trip, away from the work. Surprisingly, Jackie was *not* so thrilled with the idea. A somewhat foreign crease wrinkled his brow.

"Em," he muttered to himself, "I'm not so sure about this."

"Oh, Jackie," My mother was delighted with the idea. "She won't be in any danger. John will be there. He'll look after her."

"That's just what's bothering me!" he said. " What about the other women in the office? They don't go sailing off for a drive any old day of the week with their employer! What are they going to think?" I was dumbstruck.

"Jackie! She's one of his secretaries!"

"Yes, and you don't know John as I do! She is so like you! This stepfather business is becoming a bit of a handful…"

"I beg your pardon?" Indignation sounded in her voice.

"Dory, she is a beautiful girl. You are married, she is not!" He looked worried; "I had better give John a ring." Both my mother and I burst out laughing. "It's all very well for you two to laugh…" and with firm strides and shoulders set he made his way towards the small landing halfway up the stairs to the phone in its place on a table. At that moment Jason, our ultra sophisticated black and white cat, made a dignified entrance through the garden door. With tail held high he stalked across the parquet floor, followed his master up the stairs, sat down at his feet and gazed up into his face. Their backs held a remarkably similar stance! My mother and I glanced at each other, grinned and left it at that.

Those early days without air conditioning life was not as easy in the tropics as it was later in the decade. Ceiling fans were commonplace in every room in every building. For men in the office, shorts, open-neck shirts and knee-high socks were the order of the day and light cotton dresses for the women. When we started on our trip, John and I were fresh and comfortable for our drive. Cars were not air conditioned either, but his was large and luxurious as became that of the head of the CID. Leaving behind the *syce*, his Malay driver, we started early to catch the coolest part of the day with John at the wheel and soon crossed the causeway to the mainland and on through the town of Johor Bahru, then up the inland road.

As the jungle closed around us we might well have entered another world. Giant trees stretched towards the sky from a tangled maze of ferns and dense undergrowth. Vines clung to their trunks, winding their way along bows that reached out to each other from either side of the road high over our heads, folding us in a cloak of dark humidity—a contrast from the brilliant, hot tropical sun we left a stones-throw behind.

After forty-five miles John stopped the car, got out, closed the door and walked leisurely round to my side and bent down to speak to me through the open window. He said he had to meet someone, that I was not to worry and that he would be back shortly. To meet someone?! Out there miles from anywhere in the middle of a jungle? If he had to go, all right go! But just how gullible did he expect me to be? Cat-like he moved without a sound. Not a twig snapped nor leaf rustled as he turned and disappeared into the shadows.

I settled back more comfortably, relaxed completely and was soon lulled by the unceasing medley from the orchestra of tropical insects performing their busy chorus as they went about the daily routine of their lives. I did not move—there was no need, but closed my eyes and allowed the peace of the moment to reach into my very soul. I lost track of time, but after a while a familiar sound broke through the background chorus: the strange call of a bird that resonates through the darkness of the tropical night—one we affectionately know as the Doink-Doink bird. The only way I can describe the cry of this elusive creature is to liken it to the sound made by a human-being, who might hold their breath in an attempt to say "doink" from the back of the throat! "Doink-doink," he calls, then after a pause "doink-doink-doink," another pause and—"doink," but never the same number of doinks in a row! Some people say it drives them crazy to lie in bed on a sleepless night and anticipate how many doinks will follow! But to me it is the sound of a beautiful, elusive creature calling to his mate.

After a while it ceased, leaving the background of the insect orchestra, and the stage for another soloist. Soon one long, infinitely sweet pearcing whistle floated on the air, then there was silence. Or was it someone striking a metal pipe? I opened my eyes and looked around—they might be near, but when the second hollow sound rang out, I realized it came from the canopy high overhead.

When thirty or forty minutes had passed it was plain it was not the call of nature that had taken John into the forest; however I was not in the least bit anxious. Hadn't he told me not to worry? Still gullible enough to trust my fellow men, I relaxed and continued to listen to the wonderful sounds so alien to me, fresh from a totally different environment the other side of the world. In England the many hours spent alone as a child in the fields and woods with the rabbits and other little creatures gave me the patience needed later in life. Once again alone with nature, lulled and relaxed, I loved every moment! But then a muffled boom rang out through the jungle. "Boom!" then a pause, then again, "boom!"—the sound of heavy wood meeting wood. There was no mistake—this was man-made, and suddenly now I was very alert!

Just as he had entered the darkness, John reappeared, as silent as a ghost—standing there by my window. He spoke softly, as if reluctant to break the spell.

"Look, Annette. Isn't it beautiful?!" Between his hands lay a long cigarette case that was definitely *not* in keeping with the surroundings—it was gold, slender and beautiful. Col. Daly had kept a tryst with his former local comrades, men from the old war days. Informants? It seemed logical, but I didn't ask—it was instinct, training from days long ago, and possibly a quick mind that kept me quiet. He went round to the driver's side and opened the door as another boom rang out again.

"John, what *is* that noise?" I had to satisfy my curiosity.

"What noise?" he asked.

"Listen! There it goes again." Motionless, we sat and listened until another muffled boom rang out.

"Oh, that!" he laughed as he reached for the key, turned on the engine and let off the clutch. "You know those sarongs you love to wear? The *Hari Rya* sarongs with gold patterns running down the front?" He glanced at the rear mirror before turning the wheel, "That sound my dear, is made by the Malay women as they weave those sarongs! Heavy wood looms—wood meeting wood."

He drove on up the hill until he reached a wide stretch in the road where he was able to turn the car. I was puzzled, but he continued. "Each Malay State has its own design. Johor is the chief state so it has the more elaborate design. The silver panel is called the *kapala* and is worn down the front of the sarong. Next time you see them worn on *Hari Ria*, notice how they are wrapped round the body—men and women. The silver panel falls down the front."

"The silver panel that falls down the front!" I thought aloud. Yes, I was well aware of these strips of cloth, of glorious colors worn by the local people on their high days and holidays, or *Hari Ria,* tied in such a way that the intricate pattern of silver or gold fell down the front of their bodies. No matter how hard I had tried to tie these sarongs around myself, they slipped and threatened to leave me standing thoroughly embarrassed!

I digested this in silence. Communists or simply quiet people living out their lives in a tropical forest? But yes, indeed I did love the Hari Ria sarongs. A beautiful dress had already been made for me, exquisitely fashioned by Doris Geddes, the famous designer, well known throughout the Far East and Australia. Doris was a friend of my parents, and soon to be a good friend of mine. Her elegant salon in Raffles Hotel drew distinguished visitors from all over the world, as they passed through Singapore. But what bothered me at the moment was how on earth these gorgeous materials came to be made in the middle of a tropical forest? How did these people live?

John was in no hurry to return to the office, and decided to improve my education concerning the soil on which I lived. After a pause for a picnic lunch in the shade of the coconut palms on one of Malacca's deserted beaches, we crossed back over the causeway onto the island of Singapore, skirting the town, glimpsing some of the local life.

Near the shores where the coconut palms and frangipani swayed gently in the breeze on the left, and small waves lapping the hot sand to our right, all was peace and quiet save for the occasional bark of a dog.

We saw Malay kampongs made up of attap huts built high on stilts. Beneath the huts life went on, as chickens scratched in the earth clucking away to themselves, and scraggy dogs lay dozing peacefully in the shade. A lone infant sat nearby, drawing patterns in the sand with a feather.

Further down the road, again amongst the palms, lay another small kampong*, peaceful and quiet. The aroma of cooking mingled with the woody fragrance of smoke wafting on the air from a pot suspended over a fire beneath the floor of one of the huts—so picturesque and so peaceful that it was difficult to appreciate the hardship these local people had experienced during the Japanese occupation.

Jackie was at home from the office as we drove up, all smiles and delighted for a chance to chat with John over a drink. I left them to it. They seldom met and no doubt would reminisce—on the other hand they might purposely avoid the past. One never knew with fellow occupants of more uncomfortable places. So many of them back here on this island, living in a place they loved, they tried to forget the years of interruption. Some on their return to Singapore found their silver still intact; knives forks, spoons and other small items hidden beneath the floorboards of their homes. They desperately tried to save what they could as enemy forces fought to gain entry and take their island home. Others not so fortunate, were forced to start all over again.

When my paycheck arrived that week I decided that, despite the monotony of card indexing, this really was a pleasant way to earn one's living.

CHAPTER XX
SINGAPORE
INTO THE SWING OF THINGS

Jackie would accept nothing towards my keep, therefore my salary became my own with which to do as I please; this was generous on his part and gratefully accepted on mine. I was soon swept up into the whirl of life in South East Asia—exotic, expensive and the greatest fun. His own remarks about "the unnecessary expenditure one indulged in civilian life," before the war, and wondering "if we shall go back to the old ways when it is all over" was a foregone conclusion. In no time at all the "old ways" became the order of the day—lavish cocktail parties, wining, dining and of course, plenty of the necessary domestic help that goes with that way of life. Shops were flooded with merchandise from every corner of the world, if not as cheap as before the war, expenses did not soar to dizzy heights. Glorious fabrics from Switzerland, India and Siam soon found their way to the markets, together with Malay sarongs and other materials made by the local people. These were soon on their way to the cutting boards where, under the skilled hands of the Chinese, they were transformed into the most beautiful evening gowns for their British and American customers.

The famous Tanglin Club and Singapore Swimming Club, the hotels—Raffles and the Adelphi—and the restaurants—Princes and the Cathay (atop the only high-rise at that time)—were once again filled with glamour, color and excitement as women swirled around the dance floor to the music of many bands, in the arms of their escorts, stunning in white dinner jackets and black ties. It was into this exotic life that I was swept watched over not only by my elegant mother, but an enthusiastic Jackie who, with pride that at last having a daughter to launch into society, introduced me to all their friends, making sure I had the time of my life. Yes, we went back to the old ways.

At first, my job fully occupied my mind, but alone in the evenings as the sun went down, the warm waters of Tanglin Club swimming pool were just too inviting to resist. At that hour the club was deserted except for *"boys,"* smart in their white uniforms busily preparing the place for the evening's activities. The members were at home changing for dinner, indulging in a cocktail or two as the night creatures awaked outside with the unceasing buzz of insects mingling with the chorus of frogs who croaked happily to each other in the undergrowth. The club, within walking distance of Ardmore, gave me a chance to train my ears and mind, to savor and appreciate these sounds as I walked home, such a difference from those that I had left behind in London!

The road ran between trees whose branches dropped leaves and twigs not easy to distinguish in the rapidly fading light. So when, one evening, a twig on which I was about to step, wriggled into the grassy verge, my heart gave a leap. Since infancy I have had an inordinate horror of snakes, when, clutching my nanny's hand, I watched one of these creatures slither into my pram. It was a small one, but when you are a very little girl everything you see takes on gigantic proportions! Fortunately my doll lay in the pram, not me. The incident walking home that humid night did nothing to diminish the feeling—my stride to avoid the frightened creature was exceptionally large and my pace increased to such an extent I was quite out of breath when I tripped up the steps of the house almost into the arms of my mother. She had already changed and looked quite lovely in a long, floral skirt and mauve chiffon blouse with full billowing sleeves caught at the wrist, giving the appearance of peaceful grace.

Jackie turned at this commotion still wealding the cocktail shaker: "Good heavens! What happened to you? You look as if you have seen a ghost!"

"No, no," I said. "I almost stepped on a snake. It looked like a wriggling twig."

"A wriggling twig," he raised an eyebrow. "Did you have a drink at Tanglin?"

"No, I did not!" I retorted and in as few words as possible explained what had happened.

"Well, you had better have one now. Boy!" He turned to the boy, neat as ever in his white uniform and about to disappear into the kitchen, "Boy! *Lagi iah batu,*" Jackie called for more ice,—the never-ending cry in the Singapore heat—then rattled off something in Malay. Judging by the grin that spread across the boy's face, Jackie was expounding good-naturedly on my lack of knowledge of the local wildlife. Soon an inviting concoction, one of his *specials*, was splashing into a glass over plenty of ice.

Take it with you darling," suggested my mother, an amused onlooker. "Don't take too long changing. Dinner is almost ready, and afterwards we will de-bug the cannas."

"De-bug the cannas?" What was this about? I thought I had had enough of nature for one evening. De-bug the canas! This sounded ominous.

"You may be surprised." She smiled, seeing the look on my face. "Hurry up. I'm getting hungry."

It was a pleasant meal; the French windows open wide, as were the doors leading to the garden to catch every available breath of wind. In those days there were no windowpanes in the houses in Singapore, just open slats—air conditioning was a thing of the future—but fans spun from the ceilings as well as those that stood upright on the floor. Would I ever get used to this incredible humid heat? Jason emerged from his evening prowl, climbing the steps from the garden, the white parts of his glossy coat standing out in the darkness. The sky was filled with a miriad of twinkling stars, the heady fragrance of tropical plants wafted in the air, and into this beauty of the night my mother led me after coffee had been served.

The *Kabun* was already in place, armed with a bucket for the enemy—large snails with a veracious appetite for their favorite delicacy, the succulent leaves of the giant Canna Lilies. Their beautiful bright red and yellow flowers reached to my shoulder, and when tightly packed in their respective beds made a glorious splash of color, catching the eye of anyone driving up to the house. But humans were not the only ones to appreciate the Cannas. On tropical nights the snails took advantage of the darkness to emerge from their daytime hideouts for a feast. It was a never-ending battle between them, the Kabun and occasionally my mother! Already some of the slugs were lying in the bottom of the bucket. Although I was not sure what to expect, my mother knew exactly what she wanted me to see. Holding a small flashlight in her hand, she stepped from the damp grass onto the earth between the plants and searched amongst the blooms. Finally, success achieved, she called softly.

"Annette, come here." I followed her carefully through the bed. "Look, darling," she whispered drawing me towards the clustered blooms. "Careful! Move the petals very gently."

Curious, I reached out and drew back the red petals as she aimed the beam into the center of the flower, and there inside, lay a tiny hummingbird, sound asleep in it's soft velvety bed. I held my breath and gazed in awe, fighting the temptation to reach out with one finger and touch the little creature, but instead released each petal slowly so as not to disturb it, so oblivious to the attention it was attracting, and left him to rest in peace. I glanced at my mother, drew a deep breath and shook my head in amazement, allowing the flower to rock gently in the evening breeze. Our so-called quest for slugs totally forgotten, we searched for more little sleeping birds, and found just a few in the red and yellow blossoms, each one equally as breathtaking as the first. Then, leaving the Kabun to go about his business, we went indoors to join Jackie as he puffed away contentedly at his pipe, reading the daily newspaper.

*****

One morning, as Jackie rose from the breakfast table, pushed back his chair and made for the door where the *syce* was waiting to drive him to the office, he asked the pertinent question: "Annette, why don't you join the Stage Club? I see they are putting on "Claudia" at the end of the month—it had a good run in London. Go down for an audition. It would be fun for you!" I glanced across at my mother's face expecting a glare in her husband's direction, but strangely enough though not showing outright delight, she was not adverse to the suggestion.

"I don't mind as long as you're not paid," came the extraordinary reply.

"Em!"—Jackie looked at her over his reading glasses. And me? Well, I did manage to keep a straight face.

Thus ten eventful years were under way, first with the Singapore Stage Club (where I was not paid), and then the Singapore Repertory Company (where I was), and with it came a whole new circle of friends with similar tastes as my own. Life was about to take an exciting turn. Following a small part in "Claudia" I shot into the public eye in "The Importance of Being Earnest" and never looked back during my time in Singapore, thanks to the glorious sets and costumes of some very talented people.

I now became a night owl, frequenting the restaurants and clubs with my escorts, with an ever increasing wardrobe of glamorous evening dresses as was the custom those postwar days when we subconsciously endeavored to make up for six years of austerity during the war. We were extravagant, seldom giving a thought to expense as we dined in the best restaurants on exotic tropical foods and occasionally an overabundance of wine. As for the corsage—our beaux were generous in their floral gifts—great baskets of tropical orchids gracing my theater dressing room, a magnificent display night after night.

. . . .

The top floor of the Cathay Building, a high-rise perched on top of a hill, afforded the most glorious night view under a sky of twinkling stars. Across the town of Singapore lay the harbor, the near waters reflecting each individual light of a sampan. The large ocean-going liners lay at anchor further out to sea, their portholes a string of lights in the ghost-like forms of their enormous hulls in the darkness, reflecting on the dancing ripples of the water. Out there all was silent—strange to think it looked very much the same under enemy occupation, heart-searing for any prisoner of war gazing out across the waters longing for home, longing to be anywhere but here.

It was there on the terrace four of us met that night, for what would become an unusual evening. Sheila Snedden was a pretty girl with her long blond hair and clear-cut features, wearing a filmy blue and pink evening gown that floated around her slender form as she danced. Sheila was the daughter of my father's friend and colleague when, as pilots in the South China Seas, they chartered the waters around Hong Kong. Dennis, her dark, good-looking escort, complimented her with his six-foot two-inch height.

Our small table placed strategically at the edge of the terrace, held the glasses for our after-dinner drinks where Nobby, the shorter of the two men, stood for a moment, gazing out to sea. There must have been many memories for him; he knew this place well—how well I was not sure—he did not talk very much about it. Relaxed in my comfortable chair my back was half towards him, but I turned my head and looked up. After a moment he glanced down and smiled, then taking my hand drew me to stand beside him. "It's beautiful out there!" he said. I nodded, just two figures in white—his the white dinner jacket of the East, mine a long, slender dress with scarlet braiding round the neck and cuffs. We could hear music from the band playing softly in the room behind us where we too had danced and dined, and now the four of us relaxed and sipped our drinks. I remember that night with fondness. It was warm and fragrant; the stars above seemed strangely close, lying low over our heads. I am glad I was born into that era! Nobby and I danced for a while, a slow fox-trot before joining the other two sitting at the table. We ordered another round of drinks, which soon arrived and set in place when Nobby made a strange request—that for a pack of cards. Although curious, we didn't question *why* he wanted them, nor even gave a thought as to whether or not there was such a thing in the place, nor were we surprised when the waiter returned almost immediately and put them into the *tuen's* hand. Nobby leaned back in his chair and shuffled them, turned to his right and placed them on the table for Dennis to cut. He then put the pack in front of me, moving my glass to a safer spot, and indicating the cleared area, said "Annette, put the black in one pile and the red in another—face down."

Somewhat surprised I looked at him, but to satisfy his whim, was about to comply by turning up the first card. "No, no" he said, "don't look at it. Face down. The red on the left, the black on the right."

"Nobby, you're crazy! How can I possibly do that?" I asked.

"Try" he said, softly but quite firmly. "Black here—red there," he then sat back and sipped his drink.

I shrugged, gave a conciliatory smile, picked up the pack once more and began to deal two little piles face down, carefully, to avoid brushing them aside with my long, full sleeves. Aware that Sheila and Dennis were now gazing at me intently I decided against any serious thought, there was no possible way of knowing which was red and which was black. I dealt quite fast until I came to one particular card, gave a little laugh and dithered from one side to the other. "Any you don't know put in the middle." Nobby's voice once again. I put offending card between the two piles and continued dealing until none were left. Nobby leant back in his chair, a mysterious smile on his face whilst I reached over for my drink and watched and waited to see what my friend would do. A couple glided by to the soft strains of music from the band in the adjoining room. Well aware of the attention he attracted as the three of us gazed at him, Nobby was in no hurry. Finally he reached out and turned face up the little pile of cards on the right—*all* were black. No one said a word. He turned those that were on the left—and *all* were red. Then reaching for that one card in the center paused, held it in his fingers, looked at it a few moments longer and let it fall—the Joker!

Sheila gasped. Dennis stared at his friend. "How did you know she would do that?" he asked.

"I didn't," came the strange reply. "I've heard about it but I have never seen it done before. I thought if anyone could do it, Annette might," and added, "like to have a try?"

Dennis shuddered. "Not on your life. You're not getting me into this! Come on, Sheila, let's dance."

Laughing, my friend also rose, offered me his hand and led me to the floor.

Unfortunately our happy mood was about to come to an abrupt end. After the waltz there was barely time to return to the table and settle ourselves as the band continued to play, when across the floor, heading in our direction, a tall, burly individual pushed two waiters aside as he weaved an unsteady course between the dancing couples.

"Em, em!" muttered Dennis as the individual pulled a chair up to our table, spilling his drink and sat himself down. His presence was not particularly desirable; his speech was slurred and loud, and what we could understand of it proved that he was one of the Americans who frequented the Cathay. Clearly he held a very high opinion of himself and likewise a pretty low one of us.

"Saw you on stage the other night," was his introductory remark and presumably his right to join our company.

I glanced at Sheila—should we make a tactful exit and allow the men to handle the situation, aware their hands were embarrassingly tied in front of the ladies? But I waited as he expounded on the magnificence of his exploits overseas, which might have been more interesting had he not been so much under the influence of an excessive amount of alcohol. Soon the intruder became a bore and gave no thought to present company or those incarcerated as former POWs under the enemy. Perhaps not realizing that those in our island home had held the enemy at bay for two long years, during the blitzkrieg onslaught while London and Coventry blazed. How could I ever forget watching from our school dormitory windows so far away in the country, the ghostly red sky in the direction of London? Our two companions—what were their thoughts? These men who had flown and fought, or spent time here on this island captive of another foe?

The drunken drawl bragged on in ever increasing volume, attracting disparaging attention from the tables in the near proximity—hadn't the Americans won the war and saved us from ultimate annihilation? I looked at Nobby, admiring his restraint. At last and none too soon, I switched a steady gaze at the tormentor and looked him right in the face. With fury blazing in my eyes, but evenly and in clear tones so as only to be heard by those at our own table, I asked the pertinent question: "And what would you Americans have done had the Japanese *not* attacked Pearl Harbor?"

"Oh, *touché!*" Almost inaudible at my side Nobby breathed the words in mingled admiration and delight.

The intruder stared at me, at a loss for words, the only sound coming from the orchestra in the other room. No one moved for several moments until he staggered to his feet, gripped his glass and crossed the floor to disappear through the door. I never saw him again.

Simultaneously both men rose reaching for their wallets. "Let's go," said Nobby.

"Tanglin or the Swimming Club?" Asked Dennis. The vote fell to the more secluded of the two—the Tanglin Club—where we would be insured of a pleasant conclusion to an unusual evening amongst our friends.

CHAPTER XXI
PENANG TO ALOR STAR

"Annette, one of your admirers has sent you some flowers." As I tuned the corner from the upper flight and started down the rest of the stairs, Jackie looked up, staggering under an enormous basket of mauve and white orchids that had just been delivered by the florist.

"Oh, how beautiful—who are they from?" My mother crossed towards him as I reached the bottom step. I joined them and searched for a card amongst the blooms, without success.

"Look," I said, "a rabbit!" Sure enough a little china rabbit, white with blue spots, tied with a blue ribbon nestled amongst the flowers that wound their way up and around the tall, circular handle. "Who on earth has sent this?" I started to say simultaneously with my mother's exclamation of "Oh, no!" and Jackie's "Smooth, very smooth!" At the sight of the ornament both had guessed the identity of the mysterious donor and were not overjoyed. I was on my way to work and sensed that I had left two very uneasy people looking at my newly arrived basket of flowers in mingled admiration and disquiet. "Don't say a word Dory, it'll only rouse her interest all the more," Jackie warned his wife.

It was during the run of "The Importance of Being Earnest," when dressing rooms were filled with flowers, the daily papers with reviews and photographs that Bunny Salvesen came backstage. He saw the visitors, decided against being one of a crowd and departed with other ideas to impress. Ten years older than I, Bunny was married to an admiral's daughter in England, in the throes of getting a divorce, very much a man of the world, and what is commonly known as a "ladies" man. In the eyes of my parents he was not one of the most suitable companions for their daughter. However, there was one bright spark to the start of my mother's day. The morning after opening night—a black tie affair—the wife of the High Commissioner for South East Asia, Lady Malcolm MacDonald, called to congratulate my mother on her daughter's performance. She also heard that other people were returning to see the production a second time and decided that the stage was not so bad a place after all! But this floral offering was a bit of a worry.

Although my parents were not exactly delighted when an invitation from John Watson arrived—the young civil servant I had met on board ship—he would, indeed, appear to be a more suitable friend for their daughter. Besides, it would be a good opportunity for her to get away for a while and see another part of the country. As for me, I couldn't have been more delighted. It came between the run of theater productions and a leave of absence from card indexing—the opportunity to explore other exciting places was my idea of heaven!

Jackie drove me to the airport to board the plane bound for Penang where John, already bronzed from the tropical sun, met me in a loose-fitting Khaki uniform, the most comfortable attire for tracking down communists hiding in the jungle on the border of Siam. A gun, his constant companion, lay on the seat beside him. This surprised me, until we left the town and started to drive north, up the Malay peninsular towards Alor Star, through rough and strangely deserted countryside.

There were but few buildings that made up John's headquarters both for himself and his men, all of whom wore the same loose fitting khaki uniform and sported guns at all times. In constant anticipation of trouble a strange quiet hung heavy in the air, voices were never raised; they were prepared for the slightest sound that would trigger off a burst of gunfire.

This was all so alien to me—such a contrast to life in Singapore; no wonder my parents were anxious I should see the place, to experience and appreciate this strange way of life, so great a contrast to that which I enjoyed in Singapore. But it did have its moments. John succumbed to my repeated requests to visit the border. We drove in a convoy of jeeps filled with his men, all armed, their legs dangling over the sides—one man under strict orders to stay at my side at all times and not let me out of his sight.

First we bumped over flat, open but rugged terrain, where there appeared to have been some attempt at cultivation but abandoned when life became too dangerous. There we approached the edge of the jungle where, in the shadow of the trees on the Siam side of the border, so compact and forbidding, lurked human forms hardly discernible in the shadow of the undergrowth.

"Annette, we've gone far enough!" John spoke softly, his voice steady. "Those are not our men up there on the bank. If you want to visit Siam you must do it at a later date, some other way." I recognized the voice of authority! Although longing to cross to another country, I realized what he said was true.

We drove on a little further, turned and without tempting fate, retraced our steps to a safer place. John *did* show me around the town of Alor Star before boarding my 'plane the following day satisfied that I had seen what his situation was like in the North.

*****

Bunny Salvesen had made his point and gained my interest, and although much older than the other members of our late afternoon badminton parties, he soon became a regular visitor, despite my mother's disapproval. The younger men—especially those who flattered her—were far more to her liking, but the more she lauded their praises the more stubborn I became. The ultimate perfection in her mind for a future son-in-law, was David Montgomery, son of General Montgomery, who arrived in the wake of a couple of our friends one happy evening. Jackie was actually on the court playing. He was at one time an excellent badminton player, a member of the Champion Malay team before the war, but prison camp had taken its toll on his health, and now he played for short intervals. David sat with us watching from the sidelines, drinking one of "Jackie's specials" until the game was over, then he and Jackie sat talking, enjoying each others company, but as I pointed out to my mother David—although so charming—was only "passing through" Singapore!

It was Bunny who was the expert at organizing after-theater dinner parties, not only at the best restaurants but also on the beaches, complete with a motor—boat to take us out to sea and visit other small islands off the shores of Singapore. Those tropical carefree nights amongst good friends will always remain indelibly stamped on my memory. What finally captured my imagination were his wartime exploits. Whilst I was still at school, in short skirts and long socks, he was already on active duty fighting in Europe. His anecdotes and experiences as second in command of the Rock of Gibraltar, although no doubt exaggerated, fascinated me. Moreover, Bunny was the Deputy Commander of the Volunteer Police Force in Singapore, ready to go into action at the first sign of any uprising by the Communists. However, my parents somewhat thankfully, watched the group of boys and girls chasing the shuttle back and forth in the evenings at Ardmore Park before the sun went down. The more the merrier in their opinion.

John Payton captured my mother's fancy as a prospective son—in-law. He was a soft-spoken, eccentric young man, with a nice steady job in a bank, and would turn up unexpectedly at all hours of the day when not working. Dressed in what I considered the most extraordinary loose-fitting but comfortable attire, he appeared to be following some sort of fashion worn by the Japanese in their moments of relaxation. Charming but dull, my mother insisted he would make me a wonderful husband no doubt because she realized that that was exactly his intention. I didn't agree and when he gave up on me, finally taking the hint, and married an heiress, her irritation knew no bounds. "All that money, Annette, and you could have had him!"

"Mummy darling." I said, "had he married me he would not have had all that money—now would he?"

"Oh!" She blinked and after a moment's thought. "No, I suppose you're right. He wouldn't" We both laughed.

Soon after this there was to be an interruption to the evening badminton parties—my parents were due for "home leave." First they planned a few weeks in Australia visiting friends, followed by three or four months in England with the idea of seeking out a place to which they could eventually retire when Jackie's term in Singapore with Guthrie & Co. was complete. During their absence I would stay with their old friends, Johnny and Marion Gransden. Johnny and Jackie had known each other before the war, had been POWs together in Singapore and remained good friends ever since.

Back in England my parents bought a couple of bicycles, loaded them onto their car, and first drove around the South, visiting much-loved places by the sea in Cornwall and Devon. Then they traveled further North towards London to be within easy reach of the Home Office, staying at picturesque little pubs overnight and riding their bicycles during the day.

As these trips continued they kept an ever-watchful eye open for a lovely home and finally came across a two-storey, three bedroom, half-timbered black and white house on the outskirts of the charming little country town of Cobham, in Surrey. The property was deserted; a padlock and chain on the little wrought-iron gate, with long grass, dandelions and thistles that hid the crazy paving leading to the steps at the front of the heavy oak door. Peering over the hedge from the grassy verge they could see that the land surrounding the house and nearby garage was akin to an overgrown wilderness. They wheeled their bikes to the back gate to look up the drive where puddles from the recent rain reflected a wan sun from a cloudy sky.

"What do you think, Dory?" Jackie's gaze took in the surrounding trees. He pictured himself working in a vegetable garden at the back of the house. A finch sang a sweet song from the hedge close by whilst a large black crow, his feathers shimmering with good health, circled overhead. Without further ado they cycled into the village, propped their machines against the wall of the real estate office, sought out the agent, returned in his car and in no time at all the deal was done!

They fell in love with the place, which soon became a hive of activity of scrubbing, cleaning and painting. The wilderness was brought under control and lawns, rose gardens and herbaceous borders were meticulously planned and put into place under my mother's direction while Jackie took charge of the area behind the house; under his supervision a thriving vegetable garden was eventually born.

Rumah Ketchil means the little home in Malay, although the place was not so little, boasting two bedrooms a bathroom and an office for Jackie upstairs. A long hall dividing the sitting room and dining room, and a kitchen and bathroom comprised the area downstairs. It was their own cozy home at last in England, waiting to be occupied.

*****

As the Gransdons had no badminton court, it was inevitable that the crowd of young people diminished to a special few in my parents' absence. However one of the remaining visitors was Bunny Salvesen. We became engaged, much to the disquiet of my host and hostess, who wished to goodness Jackie and Dorothy would hurry to return. This they did and thankfully the Gransdens bade farewell to their guest, no doubt glad to be relieved of the responsibility of a non-too-welcome suitor to her hand. Once more I moved to Ardmore Park before joining my fiancée at his flat.

With Rumah Ketchil rented and in safe hands of friends, life returned to Ardmore Park very much as it was before. Although Bunny was more or less a permanent figure at my side, my parents hoped that one of the other younger men would replace him in my affection.

Late one Saturday afternoon after a long walk across the golf course, followed by a drive around the coast road, relaxed after admiring the surrounding view, we dropped by Ardmore to pass the time of day with my parents, who we discovered were not at home. Returning to the car, I heard a voice call out "Hello!" and turning to respond, found to my surprise there was nobody in sight—that the drive was quite empty. Oh well! I must have been mistaken and thought no more about it and with that opened the door.

"Hello!" Again I turned and once more saw absolutely nobody! I knew my ears were not playing tricks—someone *had* called out "Hello."

"Bunny," I said. "Someone is calling us."

He looked down the drive but it was empty. "Nonsense darling, you're hearing things."

"No I am not—someone said hello!" We both searched but there was no one to be seen.

"Hello Charlie!" It seemed a little annoyed, impatient for a response. There was no one in the center roundabout taking refuge from the evening sun, beneath the branches of the purple bougainvillea—it was deserted.

"Hello, Charlie! Hello, Charlie! Hello! Hello! Hello!" Taking advantage of the longer sentence I looked down and followed the sound of the voice, which came not far from my feet.

"Hello, Charlie!" Cajoling now, in the form of a greeting. These moods change rapidly, I thought. With his head bent low, strutting out in tiny strides with firm little steps, in danger of tripping over his toes, came a pretty green parrot! He announced his presence once more with a cheerful greeting. "Hello, Charlie!"

"Good heavens! Bunny, he's here. Look—a beautiful little parrot!" Charlie *was* there, at my feet, his head cocked on one side, looking up at me with a bright little eye. At that moment I heard the sound of a car.

"Bun," I said in some anxiety. "Stay with him. I'll stop the car." Charlie made a strange gurgling in his throat as if in appreciation as I turned and ran down the drive. Standing firmly in the middle of the road I forced Jackie to stop. "Jackie, you have a visitor! There's a parrot in the drive. He's walking towards you."

"Oh, come on darling! Don't play games!" my mother was impatient. "We have to change for a dinner."

But the enthusiastic ornithologist born in prison camp surfaced in her husband. A parrot? This joke was worth exploring. "Now wait a minute, I'll go and..." he got out of the car and followed me while my mother moved to the drivers seat, and sure enough a "Hello, Charlie!" greeted him low down on the ground as Charlie walked towards him.

His face wreathed in smiles, Jackie bent down and offered him a finger. Once more Charlie cocked his head, looked at the outstretched hand and trustingly raised a claw, took a firm grip as Jackie brought him to face level, and a friendship was formed.

The dinner party forgotten, my mother called to make suitable excuses while her husband returned to town in search of a large, roomy cage and plenty of food for the newest member of the household. As for Charlie? Well, he became a much loved member of the family, an instant hit whilst I the innocent recipient of Jackie's undying gratitude! For so long the sole recipient of his families affection, Jason's nose was a little out of joint, but with an abundant show of love on my part, despite a few hostile squawks and mutterings from the new arrival who detested cats, things were soon back to normal in a very happy household.

CHAPTER XXII
FRASER'S HILL
ANOTHER KIND OF WAR

To escape the heat Bunny decided to take two weeks local leave, planning a trip to Fraser's Hill with a stopover at Kuala Lumpur. As always, I packed with the greatest care each seam in every garment folded in place, protected by tissue paper to ensure against creasing. Bunny loaded the luggage into the car—traveling 'light' was never my forte—and there was a considerable amount to squeeze into the back of the trunk. We bade *adieu* to the staff—or *tabi,* as they say in Malay. Ah Joo An and his wife were, no doubt, glad to see the back of us for a while, and we were on our way.

We drove past the town, over the causeway and through Johor. As we approached the jungle road Bunny took a sizable gun from under the front seat and laid it between us. "Just in case we need it, darling," he commented. Of course, there was nothing strange about this—we were officially in 'a state of emergency' prepared for trouble in any form from the communist terrorists. It was becoming a second way of life and would be for the duration of our time in the East. We drove north up the West Coast Road through darker parts of the jungle, the atmosphere heavy with moisture and air filled with the ever-present song of Cicadas. Overhead an occasional monkey called out thereby advertising his presence in the treetops. On we went chatting happily, relaxed with the thought of a fortnight's respite from the heat.

After a while Bunny glanced down at the seat, thought for a moment, then said "Annette, that gun is loaded. If we run into trouble, point it out of the window and shoot. Aim high, *over their heads,* just don't kill anyone."

"All right," I replied and looked at the ominous weapon, its mission—destruction. I knew it would make a terrible noise when fired and I hate loud noises.

"You better practice," he continued. This seemed unnecessary but to please him I managed to pick it up and put it onto my lap. The weight of it!

"What is this thing anyway?" I asked.

"An old German luger," came the reply.

"A what?"

"A German luger."

"Why don't you have something British?" I muttered, it seemed like letting the side down at this stage of the emergency when we were fighting terrorists as a result of the war. "Where did you get it?"

"From a German. He was dead," he added.

"Oh! Where?" I asked, curiously.

"Fighting up the coast in Italy."

"When you were in the wrong place at the wrong time?" I taunted. I enjoyed listening to his war-time 'escapades' as I called them, particularly the one when leading his heavy tanks down a narrow lane he realized that guns were firing from his right instead of the left, that he and his men were behind the enemy lines instead of visa versa! At that particular part the lane it was far too narrow in which to maneuver and they were forced to continue on their precarious way until they came to an open field. There they performed a nippy round-about-turn to double back as rapidly as a number of lumbering tanks can maneuver and beat it in the opposite direction, everyone breathing a sigh of relief. The flask of brandy in Bunny's hip pocket proved to be a Godsend to its owner!

Now, whilst driving on that humid, jungle road Bunny said nervously "Darling, don't point that gun at me! Just pick it up, balance it on the edge of the window and pull the trigger." I smiled, shrugged and followed his directions to the best of my ability. "First you have to cock it." I dragged it back again. How does one cock a gun I wondered? Driving fast up the hill and round the bends, he was loath to stop in so desolate an area "Just pull the top part back towards you."

Holding the barrel in my left hand with the right on 'the top part' I pulled. It didn't budge an inch. Obviously a little more effort had to go into this. Pointing the gun towards the floor, gripping it between my knees I hauled with all my might. Bunny cleared his throat. "Er… never mind darling just put it on the seat and if anything happens take hold of the wheel and steer. I'll do the shooting." This seemed a better idea. Although still learning to drive, I was pretty good at steering, but I still had to take my driving test. In the evenings, in a deserted spot in Singapore, he was teaching me to reverse between two coconuts shells placed on the road. It was impossible to see them over the door—just a case of hit and miss; but if I could do that, certainly I could steer going straight ahead even if he was shooting across me through the open window. Maybe it was fortunate we didn't run into trouble.

Finally we reached Kuala Lumpur in the late afternoon as the sun set over the beautiful little town, so well loved by the British stationed in the tranquillity of its tropical surroundings. Spending two nights with friends, enjoying their company, easing into the atmosphere heralded a vacation as far as Bunny was concerned. As for me, I could study the lines for my next stage part on my return to Singapore. My Zeis Ikon camera exchanged for five hundred cigarettes on the black market in Germany was always at my side. With ample opportunity for some excellent photography, I started shooting pictures to my hearts content. A photograph taken of the outskirts of the jungle from across a grassy valley won a prize in a local competition in Singapore the following year.

*****

In the 1800s, whilst searching for gold and tin, Louis James Fraser came across a group of seven hills high up and free from the humid heat. He subsequently built a bungalow on one where he could relax and regain energy lost to South East Asia's heavy atmosphere of the lower regions. That mountain became known as Fraser's Hill, surrounded by other rolling hills, all lush green in color thanks to their heavy jungle foliage—hill upon rolling hill of rich, tropical vegetation stretching far into the distant horizon to complete a magnificent vista. One of the half dozen bungalows discreetly built into the mountainside, became our retreat for the week.

There was a startling reminder of the never-ending humid heat in Singapore. Opening the lid of the suitcase, I was in for a shock. My cotton dress lay limp on top, soggy and moist—a sorry looking mess despite my care in the packing. Bunny laughed. "That's how we live in Singapore! Everything is wet!" Each article of clothing, both his and mine had to be ironed, but judging by the grin on the *amah's* face at Fraser's Hill, it was nothing unusual with visitors from the lower regions!

Further north lay a similar group of hills known as the Cameron Highlands, beyond the tin mining area and isolated rubber plantations, all under the care of British managers and their small bands of local workers. The State of Emergency against the communist guerrillas was escalating in 1951, and driving north to the highlands the British High Commissioner, Sir Henry Gurney had been ambushed shot and killed. It worried me that as Deputy Commandant of the Volunteer Police Force, Bunny bore the dubious distinction of a place on the communist 'black list' and marked for annihilation!

Our balcony overlooking the mountains became a favorite place for me to sit and dream the time away but that first evening as the sun went down, I was startled to see columns of smoke rising from amongst the trees.

"Bunny, look!" I said. "Fires!"

He joined me at the balcony rail, "*Kampongs,*" he said, "*kampongs******darling, nothing to worry about." *Kampongs,* but whose? Peace loving village groups or terrorists? Those columns of gray smoke, silent clouds rising from the thick green foliage so far below, still seemed a little too close for comfort! However, cool nights of undisturbed sleep without mosquito nets refurbished our energy for the daylight hours as we strolled down forest tracks, revelling in new sensations, listening for sounds so alian to us made by birds, cicadas and insects that we never knew existed. Giant ferns over eight feet tall, their lacy fronds spectacular in their beauty connected by a delicate pathway of intricately woven spider webs, towering over a tangled mass of undergrowth and shorter plants on the rain forest floor. All of which combined to make perfect coverage for tiny animals out of sight from human eyes, walking on their own familiar paths made by themselves through the maze. We new instinctively that numerous pairs of eyes from creatures of many shapes and sizes were focused on us, if not exactly friendly, at least with mutual respect for each others presence.

**kampongs*—Malay villages

Monkeys overhead found our passing far more entertaining than their neighbors on the tangle forest floor.

Only a year ago Bunny's cousin, strolling down those self-same jungle paths, came face to face with a tiger. She stopped dead in her tracks—it was the tiger that skirted around to disappear into the undergrowth! We never experienced the like of that but in one short week we revelled in the folds of nature, relaxed and at peace with the world and enjoying each other's company, meeting few people at the clubhouse for breakfast, lunch or dinner. And after dinner? There is nothing like standing in the dark, on top of a mountain with rolling hills of jungle far below, silence pervading under a sky of twinkling stars.

Eventually leaving Fraser's Hill, the jungle and its flora haven to its animal inhabitants, not to mention its questionable human species, we drove south towards the area of the rubber plantations, searching for one in particular.

Michael Owen, the plantation manager and his wife Kathy were friends of Bunny's, and had previously offered to care for my two cats whilst we were on vacation. My four-legged family would be happy and we hoped safe out there in the middle of nowhere. Well aware that six months is a quite a responsibility for anyone to care for other people's precious creatures, especially in the middle of a local 'war,' we were indeed extremely grateful for their offer.

We passed a tin mine, eerily isolated and deserted. There was nothing pretty about it and Bunny did not slow down until we reached the Owen's plantation. There was an unrealistic feeling of peace driving between the rubber trees. Tall and slender, a few yards apart, each tree baring a slash in the bark and a cup on a strip of rope around the trunk to catch every sticky drip of the precious latex residue. It was quiet, deserted, not a soul in sight as we drove to the house where the door was opened by our host and hostess with their young family of two at their side.

Their over—exuberance with their enthusiasm to greet us was understandable. People were reluctant to travel in the plantations for fear of a terrorist ambush. We were the first visitors they welcomed in weeks. We were curious as to the seeming lack of workers on the estate until we learnt they were all secure in their quarters at the back of the house. With work tending the trees complete, they did not stray far, for fear of coming face to face with an armed communist lurking amongst the trees.

I glanced at the Owen's two wide-eyed children, smiling shyly as they gazed at me from the couch beside their mother, listening and obviously understanding every word we were saying. Kathy smiled down at them. "Pretty isn't she?" she said, "but don't stare darling, it's not polite." She looked at me, " You must forgive them. Visitors are few and far between. It isn't safe to travel at the moment." I noticed rifles standing within easy reach against the wall.

"What a way to live!" I thought, but understandably necessary. We returned the following year, refreshed after the luxury of a wonderful holiday and learnt of a very different six months for the Owens. They had temporarily adopted both cats, Simon and his sister, Faux Pas, much to the delight of the children who missed human companions their own age in so isolated a spot. But the adrenaline ran high for the entire household one quiet moonlit night when shadowy figures were spotted inside the barbed wire moving amongst the trees. The laborers joined the Chinese staff indoors, armed and stationed at the window. Michael and Kathy ran from one window to the other, all firing spasmodically at the 'shadows' until the sun rose in the morning and with it, the terrorists disappeared. And my two fat cats? They spent the night in the bath tub clutched in the arms of children, all locked in the bathroom for safekeeping.

*****

Bidding farewell to our friends we left the area, heading for the East Coast Road. Soon the Batu caves loomed in sight, home to the swifts—small birds that built their nests of their own saliva, attached to the roof and walls of the caves. Sadly their own little nests—their safe-haven—a delicacy, were raided regularly by the Chinese for birds-nest soup. I would like to have explored those caves, but "No dear—the communists use them as a hide-out." Bunny's voice was firm and we drove on towards our destination at a leisurely pace. We left the jungle for more open areas and found the road all but deserted. A few Malay women and children braved the heat, but when two male figures caught my attention we stopped, got out of the car and sought permission for a photograph. Tall and stately the man nodded his assent without a smile. A magnificent royal blue sarong with a silver *kapala******fastened around his waist, a sonka on his head, he stood like a statue, arms akimbo, gazing into the distant horizon over the head of his young son. The boy was also dressed for Hari Raya*, his sarong gathered in folds over his plump little tummy. They made a striking pair waiting for friends or familymembers to celebrate a festive occasion.

All was quiet on the banks of the river at Batu Pahat. An Indian—the ferryman, unhurried, in his own good time guided us in the car, easing it onto what can best be described as a fair-sized raft. Grasping a lengthy pole, he conveyed his charges slowly across the murky waters. I got out and I leant against the bonnet and watched the ripples passing by, the north shore getting smaller and the landmarks of the other appearing in the distance. The ferryman padded silently on bare feet, first to the front of the raft then, with hardly a sound, he put one end of the long, slender pole into the water and the river bed, and pressing with his diminutive weight, eased the raft and its cargo slowly forward. He continued to push on the pole passing by the car to the back of the raft—then it started all over again until we reached the far bank. We were in no hurry, time was our own.

There was another river to cross at Maur, before cruising gently south towards the sleepy little town of Mersing on the coast. En route we paused to watch a pair of tan colored bullocks with their gently brown eyes and long lashes as they lumbered on their way at their own good pace, pulling their cart, its driver seated comfortably in the shade of the Chinese-style roof. The international population of Malaya made it a land of diverse color and charm, and a land that I loved.

**kapala*—border woven in silver thread

*****Hari Raya—Malay festive occasions.

We parked the car by the side of the road and sat at for a while in the shade of a coconut palm at the edge of one of Mersing's magnificent beaches. As usual it was deserted except for a couple of crabs searching for food in the shallows, all else retreated from the searing heat to wait for the cooler hours early the following day. We loved to visit that long golden beach at that particular time, to spread a towel for a picnic and watch a lone fisherman waist deep in the shallows, he cast his net with an audible swish. Fine poles attached to either side dragged the net down to the sand, then slowly with hardly a ripple, he moved forward—all was quiet and very still. After a while, with ease that comes with practice, he hauled on the poles forcing the net up towards a cloudless sky and sprinkles of water sparkled raining down upon the surface. With a flash of silver, small fish leapt in vain to escape.

"Bunny," I laughed in delight, " that net is like a giant butterfly!" From then on, we referred to it as 'butterfly fishing at Mersing,' and made up our minds to return and spend more time on the beautiful beach where thoughts of any kind of war seemed very far away.

Back in Singapore we detoured the island to find a perfect scene to finish the film in my camera. Driving between coconut palms we chanced upon a small Malay fishing village on the shore of Tanjong Kling. There was nothing ostentatious about these people eking out a living at a leisurely pace in their humble Malay-style huts on stilts. Safe and dry as the water rose and washed beneath the floor of their single room abodes, they climbed down the rickety ladders as the tide receded, to step onto the beach below. It was a poor but picturesque neighborhood, with happy, smiling people, content with their simple way of life. For me it was a chance to get a perfect picture—two tiny tots, one in danger of losing his pants. His laughing mother, watching with her friends made a dive at the at the offending garment, caught hold and dragged them back in place, giving strict instructions to the little mite to hang on and smile as I focused the camera. I could not have hoped for a more perfect shot.

CHAPTER XXIII
RUMBLINGS OF THUNDER

Our lives were almost picture perfect at Bacchus Lodge, the beautiful house we built on the side of a hill. Looking down from a spacious verandah that connected two bedrooms on the upper floor, one could see the white blossom of the heavily scented frangipani tree to the right, and the purple bougainvillea that wound its way up the pillars to reach across the outer edge of the railing where we stood. The view across the lawn and badminton court to the valley beyond was all that one could desire, with a blaze of color from the canna beds on the far edge of the grass. Beneath the bedrooms a pink and acura colored guest and adjoining bathroom looked out onto herbaceous borders filled with glorious plant life! Ideal for entertaining, a large sitting room opened onto the terrace and garden, and down a couple of steps one side of the room, we reached a sunken dining room. The kitchen was charming with its pink and gray tiled floor, decor especially for my benefit—just in case I took a fancy to indulge in a little experimental cooking. In this I risked the displeasure of Ah Joo An, whose hostile eyes bored into my back through a crack from behind the door. Well hidden from the main house by gardenia bushes, a staircase from a passage behind the kitchen ran down the left bank of the hill to the servants quarters.

The *kabun* tended plants with his green thumbs and plenty of tender love and care, persuading them to bloom in all their glory. Slender strands trailed from a coconut shell that hung from the terrace above; each one bearing six or seven miniature white orchid blossoms, no larger than a fingernail, all perfectly shaped as a dove in flight—the head, body, tail and outstretched wings—natures delicate perfection. In contrast, clinging to a trestle, the moonflowers opened after dark as the sun went down. Their buds a full eight inches long, quivered and danced as if on cue in their exuberance to greet the moon, then finally burst open before our eyes, each pure white face the size of a dinner plate, exploding their fragrance into the air as the moon shone bright in the evening sky above.

My husband left for the office soon after breakfast served as always by Ah Ju An, whilst I gathered flowers from the garden to fill vases that decorated the walls and rooms all over the house. Giant spiders' webs spun overnight, stretched from one gardenia bush to the other, from hibiscus to hibiscus, their lacy works of art covered with magical drops of sparkling moisture from the heavy overnight due. It was a beautiful time to be up and about before the sun had a chance to reach the almost unbearable midday temperatures. With the humidity around ninety-two per cent, flowers bloomed in profusion, filling the air with their fragrance. The whole place was a heaven for birds, butterflies and insects alike—a kaleidoscope of color—and served as a mini lush green jungle for our ever-increasing feline family where butterflies in particular gave them untold merriment!

Early one morning, Lobbie, an energetic young red cat, momentarily exhausted from too much exercise romping with his siblings playing hide and seek in the herbaceous borders, snatched forty winks stretched out comfortably on the sitting-room couch, when out of the corner of his eye he spied movement not two feet away. Struck dumb with indignation he could only watch in amazement as a giant butterfly settled on the wall above his head. The browns and reds stood out as the magnificent creature held its place with the color of the wall shining green through the iridescent portions of his wings that boasted a massive one-foot span. My camera near at hand I took a chance shot, but unfortunately without anything with which to compare its size, the result was really not outstanding—just a wonderful moment to remember.

With so much peace and beauty it was difficult to comprehend communist uprisings as we settled down to a normal routine. But they were there nevertheless, and Bunny and his band of volunteer police met once a week complete with radio vans to practice in readiness for any sign of violence. I on the other hand rehearsed in a different way, amidst much laughter in a lighter vein for stage and radio productions. After the overwhelming success of "The Importance of Being Earnest" I never looked back and found myself cast in leading roles in each production. It was time consuming but enormous fun not only for me but also for my parents in the audience on opening nights as they joined the sea of white dinner jackets and long evening gowns. On occasions, we joined them with their party of friends after the show at the Tanglin Club or one of the other elegant restaurants for a late night dinner and dance. There Jackie would reminisce on amusing incidents in Changi, expounding on the excellence of productions in camp where inmates enacted such persons as Judy Garland, Betty Grable and a host of others. In this light mood, his bubbling sense of merriment—being somewhat of a performer himself—would keep us laughing with his own impersonations. "Hey! Isn't that Betty Grable?" "There goes Judy!" one camp inmate called to another during those harrowing days as a raggedy but good looking prisoner passed them by after a previous nights performance. Judging by Jackie's chuckle, the excellence of those impersonations brought much needed laughter as the years dragged on in Chingi. So excellent indeed was that production, it was staged in one of London's West End theaters when the war at last came to an end, using the original cast.

At other times my husband and I dined alone in our lovely home relaxing on the terrace over coffee after dinner, gazing out into the darkness and listening to the unceasing medley of the frogs and other night creatures—a perfect accompaniment to whatever books we were reading at the time. Often we dined at Princes, our favorite restaurant, at a table within easy reach of the dance floor. There, one or two or more of our bachelor friends invariably joined us. Frequent players at our evening badminton games, these young men were of my age, whose company my husband encouraged and indeed enjoyed. Although Bunny was an excellent dancer he was ten years older than me and thought this young crowd good for my morale! Not only were they amusing but all loved to dance, so life was never dull when they were around, especially at Christmas. With clubs and restaurants bedecked with balloons and colorful decorations, together with unceasing efforts from various bands, the mood was one of merriment as the corks burst from champagne bottles and the bubbly liquid flowed. It was a time for new and beautiful gowns for the ladies and gold braiding on white dinner jackets as the Governor's aides stood out amongst the men, with everyone relaxed and fell under the spell of the Christmas spirit during those days in Singapore and British South East Asia colonies.

Blythe, a special friend and a regular member of our group—suave, handsome and a wonderful dancer—made up our party that last Christmas. As we were dancing I remarked on the colorful balloons festooning the ceiling, and out of reach.

"Want one?" he asked as we swirled around.

"Yes," I laughed. He caught me round the waist and up I went.

"Oh!" I was taken by surprise, but reached up. Still the pretty balloons eluded my out-stretched fingertips. Then to my delight, I rose a few more feet! Someone else had stopped in his tracks and, as his horrified partner watched, he bent down and clutched Blythe around the knees, and with the strength of Goliath picked both of us up. Oblivious as to the cause, I laughed with delight as I rose even higher to clutch my prize. The column swayed as the unknown hero strove to keep his balance "Whoops!" the crescendo rose around the room as more gentlemen rushed towards us with outstretched arms. Amidst clouds of deep-pink chiffon and colored balloons my landing was assured. Poor Blythe was not so fortunate—in fact totally forgotten, he landed on the nearest table with a splash in a bowl of soup. Soundly chastised by the middle-aged lady to whom it belonged and received part of her first course full in the face, Blythe made his way sheepishly back to my side.

That was the start of a hectic Christmas season. The evening festivities went on until breakfast, followed by a quick change for a Pimm's party before lunch and a much—needed afternoon's nap in preparation for the next evening's dance. And so the festive season continued culminating in the New Years Tanglin Club fancy dress ball.

Our social list continued to grow amongst our set with lighthearted *joie de vivre* and ever-increasing tempo, both on and off the badminton and tennis courts, the swimming and yacht clubs and bachelor messes. There were also more formal gatherings, such as cocktail parties at Flagstaff House at the Naval Base, where a magnificent basket of orchids was presented to me on stage following a performance.

I had the honor of sitting on Sir Francis Fogarty's right as he presided at the head of his table of fourteen at a dinner party at Air House when a Labor parliamentary member passed through Singapore. This gentlemen sat next to me, much to my husband's displeasure—Bunny was a staunch Conservative—but nevertheless with his wife placed on the right between the host and guest of honor he didn't know whether to be pleased or otherwise until the ladies retired to the powder room and left the gentlemen to their cigars and brandy! Then, I understand, things tended to get a little heated between him and the Labor guest of honor!

At Government House where aids to the Governor numbered us amongst their personal friends, we enjoyed less formal gatherings in the apartment on the top floor of the Residency overlooking the luxurious grounds, as well as at more formal gatherings and dinner parties given by His Excellency Sir John Nicoll. Even there I felt relaxed when escorted by David Montgomery, Jim Lawler or John Forbes-Sempil, all aids to the Governor.

Beneath the lighthearted gaiety, distant rumblings of unrest could be heard amongst the local population. No doubt the entries to Mr. Corringdon's filing system had markedly increased since I left his office to get married but I gave it little thought.

Relishing the luxury of an evening alone at home relaxing on the terrace with a good book, safe and dry listening to the thunder and downpour of the rains that hit us in the monsoon season, I was surprised one dark night, by Ah Ju An ushering in a Malay police officer in uniform.

"Is everything all right Mrs. Salvesen?" I recognized one of my husband's men.

"Yes!" I replied, somewhat surprised. "Is something wrong?"

"We tried to call you but your line was dead. May I use your 'phone?"

"Of course," I said and got up from the chair, crossed the terrace and joined him in the sitting-room. "Is there trouble in town?"

"Yes," he answered as he went to the 'phone. "Two gangs are converging on one area and Mr. Salvesen was worried when he couldn't get through to you." He smiled, replacing the receiver on the 'phone "All seems well. I'm sorry to have troubled you."

"Not at all," I said "thank *you* for your trouble. My husband will be late tonight?"

"Possibly," he replied, and with that went out into the soaking night. Through rain that sparkled in the light of the porch, I watched the rear lights of his van disappear in the darkness up the steep incline to the top of the hill and then turned to go inside making sure the servants were indoors. We heard nothing more of the troublemakers until the following day. Despite a lot of noise there was little damage but this served as a warning that unrest lay beneath the surface of the times in which we lived.

The monsoon rains brought out other members of our wildlife and not all the creatures of our tropical beauty were friendly. Far from it. Some exploited their color in warning, as a danger signal, not that it was in every case effective. The day following the policeman's visit I went out through the front door when, to my horror saw a snake curled round a canna lily asleep in the bed beyond the porch. There was no mistaking its black and orange markings so brilliantly displayed. A creature of beauty but too close for comfort! I called Ah Joo An and at the sound of my voice all four of my beautiful cats strolled out—Lobbie followed by Simon, his black and white father and the multi colored Faux Pas, with her daughter, Fifi. Pandemonium! The snake awoke its bright colors shimmering in the sun, went shooting up the drive with all four cats streaking in its wake. My frantic calls were lost on the air—not one member of my family took the slightest notice as I raced in hot pursuit with Ah Joo An, *amah* and the *kabun* following hard on my heels, all attracted by the noise.

The object of this nonsense had had enough and seemingly with the ability to fly, shot up the perpendicular bank one side of the drive, disappearing in the *lalang* beyond. He left four frustrated cats, one female horse with yelling, a Chinese hopping painfully from one bare foot to the other on the burning tarmac and a giggling *amah* who thought the whole thing a tremendous joke. Only the *kabun* retained his normal calm, putting the rest of us to shame.

By 1955, the insurgent activity had increased on the mainland and crossed the causeway onto the island. It coincided with the second South

East Asia Film Festival due to be held in Singapore, with participants from the Philippines, Malaya, Japan, Formosa, Thailand, Macao, Indonesia and Hong Kong—an impressive affair with His Excellency the Governor of Singapore Sir John Nicoll, K.C.M.G. in attendance at the presentation banquet on May 15th 1955, at the Sea View Hotel. With preparations under way, Bunny and I were not altogether surprised when our good friend Jim Lawler approached us with a request—would I take charge of the Japanese delegation? They were to be present in force with an impressive array of female stars, gracious and charming in their colorful kimonos. The other main contingent came from the Philippines who sent one of their best, Rohellio de la Rosa—their leading actor.

It was an uneasy time to hold a festival but fortunately all went well as we shepherded our charges from one place to another, avoiding spots where trouble arose. When news of a car being overturned in one street at night—unbeknown to Joan Lawler, my co-hostess and I—our respective husbands made sure we took a safer route with our charges in tow, all blissfully unaware of anything but films and banquet planned for the evening. By day we escorted the ladies and de la Rosa around Singapore posing for photos and chatting with the press. The whole event was much publicized, and with an easy carefree attitude we made good friends amongst our visitors, who were fascinated by all they saw and in love with our beautiful island.

One movie was of particular interest to Bunny and me after the adventures experienced by Simon and Faux Pas up-country on the Owens plantation. Filmed on a large estate and titled "Rubber From Malaya" it recounted the delicate planting of the seedlings, latex tapping to the manufacturing of the rubber—all most interesting—but did not include the dangers that went with it at that time, the constant anxiety of impending communist attack such as the Owens had experienced.

The last night of the Festival finally arrived. With delegated hostesses waiting for their charges at the various hotels to escort them to the final gala dinner, Joan and I, both in the spirit of the occasion, took the opportunity to press our respective husbands into giving us new evening dresses, the most splendid that we could find—Joan's a golden satin, mine a cloud of pastel lemon tulle. Vanity, oh Vanity! I wanted to be taller and as luck would have it, thanks to Hollywood's movie star Carmen Miranda, the fashion at the time was for high-heeled platform shoes! Chinese cobblers are masters at their craft,—they measure, fit and press the leather into place, and oh the comfort of their miracles! As a result, I gazed at the world five inches above my normal height.

We stood in the foyer of the Raffles Hotel waiting for our limousines amongst our charges—eight dapper Japanese gentlemen in full evening dress, silent in anticipation of the evening's proceedings. Eventually one turned to me and said, "You know, I've been here before."

"Really? When was that?" I asked politely.

"Oh! During the war," came the astonishing reply. "I was a guard at Changi Jail."

Now as tall as he, I looked him straight in the face and hoped my voice was not as icy as my gaze. "How interesting," I said, thankful that at that very moment Jim emerged from the outer realms to announce the arrival of the cars. I swept past the man leading the way, grateful I did not have to suffer his company for the drive to Sea View. That was the last we saw of our charges.

Next day, visiting my mother at Ardmore Park, I relaxed over tea in the garden and told her what had taken place. Horrified, she said "Annette, for heavens sake *don't tell Jackie.*" She paused, deep in thought then said again "Just don't tell Jackie." My poor mother need not have worried—I would never say a word of this to Jackie—but it is something I vividly recall—and with distaste. Can we never get away from the effects of the war?

*****

It was with mixed feelings my parents eventually left Singapore to take life more easily at *Rumah Ketchil*, their house in Surrey. Years in South East Asia had made them life long friends, many of who would also returned to England whilst others departed for Australia. It was a wrench for Jackie in other ways, leaving local friends, many of whom helped him in those difficult times during the occupation, providing food from their own meager provisions as he searched for extra food to keep his fellow inmates at Changi alive. As for my mother, she was so proud of the garden and sad to leave it behind. After all, when asked by her husband what she would like for her birthday—a beautiful evening dress perhaps—who else would say, "Oh no! *Tilimbu* for the garden please!" On 28th November a bullock ambled up the drive drawing a cartload of manure. It came to a halt outside the front door with his Indian master standing dutifully by his head.

But when it did come time to leave she was as happy as a sand lark. Four years a POW had inevitably left its mark on Jackie—a quieter more peaceful way of life for her husband was uppermost in her mind. He would still have interest in his job with Guthries, working out of London, and she with her artistic touch, the joy of transforming *Rumah Ketchil* into an elegant and delightful English country home.

Eventually, we too wound our way home on board the *Hamburg*, landing at various ports of call to explore in different ways. We stepped off the launch and onto the shore at Suez, then turned to see Onassis' latest tanker preparing to enter the canal. Shimmering white from bow to stern in the tropical sun, it was hard to believe that she was laden with oil; that everything was movable aboard, including the crew's bunks was jettisoned to raise her in the water before she made her way slowly down the canal!

There was also a surprise in store for me. A visit to the pyramids—by camel! Once used to the unfamiliar gait! It wasn't too bad until the next day! Then I realized there were muscles I never knew existed. It must have been a somewhat incongruous sight—Bunny, immaculate as ever wearing navy shorts, crisp white shirt, and spotless white knee high socks—perched on top of Cleopatra, his ill tempered mount. As for me, I endeavored to ward of the scorching sun and a cloud of flies with a pretty little Japanese parasol—a gift from one of the Japanese ladies at the Festival.

A picturesque oasis in the desert deserved a visit—so enchanting, it seemed like something out of a Hollywood movie. A donkey had just given birth and the new arrival stole my heart. However, it was tabu to take photographs of the little creature, for fear the camera might cast an evil spell. Well guarded by the family this was a major event and warranted a guard from the local police, a man in uniform armed, not with a gun but with a stone and sling. Bunny was fascinated by this unusual weapon, and given a demonstration by the friendly officer as to how it was aimed and used.

Browsing through baubles and rings in the bazaar at Cairo would have kept me happy for hours had Bunny not hailed a taxi for a hair-raising drive at breakneck speed down the road to Port Said. There we were due to board our ship once more. However, *en route* we came to a screeching halt by the side of the road at the sound of heavy rumbles from ahead—mettle on tarmac. We waited, anxious about loosing precious time until a column of giant tanks approached. Bunny let out an astonished roar—six or seven mighty Churchill tanks, once our own then sold to the Egyptians following World War II now to be used against us in the Suez Crisis! A number of official cars followed, one bearing President Nasser.

The *Hamburg*, a picture of unconcerned peace, lay at anchor beyond the harbor, awaiting our arrival at Port Said. But there was still one more stop—a visit to a jeweler's shop where Bunny bought me one last gift from the East, a magnificent deep-toned 25carat topaz ring. With that we stepped on board the launch alongside the jetty and sped out to the waiting ship, walked up the gangplank and onto the deck—homeward bound for England.

Standing alone at the rail, at one with the motion of a ship, gazing into the distant horizon unmarred by human clutter, is food for the soul. Nothing can equal the joy of a long sea voyage nor bring such peace to the senses as the sound of the waves that wash against the bows in harmony with the vibrations of a ship's engine, or the feel of the spray on ones face and smell of the good salt air. In tropical waters, we watched the flash of silver as schools of flying fish rose from the waves and flew through the air before descending to their watery home. Although smaller than the big ocean-going liners of the P & O and White Star lines, the *Hamburg*—based in Germany—by comparison was more intimate equally as comfortable, with exceptionally good personal service. Our last voyage was one to be remembered with carefree happy days and festive nights.

*****

My mother and Jackie's excitement increased each day with the knowledge that we were on the way nearing our destination. Rumah Ketchil was a hive of industry—polishing, cleaning and tending to the garden in readiness for our arrival. Early one glorious Spring morning, my mother looked out of an upstairs window to call her husband indoors for breakfast already on the table but she was in for a nasty shock. "Jackie!" She screamed, shaken out of her normal calm. "What are you doing?" her husband, a soft mat under his knees, a basket by his side and trawl in his hand, looked up from the crazy-paving between the rose bushes, "I'm pulling up the weeds between the stones to make it look neat for Annette" he replied. "Those are not weeds!? Her voice unsteady, "they are Forget-Me-Not's for her return!"

"Oh Dear!" Jackie tried to suppress a giggle as he started carefully to replace the seedlings between the slabs.

*****

Sadly, Bunny and I parted ways after ten years of married life that came to an abrupt end in 1960. *Rumah Ketchil* eventually became my home, until my departure for America in 1962.

Jackie's last words are indelibly stamped upon my memory. "Annette," he said "just remember you will *always* be welcome here if you are not happy in America." Then repeated, "You will always have a home with us."

But his past experience as a POW took it's toll in spite of every care my mother could give, leaving her with her beautiful home and a life full of memories. He died of a stroke on August 8th 1968. She followed Jackie at the age of ninety-six as she lay in bed preparing for a good nights sleep. That was twenty-six years later. Now she lies at rest beside her husband in a quiet little country graveyard at Wetheringset, in Suffolk, away from the hustle and bustle of their former life.

But she is not forgotten. Her credentials are safely treasured in the archives where she once worked as Deputy in charge of 200 girls in her department, at Bletchley Park during World War II.

Now recreated into a museum in honor of all coders who worked in that extraordinary place, I too have the honor of joining others of my kind. Although a very insignificant and humble little coder at that time, it is awesome to think that my particulars already rest in the shadow of the grates, such as Alan Turing and those connected with him—all people working in the background to bring suffering and horror to an end.

BLETCHLEY PARK

Fifty years went by—the jubilation of Victory Day at the end of World War II was almost forgotten, remembered only by those who had lived through those six harrowing years, 1939—1945. The youth of today in America knew little or nothing about it, and indeed appeared totally disinterested, dismissing it as something of no concern. But for those who had lived through those terrible times as codests at Bletchley Park in England, it was fifty years of close-lipped silence, with secrets to be held in the mind and memory.

My mother passed on to happy oblivion, no longer beset of thoughts of war, for she too held many a memory—many secrets of years gone by. She had worked at Bletchley Park, the worlds great coding and Secret Service center. Indeed she was deputy in charge of a section run by WRNS, though what they did she never divulged to me and I never discussed our method of coding in *Hut 10* sent to our agents behind the enemy lines.

Again browsing through her file I read the letters of recommendation for work well done—but even those were cloaked in secrecy!

Mrs: D. Wainwright

Mrs Wainwright has worked in a section of the Foreign Office under my control from Nov: 1944 until 1945. I am precluded by the Official Secrets Act for giving particulars on the work on which she was engaged.

During that period she was deputy head of a group of about 200 girls engaged on various forms of clerical work .She is most conscience and hard working, was a very loyal and valuable second in command fully capable of taking charge when the head of the group was away She was excellent with people, firm and tactful in dealing with the girls and universally liked by them. I can recommend her for any similar job.

It was signed by *CHO'D Alexander*

1-12-45

There were more letters along the same vain, which I would eventually present—in the correct manner—to the Bletchley Park archives where she is for ever remembered. The beautiful old building I knew so well is now a Museum, dedicated to the honor of all the codests who worked within its walls. I smiled as I realized that too included me!

Turning the page I came across a flimsy sheet that had previously escaped my notice, its color aged with time. A casual glance I suddenly caught my breath—this was directed to *all* who had worked and served at Bletchley Park which, of course, included me. I took it to the window for more light and further scrutiny, and realized it was a message from the Director General, with *Words of Gratitude.* Gratitude for all that had been done by so many in that Great Organization!

"Words of Gratitude" I could hardly believe my eyes. *Words of Thanks* after so many years! We *the silent ones* who sat with our heads bent in silence pouring over thousands and thousands of five figure groups, hour after hour, day after day,—the days turning into weeks and then into months followed by years! Why had my mother held this from me? Just a slip of the memory no doubt, but it would have meant so much!

We codests never spoke of what we did—no one outside our hut was so tactless as to enquire although many a one of the opposite sex would dearly have liked to get to know those strange, quiet women a little better. But the codists of *Hut 10* eventually moved to London! Husbands and wives in that Organization held secrets each from the other in Bletchley Park, information all bound up inside our minds and memories.

After six long years the War eventually came to an end and with righteous jubilation we celebrated and with gusto. We hung precariously out of windows in out excitement, screaming ourselves hoarse as the heroes passed us by in the street below, to the sound of marching bands in the victory parade—the army, the navy, the air force along with many others. It was the Poles who received the most rousing cheer, their bravery in World War II never to be forgotten. But there was never a thought for those in our profession—it was as if we had never existed.

Falling over each other in our excitement we tumbled down the stairs to reach the street, and made our way amongst the crowds to

Buckingham Palace. It was an orderly crowd; even the men had tears of joy running down their cheeks. Everyone respected the right of their neighbors to have a perfect view of the balcony as the Royal Family stepped out time and time again to acknowledge the cheers of their exuberant people—the king, the queen and the two princesses—Princess Elizabeth in the uniform of the ATTS with whom she had served. Then when a beaming Mr. Churchill appeared, the man who had lead us from a possible iniolation we went wild with joy!

After that wonderful day we returned to work, to puzzle over our mathematical problems. Not everyone—for many their work was done—the War was won. But for the *"Hut 10"* codests messages still had to be received and sent to those whom I considered to be he greatest heroes of all, the people behind the enemy lines—the resistance fighters of France. These I longed to emulate, dreaming in my childish mind, rescuing our men shot down, to hide and plan their escape. They watched troop movements from behind hedges and dark corners, encoding their messages to England which eventually came to us at Bletchley Park. It takes a certain kind of courage to perform that sort of work.

At Bletchley Park the lovely old building that had housed 8,900 people was itself to be demolished until a few discerning soles remonstrated and said "NO" and then fought back for the memories of those who had given years of their lives to the place. Now we too are honored at the Bletchley Park Museum.

I held that precious piece of paper in my hand and as I read the words I felt a catch in my throat, my tummy tightened as my eyes clouded over, such was the emotion to be felt after all those years. The message was simple and to the point…

MESSAGE FROM THE DIRECTOR GENERAL

The following message has been received from the Director General—

"On this memorable day, I desire that all who are doing duty in this Organization should be made aware of my unbounded admiration at the way in which they have carried out their allotted tasks.

Such have been the difficulties, such has been the endeavor, and such have been the constant triumphs that one senses that words of gratitude are perhaps out of place. The personal knowledge of the contribution made towards winning the War is surely the real measure of the thanks, which so rightly belongs to one and all in a great and inspired organization which I have the privilege to direct. This is your finest hour."

(Signed) S.G.M.
8th May, 1945.

From America I called my friend Peter Wescombe, formally of the British Foreign Office and Founder of the Bletchley Park Museum.

"Annette! Don't you realize who that is?" He almost *shouted* into the phone from England! " Menzis, pronounced Minzis—he was Scottish!" he added dryly, "S.G.M? Menzis! Was the head not only of those 8,900 people who worked or past through the gates of Bletchley Park, but the head of MI5, MI6, SOE and SIS. In fact every secret organization working to beat the enemy, was under his direction! You were working for MI5 and SIS. Don't you dare hide that letter away. Frame it, and hang it on the wall with pride. It is yours!"

Little did I know at that time my future husband had already spent several months in that area. As commanding officer in charge of training men in the so-called art of winter warfare, namely to fight the enemy on skis, "Bunny" Salvesen requisitioned the famous Cristala Hotel as his headquarters. A stickler for what was right, he demanded of his officers that no spoon, knife or fork, or any other object would be stolen and no damage to the property would be tolerated. As a result, when we arrived unannounced on our honeymoon in 1952, the grateful owner, Leo Menadi threw his arms around my husband and greeted us with tears of joy. We spent two glorious weeks as guests of the Hotel Cristala, made famous by the movie *The Pink Panther*; champagne flowed like water, mouth-watering food, and the bridal suite—all at the expense of our generous host.

Exploring the Dolomites in the snow on a glorious sunny day, Bunny reminisced on one perilous run that he had made on many occasions. As I stood beside him gazing up at the vertical slope, he told me of a platform built out of railway sleepers about four feet in width that traversed the circumference on one side of the cliff's hazardous drop. Standing beside him in the snow gazing up at the perilous drop, I tried to picture the narrow platform slung out on wire, I to imagine what it must have been like for those men to ski from the summit towards the entrance of that platform, knowing full well that if they miss-timed the descent they would go flying over the edge and plummet to an inevitable demise amongst the trees far below. According to my husband, only one man, a daredevil Polish office, plunged to his death in this way. The platform torn down after the war had served its purpose and made some expert skiers out of a number of very brave men.

CPSIA information can be obtained at www.ICGtesting.com
Printed in the USA
BVOW042240220911

271937BV00001B/16/P